THE
MOLTEN
SOUL

THE
MOLTEN SOUL

DANGERS AND OPPORTUNITIES
IN RELIGIOUS CONVERSION

GRAY TEMPLE

Foreword by Walter Brueggemann

CHURCH

CHURCH PUBLISHING, NEW YORK

Library of Congress Cataloging-in-Publication Data

Temple, Gray, 1941-
The molten soul : dangers and opportunities in religious conversion/
Gray Temple.
      p. cm.
  Includes bibliographical references.
  ISBN 0-89869-335-7 (hard cover)
  1. Conversion–Christianity. I. Title.
  BV4916 .T44 2000
  248.2'4–dc21

                                00-065583

Church Publishing Incorporated
445 Fifth Avenue
New York NY 10016

http://www.churchpublishing.org

5 4 3 2 1

DEDICATION

To the men, women, and children of St. Patrick's Episcopal Church who for twenty-five years have nourished me and these thoughts.

TABLE OF CONTENTS

FOREWORD

In Gail Godwin's early book *The Finishing School* (Avon, 1966), the lead character, Justin's tutor, says to him, "Do not congeal too quickly." To congeal is to get settled in a fixed, stable, durable form, a process too much identified with "growing up" and "maturing," much encouraged by "adult culture." In *The Molten Soul*, Gray Temple discusses the propensity of "congealing" in every phase of the church's life and shows in clear, passionate, specific ways why "congealing" is deeply against God's gift in the gospel.

Against the broad inclination to congeal, Temple urges "moltenness," the process of being melted down, liquefied, rendered supple and open for new congealing that must not be too firm or full, but that readies the soul, in good gospel fashion, for the next melting which is the good work of God.

The book is a careful, rich exploration of the metaphor of "moltenness" that is carried into every dimension of Christian life and faith. It is a deeply moving combination of *personal testimony* and *critical thought* concerning ecclesial, institutional matters. I suppose the genre is "spirituality," except that the term hardly prepares the reader for the penetration and candor that Temple brings to the task.

The personal dimension of the testimony is Gray Temple's self-announcement. He is the rector of a working Episcopal parish. But what he really is, is a "Spirit-baptized" Christian who easily embraces charismatic qualities of Christian life. He nicely refers to the charismatic as "democratic mysticism" that I understand to be an "ordinary" (not elitist) access to God's Spirit in an immediate way that can happen to those who present themselves to the Spirit. Temple is not preoccupied with the mechanics of his "Spirit-baptism," exhibits nothing of the "bizarre" that usually defines charismatic, and has nothing of the shrill, authoritarian tone of the newly converted.

Rather Gray Temple is molten himself, open, ready to be reconfigured according to God's purpose in his life, a purpose that variously exhibits traits easily termed "conservative" and traits readily taken as "liberal." His apt observation of a Spirit transformation that has durable markings is that "all brushes with God leave us molten." Temple has had such a brush and it has opened his critical horizon on the life of the church.

His strictures against "religion" are as deep as those of Karl Barth, for he sees religion as inescapably tending to either commercialism or manipulation. His pervasive critique is of a combination of rigidity and hypocrisy for which his pioneering reference point is Ernest Becker. Temple finds that rigidity and hypocrisy of a deathly kind pervade the church, but offers as an antidote openness and candor that need hide, defend, or attack nothing. His suggestive metaphor for the molten and the congealed is the contrast between Edgar Bergen, the ventriloquist, and Charlie McCarthy, the puppet. Bergen grew and changed like any human being, but McCarthy never grew and never changed and when "broken" needed only to be "fixed." While the book does not carry the metaphor of Bergen and McCarthy beyond a mention, Temple surely implies that every aspect of the church readily takes on the image of a dumb puppet without life, growth, or change.

From that vantage point *The Molten Soul* considers a molten Bible, a molten church, and a molten Christology. In every case the book cites heavyweight examples of congealing that turn the immediacy of experience into a managed formality that leads to going through the motions of faith. The critique offered here is not exceptional, except that it is kept close to the defining metaphor of moltenness. The author shows himself to be an informed and thoughtful student of Scripture and of the faith of the church. His extensive review of "theories of atonement" is an illuminating study of historical emergence in the life of the church of metaphors and theories that have been frozen into hard formulations that, not surprisingly, have no real power.

Becker's focus on *fear of death* informs everything for Temple. It is fear of death that causes congealing. When freed from that fear, as the Spirit may do, a rigid Bible, a closed church, or a shrill doctrine is no longer necessary.

Temple renders a remarkable service by bringing into question the conventional characterization of the church. After a penetrating discussion of the Book of Job that concludes with a view of Job as a newly created molten soul, Temple raises the demanding, suggestive question, "Where can Job go to church?" Too many—almost all—churches are operated by and for Job's friends who know too much, who explain too much, and who supervise too much. Job has tried their churches, but did not stay because he needed a community—that he never found—that would host his riskiness. I can imagine that Temple would be a proper priest for Job, standing with him in the wind, and urging him not to give in too soon.

The Molten Soul has surely grown out of deep struggle with appropriate measures of fear and frustration and anger and rejection. But here speaks now a priest of freedom, a man of joy. In his freedom and joy, Gray Temple offers Job a vision of the church he needs:

> Where could we look for a list of congregations that readily accept, support, and deploy Job? Such groups would need to live comfortably with ambiguity and paradox. They would need non-repressive and non-capitulative norms for conflict management. They would need a purchase on the Bible, the Creeds, essential doctrines, and the imperative for justice, which is respectful, exploratory, grown-up, and non-idolatrous. Such groups would foster group norms within which members could seek and discuss mystical encounters with God—without experiencing embarrassment or incurring scorn. They would need to be committed to justice and charity—while remaining merry. Their worship would need to reach eternity and the depths of contemporary souls simultaneously. They would need to be conversationally candid, as interested in actual personal reality as in ideal personal profiles.

The molten voice, not unlike that of Job, has "spoken of me what is right" (Job 42:8). Thanks be to God!

Walter Brueggemann
Columbia Theological Seminary
October 16, 2000

ACKNOWLEDGEMENTS

Various dear friends have read and made helpful comments on the manuscript. I would love to say, "If something looks stupid, complain to them." But without them it could not have escaped the tight orbit of my personal musings and idiosyncratic codes. So thank you, Anita, Becky, Betty, Cheri and Tom, Doug, Evy, Evelyn, George, Holly, JoAnn, Kent, Martha, Sherie, and the Not-As-Young-As-We-Used-To-Be Sunday School class—may God accompany and prosper you in every endeavor.

Three teachers form an internal council of elders in my head, an intellectual conscience:

Harold G. McCurdy, Kenan Professor of Psychology at the University of North Carolina at Chapel Hill for many years, demonstrated a tough-minded allegiance to truth that cleared room for wonder. The textbook he authored, from which he taught Personality Psychology, is characteristically entitled *The Personal World.*

Kenneth J. Reckford, Kenan Professor of Classical Languages at Chapel Hill, now only corrects my Greek and Latin—and English syntax, and theology, and logic, and taste—when I ask him to. He is a model of merry, faithful wisdom.

The Right Reverend Bennett J. Sims (in addition to his sparkling clarity with words) has always modeled utter charity in serious debate, dignifying every person and idea with which he differs in public and private discourse by a courtesy integral to godly understanding.

Every writer should have an editor like Joan Castagnone—one who understands your intention, shares your passion for it and insists on your striving for perfection. On any number of occasions my thoughts were clearer to myself in the wake of Joan's perceptive suggestions.

It remains to thank one other person who is deeply part of this project. The influence of my wife, Jean, a psychotherapist in private practice, will be discernible here to all who know her. Her guardianship of my privacy, her encouragement, her wit, and her frank and clear opinions made it all possible. She typed the first embryo of this manuscript on an idiosyncratic typewriter thousands of miles from any repairfolk when we were on sabbatical in western Kenya.

INTRODUCTION

We're about to look together at some specific problems to which people expose themselves when they try to be religious—and what can be done to forestall or correct those problems. Because I'm a Christian, I confine my discussion to the Christian church, though participants in other religious systems could possibly apply my analyses to their own faith expressions. I'm a congregational cleric, not an academic theologian, so this discussion is not especially technical.

A POLITICAL AGENDA

An astute friend asked me, "What question produced this book for an answer? Who is on the other side of the conversation?" For me, the question that spurred this discussion is "Why is American Christianity so divided against itself?" And the book is for the folks I would like to have this discussion with—passionately serious Christians of all stripes.

Specifically, this book looks at problems and opportunities in intense religious conversion in the context of the polarized state of American Christianity today. What makes that political backdrop necessary? The answer is deceptively simple. People on the right-hand side of our religious polarity sometimes assume that they are the only ones much interested in conversion, in getting "born again." And people of the left-hand side of the polarity sometimes look with suspicion at anything smacking of a conversion, hearing phrases like "born again" with visible distaste. Conversion in our day has become a political issue, God help us.

Within one generation, the public religious discussion has moved from the gospel-based impulses for justice that accompanied the Civil Rights Movement, the War on Poverty, and the critical discussion of the Vietnam War to its present Bible-based emphasis on personal salvation, sexual morality, and political conservatism. What effect this shift has had on those of us who just go to church is not always easy to gauge. But there is little question that we're hearing a different message over the loudspeakers. Neither of these emphases has derived much conspicuous benefit from the other.

Rather than fake a balance I do not possess, I'm writing primarily as a "liberal" who has learned to value "conservatives" and to share their deepest commitments, asking "conservative" brethren and sisteren to consider how embracing certain "liberal" commitments might serve God more faithfully.

Since becoming a "Charismatic" (something you become by "conversion") I've spent a lot of time with people vastly more conservative than I am—because Charismatics tend towards biblical, political, and social conservatism. My experience during that time has been alternately troubling and rewarding. In many of these settings, where it was assumed that we would all vote Republican, I felt like a spy in an enemy camp, about to be discovered at any moment. The richest times in those circles have been those when we were worshiping together, when we were enjoying—or at least discussing—actual encounters with God. Yet much of the time has been frustrating. A lot of energy gets wasted trying to solve non-problems (e.g., the timing of "the Rapture") and overlooking real ones (e.g., God's "preferential option" for the poor). My companions have seemed terribly fearful of modernity—as though God were not involved in current history. I've noticed a lot of unrealistic idealization of the distant past—as though all history from the time of Constantine to this minute were regrettable. I notice much labor to maintain a sense of previous blessing or of doctrinal confidence.

Some of my participation within the Charismatic Movement has been conflict-laden, one or two occasions spectacularly so. This is not the place to reopen those fights—and you would be unwise to trust my report should I attempt it. (The effort to put these thoughts to paper without querulousness has proved a healing personal discipline.) The primary connection between those old fights and this discussion is that if all of us—me included—had heeded these understandings, those differences of perspective would not have led to quarrels.

At this point in the national religious discussion what gets called "liberalism" has little voice, a reversal from the '60s. So thoroughly has the very word "liberal" been discredited that vast treasures from that earlier period have become less approachable than toxic waste. In this book I am eager to offer some "liberal" understandings I gathered "from back before I got saved," which to my way of thinking urgently deserve fresh consideration—by all of us.

A similar reversal could happen to today's religious "conservatism." If so, I guess I'd attend the liberal victory party—but nervously. Americans are not stupid. If there were no value in conservative religion, it wouldn't enjoy its current popularity. A shift away from it would cost us all much of abiding value. Among the treasures religious conservatives can offer are procedures for an experiential encounter with God. So I'll be stressing some understandings I want to see survive when the wave function of religious conservatism eventually collapses to a particle. I'll also be suggesting how these understandings could be expressed and recommended by those who treasure them right now in ways that might assure their survival.

I am putting these thoughts on the table, despite my fear that they are too conservative for my liberal buddies and too liberal for my conservative buddies. Even if they launch no fruitful discussion, I will be delivered of them and free to think about something else.

Some of the discussion is offered more to conservative friends than liberal ones—discussions of faith development stages, of the Bible's real authority and proper interpretation, of how we apprehend Jesus, to name the main points. Some are addressed more to liberal friends than conservatives—discussions of how to kickstart a personal relationship with God, how faith communities might constitute themselves, and some nourishing ways to engage the Bible. But the analysis of what makes a straight relationship with God frightening, and why we polarize over rival religious notions, and how to get braver than all that—is addressed to everybody, myself included.

So who is this book for? This book is for committed Christians—lay as well as clergy—with a passion for God. The desired outcome is enhanced religious citizenship.

SOME EXPERIENCES THAT LAUNCHED THIS PROJECT

The thoughts in this book result from three decades of ordained ministry, including much lecturing and consulting about spiritual renewal in Christian congregations over most of that time. If somebody asked me, "What do people most need to know about being religious these days?" this book would be my answer.

In 1973 I underwent a formative experience I claim as "Baptism in the Holy Spirit." That left me not only the liberal, existentialist pacifist I had been, but also a "Charismatic"—a mixed identity whose every element I continue to embrace.

My own congregation, though containing few liberal pacifist existentialists, is often termed "Charismatic" and does not mind the title. We have church fights from time to time like any congregation, but being "Charismatic" is rarely at issue in them. For us, that identity is settled.

That development in our parish—during peaceable periods, at least—used to prompt clergy and lay leaders elsewhere to ask what we were doing and how they themselves might go about it. In response to such inquiries, I visited many congregations and groups—upwards of a hundred—and several visited us.

When I'd done such consultations long enough to start seeing patterns, I noticed client groups were rarely all that "happy in Jesus." Some would be standard-brand congregations that, upon experiencing Charismatic stirrings among themselves, had sent for a bilingual Charismatic to help them make sense of things, hoping to maintain order and unity. They felt the need because they knew that where people increase the voltage of their spiritual commitments and bring that higher voltage to church with them, somebody's going to get hurt—real bad. Others already saw themselves as "spiritually renewed"—a not-altogether-modest way we Charismatics refer to ourselves. These congregations experienced difficulties and conflicts which standard Charismatic teachings do not fully illuminate or resolve. In other words, people were getting hurt—real bad. Eventually, I discovered that all these people had one characteristic in common—dissatisfaction with intense Charismatic spirituality. Worry greatly prevailed over interest. People had come to expect harm from each other while actively pursuing the things of God.

I'm embarrassed at how long it took me to catch on to that dissatisfaction. Those of us who have undergone Spirit-baptism think it's a good thing. We're reluctant to entertain criticism of it. To be honest, we wish everyone would line up to receive it. And if being a Charismatic individual is good, belonging to a Charismatic congregation must be better. Yet the common element in client groups, at home and at church, was anxiety and strife. Why did an energetic spirituality that retails itself as God's own solution to so many difficulties produce such trouble and pain on its own?

At first, each time an invitation to address another congregation arrived, I thought I was being asked to describe and point to the encounter with the Presence of God. Only gradually did I realize the audiences needed to talk about difficulties and disappointments, wounds and divisions incurred in that pursuit.

Detailed discussions of the Charismatic Movement appear in many other books devoted to explaining it. It's not my purpose here to argue for the Charismatic Movement—as shrill and partisan a pressure group as any other. But taking Charismatic spirituality seriously for two decades has taught me things that apply to other spiritualities. The dynamics of Charismatic spirituality resembles that of Evangelicalism, devout Catholicism, Christian peace groups, or Jungian Christian groups. In effect, the need to reflect upon how it all went so wrong is common to several approaches to spirituality.

The dynamics are common to several spiritualities: The initial "Aha! Experience"; mastering the group's lore and norms; emotional highs followed by emotional lows occuring in a sigmoid pattern; doubts ensue; revival procedures, with their momentary relief, are sought out; increased energy is allotted to forestall cognitive dissonance. Equally common is the smug posture that our own cognitive community is superior to everybody else's. All this occurs within the Charismatic Renewal, but is hardly confined to it. Consequently experience in the Charismatic Movement forms a protocol for understanding what goes on with other religious conversions of detectable strength. The elements that make some people fear the entry of neo-Pentecostalism into their congregations and make others disappointed in its unfulfilled promises are visible in other intense expressions of the Christian faith as well. For example, when a suburban congregation discovers how to staff a homeless shelter and makes that ministry a conspicuous element of its identity, it will experience much the same turbulence—only the vocabulary is different.

Intense religious conversion is simply scary—for good reasons.

SOME SOURCES

The analysis of the problem and the remedies proposed here derive from personal experience and the thoughts of wise friends. I also owe an obvious debt to many writers. Devout readers will recognize familiar authors and titles, standard fare for the Christian bookworm. Those who know C.S. Lewis will not be surprised to find G. K. Chesterton, Dorothy L. Sayers, George MacDonald, or Lady Julian of Norwich nearby. Whoever knows any of those writers has at least heard of Augustine, and some of the saints: Gregory, Origen, Anselm, Abelard, Luther, Calvin, and Kierkegaard.

This discussion also draws heavily upon sources that are too little known among Christian readers. Chief among them is the work of the late anthropologist Ernest Becker, the earlier writings of Peter Berger, and the contemporary work of James Fowler.

My selection of these sources has not been entirely deliberate. It was more internal discovery than choice. These materials more than any others have repeatedly bubbled up from my pre-conscious memory when I have fielded questions from the audience following talks in countless sanctuaries and undercrofts on the lecture circuit. Such sessions often make me feel like a goalie practicing on a hockey rink, pucks flying at me from all directions at once; responses have to be largely reflexive. That sort of setting exposes me to my governing assumptions, since there is rarely time to be slick when questions and contrary ideas are flying all around the room. For me, the writers I cite—especially Becker— pop up consistently more than any others. What connects them, I wondered? Why do they seem to hold out recognizable hope to the frustration, fear, and disappointment of people who are giving religion their best shot?

I have concluded that their tough-minded insistence on the priority of demonstrable truth over personal whim makes them essential allies in the project of *being a Christian in the setting of modernity*. If being a Christian requires that we pretend to prefer the thought-forms of pre-modern eras, then it becomes toxic, in its very divisiveness a form of "sin." But as we discover in modernity a congruence with the deepest aquifers of our faith tradition, we come to trust that Truth is both friendly and bomb-proof—that the encounter with the Other described in the first chapter does not require that we dress up as pseudo-Israelites (to borrow Sam Keen's haunting phrase from the chapter title, "Confessions of a Pseudo-Israelite" in *To a Dancing God*). Daily life confronts us with more than enough cognitive dissonance without our having to send out to religion for more. *Sufficit religionem malitia sua.*

To grasp this perspective, to open up for a deeper conversion, requires no particular cleverness—only a little courage, only the God-given trust that " . . . all will be well." Nor is there anything exclusively Charismatic about this perspective. Readers who object to what they perceive as the intellectual imprecision and emotional frivolity of the Charismatic Movement will get no argument from me—not on these pages at any rate.

Yet my frequent mentions of the Charismatic Movement stem from one consideration that is an outright recommendation for what it could offer. That is, at its best, the Charismatic Movement was passionately serious about our not settling for anything less than a personal, experiential relationship with God, a relationship analogous to our dealings with the people closest to us. It's both futile and toxic to try to be religious without going the full distance into mysticism, into the felt Presence of God. And the Charismatic Movement used to be able to mediate such a relationship—think of it as "mysticism for the rest of us." On lesser, submystical terms, religion becomes a means of repressive social control that generates its own counterreaction.

Now the abiding problem with mysticism is its apparent elitism, an observation almost as true today as when Christians first confronted elitist Gnostics with it. Though any numbers of conspicuous mystics have been plebeians and peasants, mystics are often thought of as spiritual aristocrats. So how can mysticism become democratic? I know first hand that the (admittedly flawed) Charismatic Movement offers—or once offered—an answer to that question. The procedures Pentecostals and Charismatics have discovered for introducing people to God are quite simply the fastest and surest we have. Purists may disapprove, just as real Internet jockeys may spurn and despise America Online or CompuServe. However, few of us would be enjoying the Net without those points of departure. So it could be with Charismatic Spirit-baptism.

I yearn to see everybody gain access to God's palpable presence, which Charismatic procedures readily offer, if those procedures are stripped of the jejune Fundamentalist accretions for which so many have sold out their intellectual consciences.

Spirit-baptism has no manifest theological content. You can be a Spirit-filled Bultmannian Bible critic as easily as you can occupy a place on the 700 Club mailing list. You can be a Spirit-filled, tongues-praying Liberationist/Feminist—and some of my favorite buddies are. There's no reason for non-conservative Christians not to use these procedures and there's every reason to do so. They can do so without detriment, harm, or loss of membership in the company of the bright and the beautiful. The resulting personal fellowship with God can bridge all manner of partisan chasms. Can a Democrat get to be a born-again Charismatic without forfeiting her principles? Yes indeed. Can a Republican benefit from rigorous biblical/historical scholarship and psychological/sociological research without dropping out of the neighborhood Bible study? You bet.

As to the effectiveness of the approach taken here, I put forward the experience of St. Patrick's Episcopal Church in Atlanta. This merry congregation has persisted as a consciously devout community for three decades. Its members live the principles this little book sets forth, and they do so with a grace and charm that makes our Lord apparent to the most cold-hearted visitor. I trust the thoughts in this book because people I trust live them fruitfully. They taught them to me. This congregation is much too headstrong and diverse to settle for a "system" of my own or anyone else's contrivance. Only a tested reliance on our Lord's faithfulness in all circumstances will prove viable among them, and an experienced-based trust that what gets called God's "transcendence" is not a matter of distance. They know God is deeply friendly to us, if a bit scary. Their generosity with money, prayer, and time away produced this book. Their lives are its substance. Their courage and honesty have constantly shown me hopes for authentic spiritual life being lived in a normal congregation.

So if intense religious conversion is scary, there are nevertheless fruitful directions we can investigate that maximize the promise while reducing the risks.

NECESSARY APOLOGETIC MUMBLES

A necessary word about gender-specific pronouns. The easy decision is how to talk about a human population whose members roughly divide between two leading sexes. Rather than say "he or she," or "she or he," or "s/he/it," etc., it seems most graceful simply to refer to undesignated individuals alternately as she or he. The reader will meet female dentists and male nurses.

The more strenuous decision has to do with sex-specific pronouns referring to God. I embrace the doctrine of the Holy Trinity as abidingly fruitful, the best portal I know for entry into the Presence. That doctrine confronts us with the historical title "Father" for the First Person of the Trinity. Where the context permits, I say "the First Person." Occasionally I say, "Father," where it seems necessary that we be good sports about the eons-old scandal of linguistically disregarding God's femininity. I do not say "Mother"— though that would be congruent with much of God's self-disclosure in the Bible. To do so would stir conflicts and resentments that must be explored on other pages than these. Those conflicts would usurp this discussion's agenda. I avoid "parent" from the sense that as a title it drifts more towards function than person; "Father" contains at least some of the warmth of a proper name. In most instances, simply saying "God" dispenses with pronoun, though it occasionally sounds awkward. Occasionally I use the pronoun "she" in reference to the Holy Spirit, inasmuch as the Hebrew word *ruach* (spirit) is feminine.

I refer to "the Old Testament" rather than to "the Hebrew Scriptures" because, given their somewhat different contents, internal arrangements, original languages, and interpretive histories, they are not identical. I hope a Jewish reader would detect my profound respect for Judaism and its sacred writings in that very distinction of nomenclature.

Biblical citations come from the New Revised Standard Version. I occasionally modify the wording to highlight some element in the underlying Hebrew or Greek texts pertinent to the discussion.

The copious footnotes reflect the hardened bad habits of an extemporaneous public speaker whose faithful audience, being used to him, has despaired of correcting him. Footnotes often occur at all the points where, if this were a vocal presentation, I would chase a rabbit.

CHAPTER ONE

A PROBLEMATIC CONVERSION

THE ENCOUNTER

You often first notice the experience with your physical senses before its emotional impact kicks in. Your skin feels fresh, as though a pleasant breeze were stirring you up from lethargy. You may become aware of an energetic warmth progressively covering you like poured oil, bringing heightened awareness and vitality— sometimes triggering your body's or your mind's recuperative powers, remedying physical ailments. Sometimes the warmth wells up from inside you. Or you may become curious about a halo of light in an area of the room where you had been aimlessly looking.

Gradually you become aware that you are in the Presence of a Person—One of unquestionable authority and boundless affection and goodwill directed at you. You see yourself as though for the first time with absolute objectivity—yet without psychological annihilation—because the Other holds you safe and precious.

It may happen during the course of a meditation time, or at the peak of intense weeping or laughter. Mostly it comes on you unannounced and unsummoned.

Any worry you were experiencing feels eradicated—regardless of possible outcomes. Any sense of enmity towards another is swallowed up in forgiveness and understanding; you feel little concern about any future harm from him. Generous courage seems your natural state. Perhaps for the first time in your life, you feel *normal.* The thought of your own death or that of a loved one feels calmly manageable just then; during such an encounter *real* life feels somehow permanent, invulnerable to death. You sense that who you are at this precise moment is your true eternal self. You anticipate a future of facing every person and vicissitude with affectionate, wise serenity.

Relieved or delighted weeping is common—or even merry, unrestrained laughter.

The thoughts and affections of the Other are available to you without words or images. Your own thoughts and feelings are clearly available to the Other. Though this may be the first meeting of its kind, the Other is clearly One who has always known you and whom you have always known. The universe itself seems momentarily coherent, intelligible, and deeply good—friendly, perhaps even jolly.

Those reared within a Christian framework suddenly know the experiential basis for all the theological abstractions, catechisms, creeds, and doctrines. You recognize the Other as a shimmering alternating blend of two Persons: Jesus in the room with you and the First Person in the room with you and simultaneously everywhere. Paul's experience traveling to Damascus, were you to think of such a thing just then, would make perfect sense. So might Gabriel's Annunciation to Mary; you too would want to do anything that the Other wants of you, regardless of cost or effort.

Your soul feels *molten* in the wake of such an encounter. You feel supple in God's hands. You feel able to undertake whatever changes the experience invites you to.

Later, if you dare describe the event to others, their reactions fall along a predictable range: from twinkly-eyed, joyous recognition that someone else understands; to awakened yearning curiosity; to nervous insistence on cramming your report into their own dogmatic framework; to reserved, self-withholding congratulation; to concern for your mental health; and finally to open hostility and opposition.

Subsequently, the memory of the encounter serves you in several ways. The quality of the Presence draws you into frequent periods of silence in which you are attentive to the Other—prayer, in effect. Momentary flashes of the original sensations confirm that your present prayers or thoughts are congruent with it. Such flashes can occur at odd moments and in unexpected circumstances, alerting you to the thought, "This too must be holy ground," or "This must matter, this must be important." Recalling the experience helps you make choices: you choose whatever comports with the Presence, you choose against whatever feels inconsistent with it. Your dealings with others may or may not involve speaking of the Presence—but those dealings seek to convey its quality. And the occasions when you are with others who know the Presence are deeply fruitful and memorable.

I think something like that is what real spirituality is supposed to lead into and derive from. In general, terms like conversion, mystical experience, getting saved, getting born-again, getting Spirit-baptized, spiritual consolation, enlightenment, peak experiences, oceanic experiences, satori—are different expressions from various faith communities that refer to it.

You'd expect that such encounters would enrich life immeasurably. But that's not always the case. Sometimes such an encounter—or its wistful counterfeit—actually slows your personal development and complicates relationships with others. Those difficulties aren't always other people's fault. Often they result from what we permit to happen to us following such a breakthrough experience. A conversion can all too readily point you in a direction that's bad for you and bad for those around you. This often results from your allowing your molten self to get poured into somebody else's ice-tray. On the other hand, a conversion can also result in unambiguous personal growth and improve the lives of those upon whom yours impinges. It all depends on keeping the Main Thing the main thing.

THE SUBSTANCE

People who start out in the joyous molten state described above all too often wind up in religious bondage, bondage leaving them personally lifeless, their testimonies notwithstanding, and they often start behaving in ways toxic to others. Why does that happen? What are some alternative scripts? How could we arrange our faith communities to avoid that hardening?

Importantly, the difficulty inheres in the manner of apprehension more than what is apprehended. Conversion is usually good for us; where we go with it, what we do with it often is not. The mere fact of being "born-again" is no necessary certification. All brushes with God leave us molten. Then we harden. Virtually all hardened spiritual states are, in the long run, bad for us—and tedious for our neighbors. We urgently need to prefer the molten state to the hardened state. As I shall suggest shortly, that preference is not for sissies.

Religious bondage originates in deep strata of the human psyche, not simply from the group or party you belong to. It's not just something other people do to us. We carry the propensity for bondage into our conversions and out the far side. Religious bondage results in our loving God considerably less than we report—and refusing to face into that truth—and dreading or resenting God more than we admit. Much that passes for active religion is a series of ploys for keeping God at a safe distance.

There are mental factors in this bondage at the levels of hardware (the human brain) and software (temporal data). Our hardware does not work very well with our software—we think about objects in space with much more clarity than we think about processes in time, so we are impatient with our present states, not seeing them as points on a trajectory, striving in fruitless ways to alter or freeze them.

At the level of software, many of us don't know enough history to avoid proven mistakes in thinking about ourselves, others, and God. And we all too readily lose sight of the purpose of symbol and metaphor—so we literalize figures of speech, then construct grotesque worlds within which to house them. So in this discussion we'll often need to focus how we develop spiritually over time, the pitfalls we encounter when we draw on the Bible in wrong ways or on traditional theological categories. Religious bondage gets reinforced by defective, if orthodox, understandings of the Bible, approaches that squander more energy in their own maintenance than they leave for worship, service, or growth. And there are some conventional approaches to Jesus Christ which need re-examination if his ministry to us is to be unimpeded by religious bondages.

I think some of our standard spiritual classifications, whether from the Catholic traditions of spiritual direction or from conservative Evangelicalism and neo-Pentecostalism, get in our way: they often sound like static categories and types rather than developmental mileposts. So we'll need to find fresh language to describe old familiar religious phenomena, drawing on lots of anecdotes and observations from the behavioral sciences.

I insist that if people want to be religious at all, they do well to go the full distance into mysticism—since any energetic attempt at religion which falls short of real mysticism results in religious bondage. I say this because we fall so readily into sets of rules and laws for ourselves and for those around us, that our religious identity becomes the equivalent of a military uniform. Getting swept into the personal presence of God melts most of that away, and transforms the meaning of whatever rules manage to survive it.

Struggle accompanies the attempt to figure out what to do with a religious conversion. As I have pressed the project of understanding that struggle, some helpful conclusions have emerged. The problem has focused itself *as an alliance between energetic religion and the construction of a false self.* The false self begins to emerge as people refuse to face into the cognitive dissonance* generated by clutching our metaphors and figures of speech too tightly, by thinking they describe the way things really are. Anxiety to pin things down and keep them pinned replaces the initial eagerness to explore. All too readily, new converts assume the ways and manners of some new community rather than courageously exploring the divine invitation to develop parts of themselves that had previously languished. The voices of the faith community come to supplant the voice of the Other. Our vestigial dread of being absorbed by God impels us to collude with those voices. If you really aren't a "sunbeam," if that sort of imagery does not come to you naturally in other settings, then falling into asserting that "Jesus Wants You For A Sunbeam" is tantamount to saying Jesus wants you for a phony. Phoniness—even in the name of God—is bad for you.

Conversion puts us in a molten state. And in that molten state we easily—too easily—get poured into somebody else's mold, into

---

* This term will come up a lot. It refers to the tension we feel either when our behavior does not reflect our values or when two matters we hold for truths are in collision with each other. Cognitive dissonance is difficult to acknowledge and face into—we usually seek some plausible yet spurious way to pretend that there's really no problem.

the old project of self-justification. A hardened false self is what remains when the problem—the fear that your present self is not viable takes control of the solution—the Encounter with Abundant Love.

One who cultivates a religious false self is like a drowning man seizing an approaching lifeguard around the neck, hoping to stay afloat. He makes the solution part of the problem. He cannot yield himself to it. He must take control. A deeply converted person can float and perhaps eventually swim.

The tragedy of the alliance between religion and a false self is that no one seeks it consciously. To the contrary, we gravitate to the religious expressions that attracted us in the hope of discovering our real selves. But Baby Bear's bed, that felt "just right" to Goldilocks, turns out to belong to Procrustes.*

The remedy to the problem of religious bondage and our false religious self is a deeper conversion than most of us will allow, one that reaches the level of our deepest fears, that gets past our lust for self-justification, that overrides our self-deception, that flows outside the frame. That conversion must produce courage. We will need to shed our craving for approval and the terror of "knowing what we know" that rigidifies the religious mask. The problem is that as the Spirit plumbs the depths of our resistances, we must accompany her. That takes a lot of courage of a kind we usually don't practice. An exploration of the means to nourish the deeper conversion, which produces such fruit and the courage to stay with it, is the aim of this book—to remain constantly expectant in the face of the more that is to come.

Where We Are Going

In our time, Christians in Africa have walked to martyrdom singing a gentle chorus:

> We have another world in view, in view,
> We have another world in view.
> Our Savior has come to prepare us the way,
> We have another world in view.

---

* The legendary robber-innkeeper whose hospitality offered only one bed: if you were too tall for it, he lopped off your feet; if you were too short, he stretched you out to fit it....

Contemporary spirituality needs such roots as this, the ability to view another world from the vantage point of this one, content to stay patient when the terms of one do not fully translate into those of the other. Our doctrines, our rites, our manners, our teachings, our preachments can indicate the wonder of the Presence—but no combination of those can summon or contain it. If that patience leads us somewhat to distrust the self-absolutizing culture of whatever Christian community we enroll in, it can still be an affectionate distrust, based on a finally ineffable vision of splendor rather than on despair, relativism, or cynicism.

One of our higher spiritual longings is for a community united in adventurous celebrative exploration—in contrast to a crowd huddled together for warmth, self-assurance, and safety. Rigid dogmatic positions and groups—of any stripe—that coalesce around them betray a dearth of actual experience of God. Dogma properly serves as binoculars and microscope, not sunglasses, an instrument of perception, not of self-protection. To reappropriate our roots in the vision of God's merry, generous splendor, indicated to us in the same Bible from which so many saints drew it, reopens the gateway into the Promise. Oddly, a tough-minded apprehension of human reality clears our vision to see more clearly into the world to which God is drawing us. So the insistence that we heed Ernest Becker's psychoanalysis and Christian existentialism seriously, or Peter Berger's sociological critique of religious systems, or James Fowler's developmental matrix, or the Higher Criticism of the Bible is not a Trojan Horse betraying us into the hands of "secular humanists." It is the direction necessary for becoming Christian grown-ups. It is the possibility of becoming a real self, not a false self, capable of walking with fellow explorers into God's reality.

Let's have a look at how all that plays out.

TWO INCOMPATIBLE CONVERSIONS

A number of years ago a man I'll call George sat in my office weeping with rage. He was younger than he appeared, his youth fractured along with his family, costly sacrifices to his alcoholism. For the past several years he had been sober; after a long struggle and with much help from Alcoholics Anonymous and "God as he understood him," he had "come to Jesus by the scenic route," as he told me.

That was not what he wanted to discuss with me that day. Instead he needed to understand his deteriorating relationship with his 19 year-old-son (I'll call him Sam), a student at the university where I was a chaplain. The previous year, George reported that something had happened to the boy called being "born again," following which event Sam announced that he was "saved." Because George had received his sobriety back as a gift, he figured he knew a lot about being saved—but the boy meant something else, less palpable if more strident.

Sam's "Baptism in the Holy Spirit" followed shortly afterwards. He announced that he was "filled with the Spirit." That scared George initially—he had filled himself with a lot of spirits in his prime, but his son meant something different.

None of that was familiar for the boy's dad,* but he had tried to be a good sport about its importance to his son. He'd naturally expected that they would discover together some spiritual commonality, and in that hope he had been patient with Sam's new enthusiasm. Yet Sam's two-tiered conversion did not draw him closer to his dad, nor did it help him appreciate, or even comprehend, George's victory in maintaining his sobriety. Instead it licensed him constantly to criticize his father's chain-smoking and frequent profanity. As far as the boy was concerned, he and his dad belonged to different spiritual species, his own, if more recently created, by far the more highly evolved.

"I guess I don't mind God making my son a saint," George wept, "but did he have to make him a *bigot*?"

Notice something about this anecdote. The conflict took place between two people who in their different ways were passionately serious Christians. There was nothing lukewarm about either of them. Each was a "convert," having experienced a life-changing encounter with God. Each represented spiritual victory. Each understandably might have thought of himself—as their respective communities might also have encouraged them—as occupying a spiritual apex, as standing at the top of some spiritual hill. Yet each regarded the other as harmful—and behaved in ways hurtful to the other.

---

* For readers also unfamiliar with this terminology, there is a brief description of it in Appendix A.

Notice a subtler point: the trouble is not that one (George) is liberal while the other (Sam) is conservative. Dogmatism is not under patent to the Right Wing.

Now the answer to the dad's question—"Did God have to make him a bigot?"—then as now was of course "No." God's Holy Spirit does not manufacture bigots. We could argue that God loves bigots as much as God loves any other kind of sinner; that is not the same as identifying conversion with bigotry. Where we see bigotry, even in the name of God, we assume God does not yet fully reign.

Still the question is plausible. Any reflective reader knows what he was lamenting. Religious conversion had allowed one type of sullen youth to become another type of sullen youth. That is not what religion is supposed to do for you. That was not the promise implicit in his conversion experience.

We might also notice that little in George's own miraculous recovery equipped him to intuit the inner struggles of a young, late-adolescent male living with a grown-up, worldly adult, notwithstanding the man's being his father.

There was stuff rumbling around inside both of these religious converts that their conversions had not yet reached, as though something within them was holding them stuck—and using their respective religions to do it.

According to ancient records, the transformation evident in church folk drew Greco-Roman pagans to the church. "Behold these Christians, how they love each other!" was the report as it reaches us over the centuries. In those days, people saw Christians' manner of dealing with each other and with the outside community as a much-needed resource. The reports suggest that the church had found a way to protract the changed personal state people experienced post-conversion. That state persisted into the very gladiatorial arena. Paul's writings and those of the Johannine Community, especially Revelation, struggle with allowing God's Spirit to inhabit more and more of the converts' hearts over long stretches of time.

Yet that struggle was unfruitful as often as otherwise. It's a mistake to romanticize the early church as an ideal that we've lost sight of. The vaunting pride of James of Jerusalem reflected in Acts of the Apostles (and the subtle suggestion that James set Paul up to be arrested!) or the shrill resentments of the author of 2 and 3 John should set the record straight on that.* Most of the Epistles were written to address some problem of human cussedness you'd think the Spirit would help people transcend. If, as Augustine thought, there is such a thing as Original Sin, it's distributed pretty evenly across history.

RELIGIOUS BONDAGE

Many of us perceive and regret the cooling of enthusiasm. Most critiques of Christian behavior focus on the lukewarm, on the spectacle of people who acknowledge Christian identity without manifesting Christianity's excitement, its ethical teachings or its thought structures. It is easy to assume that the problem is that not enough people are Christians—and those who are Christians are insufficiently enthusiastic.

Yet enthusiasm itself is problematic. Some entries into energetic Christianity are subtly skewed in directions which, if intensified, will produce internal and social pathology rather than dispel it. A person freshly immersed in God's Presence is in a molten state that can cure into any number of rigid forms, some of which contain regrettable elements. The more "Christian" Sam becomes the worse it may get between him and his father. The more inculcated into "disease process" the dad gets, the wider the gap he'll perceive between himself and his son.

Many of us have been in the same shape as the father and son in the story, to the confusion of those around us. The undeclared message underlying most of my own reports to old friends after my Spirit-baptism was, "You no longer suit me in your present spiritual condition; you'd better change—as I have—or I will have less to do with you." Before my conversion, I was one kind of snob. Then I changed. I became another kind of snob. A curious way to recommend the gospel, is it not? No wonder that the world rejects, with annoyance, most attempts at evangelistic witnessing.

---

* I've sometimes tried to sit still for teachings in which the attractive pictures of the Jerusalem church in Acts 2–9 were brandished as a lost but recapturable desideratum. The teachers normally appear blandly ignorant of Luke's subtle point: the ecstasy of those days seduced them into taking their eye off the ball, enticing the Apostles to stay put rather than be itinerant missionaries, allowing the Council in Acts 15 to proceed without recourse to prayer or prophecy, finally leading to their sly disposal of the troublesome Paul.

The world has learned to expect hurt from such assaults. If my friends and family saw me getting more Christian on those terms they would not likely remark, "Look how serene he's becoming!" More likely, reflecting on my new smugness, my assurance of membership in a superior cognitive community, and my grabbing the moral high ground in every discussion, they would say, "He's getting worse."

The world is not the only victim. The no-longer-worldly convert catches many ricochets from her own gun. If she criticizes the world's behavior and attitudes, she then has to monitor her own carefully lest she slip into something equally objectionable. If he judges the world as licentious, he has to be careful about what sort of book people find in his possession, what music stations his Christian friends discover punched into his car radio, what movies he gets seen coming out of. Such is the anguish felt by religious converts seeking to stay consistent with their calling that we sometimes have the feeling we used to get when speaking to a Soviet Russian who knew someone was recording the conversation. Converts victimize themselves as well as others with the effort of having to look good. Being a red-hot convert does not guarantee freedom from bondages destructive to self and others.

Religious bondage takes forms that range from silly to quite serious indeed. It's not too lengthy a step from editing our own lives to editing others around us. Consider religious iconoclasm, for one example, an impulse characteristic of several periods of Christian history—especially the history of Christian missions. Iconoclasm in its true meaning is destroying the art, altars, artifacts, and literature of one's doctrinal enemies. It is no trivial matter. Any tourist who compares the color and gaiety of European cathedrals with the bleached-bone sterility of their English equivalents will sense the tragic destructiveness of this impulse, longing to see restored the many acres of irreplaceable stained glass and the statuary.*

Some American Christians are becoming shamefacedly aware of the irreparable damage missionaries inflicted upon Native American, Mexican, Latin American, and Polynesian cultures,

---

* The Puritans deliberately gutted most English cathedrals and churches, seeking thereby to eradicate what they viewed as the idolatry of Catholicism. They were deeply suspicious of beauty.

often unable or unwilling to recognize dynamic equivalents for the gospel in the artifacts, narratives, and rites they destroyed. Now you can sometimes identify various flaws in particular missionaries; but did you ever meet one who was lukewarm? Iconoclasm is not a sign of thoughtless or uncommitted people. It usually reflects passionate allegiance to God. Yet iconoclasm is far from the actual experience of the Presence described previously. All too quickly the enthusiast has kept the fervor, but forfeited the discernment, kept the energy but lost the aim.

A survey of cultural history leaves us with the impression that iconoclasm is nearly never the impulse of an emotionally healthy adult. We associate it with the Inquisition, Nazism, and Soviet censors. Yet iconoclasm remains a chronic element in Christian conversion.*

In our story, Sam became iconoclastic, a characteristic revealed when his father described his emptying his room of all rock music, posters, centerfolds, and other icons of teen culture.

An ancient account reports that the Caliph Omar (582–644), on entering Jerusalem with his Muslim troops, was guided through the Shrine of the Sepulcher by the local bishop. During the tour the hour for prayer arrived. The bishop respectfully invited him to use the Shrine as the site for his prayers and his servant brought his prayer rug and began to unroll it. Omar ordered the rug taken outside again and made his devotions under the sun. When asked his reason, he replied, "This site is sacred to the Christians; if it were reported that I had said my prayers here, it would become a Muslim site. To pray here would be an act of

---

* Iconoclasm is a way station on the road to outright religious persecution. It is said that the inscription at the grave of Torquemada, the Inquisitor, makes it clear that his life's purpose and sole desire was to serve and glorify Jesus Christ. It is chilling to consider that he and the stonecutter may have meant it. We would expect and hope that an energetic commitment to Jesus would produce a patient love for others. All too often it seems to unleash sadism. History tells us that pattern is not confined to aberrant exceptions. Luther's intemperate slatherings against Jews and peasants have proved deeply costly through subsequent centuries. Calvin found it an urgent doctrinal necessity to burn his wife's former suitor Servetus at the stake, causing the faggots to be wetted so as to protract his victim's misery. English spiritual leaders of all parties burned and beheaded their theological antagonists with dismal frequency. Yet who in Christian history has ever written of God's grace with such persuasiveness as have these?

theft." Try to recall an equivalent story told about a Christian.*

It is facile to assume that religious conversion most readily goes toxic among conservative Christian groups, who use biblical-sounding words like "conversion" more readily than the rest of us.+ To be sure, Evangelical Christians have exhibited destructive suspicion towards things artistic and cultural ever since the early days of Calvin's Geneva, the Calvinist Netherlands, Knox's Scotland, and Cromwell's England.♦ Until fairly recently, Catholics were required to check their reading and movie-going with official lists of approved materials. Present-day Southern Baptists aren't supposed to visit Disney parks or attend Disney movies.

More liberal Christians committed to a Social Gospel or Liberation Theology have our own canons—tedious, if unofficial, lists of products not to purchase, books not to be found with, expressions and pronouns not to employ. The impulse beneath such proscriptions often seems more connected with status anxiety than social ethics. Again the impulse to community formation and maintenance gets worked adversarially—and humorlessly.

I recall an episode in a society of liberal religious pacifists to which I belonged in the late '60s and early '70s. One of our leaders, a conspicuously handsome man, reported to us one evening—writhing in a paroxysm of embarrassed ambivalence—that someone had offered him a lucrative contract as a male model! In our cultural/political/religious dogmatism we heaped abuse on him for not spurning the offer instantly, accompanying

---

* If you cannot, let me tell you one. During a meeting of the World Council of Churches on Cyprus, three Southern Baptist observers were invited to the home of a Greek Orthodox priest for dinner. They naturally refused his offer of preprandial *ouzo*. Nor did they partake of the *retsina* he offered at dinner. Nor the *metaxa* following dinner. The flummoxed host in desperation passed around a box of cigars. One of the Baptists took a cigar, lit it, and struggled manfully to smoke it. Later in the homeward taxi his colleagues upbraided him for being a bad witness. He replied, "But *one* of us had to be Christian!"

+ Though more liberal religious groups exhibit restraint in discussing mystical conversions, private conversation demonstrates that the phenomenon is equally common in those circles. Over the course of three years with 55 seminary classmates of all theological hues, I discovered that each had at some point had some such encounter.

♦ These were deeply cultured, broadly educated people. I suspect they got their antipathy to the arts from Plato's *Republic* rather than the Bible.

that refusal with a diatribe against dehumanizing frivolity in the service of the establishmentarian consumerist ideology. The urgent task of raising the consciousness of others left no space for selling out even in small matters. Our passionate commitment to one view of social order rendered us incapable of discerning and sharing the delight of a friend who was about to get some mileage out of his looks.*

A prominent theological educator once let off a blast at me after I reported to him that I had "gone Pentecostal" in the face of a dramatic conversion experience. I paraphrase it here from unfaded memory:

> "Just when the churches have begun to uproot their authoritarianism, you people have reintroduced a sheep-like conformity that would make a Soviet commissar blush. Just when the churches have begun to forge the results of critical biblical scholarship into a deeper piety and a more radical service to the world, you people have reintroduced Fundamentalism. Back go women down into molds that suppress their talents for leadership and teaching. Back comes the naïve identification of cross and flag. Back comes the old distrust of physicians, lawyers, college professors, seminary professors, scientists—of anyone who wrestles with life's complexities in a disciplined way."

I naturally answered that it was not cultural bigotry that drew me to the community within which I had experienced "Spirit-Baptism." But the man had a point, did he not? Some of that really did describe my adopted community—and still does—as well as myself within it.

Each of us, even the "born again," has such a collection of episodes and observations that we understandably prefer to apply to those to the right or left of ourselves. Yet "the customer is always right," applies to more than commerce. If the world, the client group for evangelistic efforts, the intended target for religious conversion, objects to religious converts as lowbrow, anti-intellectual obscurantists, as intrusively unmannerly, if it

---

* He crept away from us later, took the contract, and made a stash of money. He now votes Republican.

describes us as "hung-up" or "repressed," it may have a point.*

Rarely and seemingly temporarily in any quarter of the church do you see truly Spirit-liberated people, radiant with godly self-acceptance, unselfconscious in worship, requiring neither self-control nor self-display, able to love the unlovable with energy and candor devoid of condescension, able to ignore their own preferment to the advantage of the disadvantaged. We hear the claim of inner freedom more than we see the reality. These liberated few are conspicuous if attractive exceptions—even in Charismatic or Evangelical gatherings where we claim such liberty as our distinguishing common possession.

Religious conversion appears to liberate us from one set of bondages only to make us susceptible to another. As far as I can tell, this difficulty afflicts Charismatics, Evangelicals, Catholics, and Social Activists alike as the fallout from our most intense spiritual commitments. Some force which was at work in us when we were still "dead in our sins" gets us. It is clearly more than old habits popping up, such as a bad temper or reading smutty magazines. A need to hold ourselves restricted, to indenture ourselves to someone else's pattern of acceptability, remains unchanged beneath a change of religious garb. Just as Sam did not lose his rebellious sullenness in

---

* A case in point concerning repression: My wife and I were once invited to observe a large international gathering of conservative Evangelicals in Nairobi, Kenya. On the third evening, the hotel produced an "Africa Night" for our entertainment. The gathering reacted to the different acts fairly comfortably—until an elaborate pattern of rhythmic thumping (iron spear-butts on the floor), jingling (bell-festooned anklets), rattling (bead necklaces), and throaty groans drew our collective gaze to the back of the banquet hall. A sinuous line of Maasai warrior dancers was weaving its way down towards the front. How can I describe that dance? Its physicality, its collegiality, its beauty, its wildness in restraint—its (dare I say "masculine") authority—took my breath away. I turned to my wife, Jean, saying, "Isn't this marvelous!" She whispered, "If you want to see something really strange, look around this room."

As I surveyed the banquet hall I was startled to realize that, other than Jean, myself, and the dancers, every person present sat frozen, immobile, moving only their eyes furtively from side to side to see if any were scrutinizing them for their reactions. They hardly breathed while the dancers were present. They appeared to think the dance was sexual. It was not all right for them to respond to it in any manner whatever. None dared be seen enjoying it. No nodding, no foot-tapping, certainly no smiles or applause.

Had I not known that it was the gospel that drew these people together from all parts of the world, I would have assumed they suffered from a soul-crippling illness.

spite of becoming a Jesus-freak, just as the dad did not move past his defensiveness once sober, all too few of us do much more than reupholster our former bondages when passing to the far side of conversion. This is more than the simple result of falling among bad companions—though that never helps.

Medical practitioners alert to psychosomatic aspects of physical illness speak of "syndrome shift," in which a patient apparently cured of one malady quickly gets another. It is as though "illness" remains present, seeking fresh expressions. Whatever that "illness" is, wherever it lurks, clearly no medicine, no matter how expensive, has yet soaked down to it. Maybe indeed the problem is not medical in the usual sense—though it can kill you just as dead.

We are learning that the same syndrome shift is readily evident in family systems. If a "good child" dies, another child reforms and attempts "goodness." When a "bad child" leaves home, a "good child" turns "bad." The roles are more stable than the players, the system sturdier than its constituents.

Something like "syndrome shift" is common in spiritual life. Released from "bondage to sin" we succumb to the "bondage of religion." The period of freedom and relief between the two bondages is often brief indeed.

A group of clergy was once expressing relief to our bishop that a vocal critic of an education program we promoted had become a shrill vocal supporter of it after grasping its purpose. "See how the man has changed!" a friend exclaimed. The bishop chuckled at us and remarked, "*He* hasn't changed; his point of view has."

So it is all too often with any sort of conversion. We change our software, but load it onto the old hardware. Our operating system still freezes the screen when we play Solitaire or Tetris; our hardware still rattles and smells hot.

I think this lingering bondage accounts for the despair just beneath the surface of the most ebullient Charismatic meeting—a setting I regularly haunt, this discussion notwithstanding. From clues like greetings prematurely cordial and intimate, laughter a little forced and a stiltedly religious vocabulary, a contrived pulpit-driven enthusiasm, you sense a suspicion among the participants that the emperor has not finished dressing. We hear testimonies that exaggerate the extent of visibly incomplete personal transformations, reporting joy with eyes still hollow, jaws and lips still tight. Such testimonies are a distinct genre with their own identi-fying narrative structure, a pre-formed matrix. Reporting partial-ly complete processes through that narrative structure, people get drawn into involuntary inauthenticity.

The problem is, such reports are partially true. The hope we responded to has not fully eluded us. Much in our lives has indeed changed. The Encounter was a fact and it truly recurs periodically. Spiritual conversion experiences really make a dif-ference. When we give our testimonies to the glory of God, with their glowing reports of victory in areas where we suffered defeat in God's conscious absence, we are not being untruthful—only incomplete. But the fact that we have no graceful way to qualify such reports accurately—it would not be understood, we sense—suggests that we are jammed in some sort of mold.

This mold affects our perceptions harmfully. Many religious models of what kinds of things can happen in our shared world do not embrace enough of our ordinary experience to be of reli-able service. Conservative groups tend to exaggerate the com-monalty between biblical times and our own with a strong prefer-ence for ancient categories over anything modern.*

For example—to pick on my own tribe again—some Charis-matics reject, on dogmatically blinkered principle, the notion that a Spirit-filled person can commit a deliberate sin. That notion will complicate your life with trouble you could have seen coming. Read the newspaper.

The same groups typically reject the notion that a "real Chris-tian" can suffer depression. Only brief observations should be suf-ficient to stretch that notion out somewhat, preferably in time to keep a depressed person from doubting her Christianity. Such maps of reality do not allow for the free discussion of the way things really are. Thus our religion, far from delivering us from sin or depression, encapsulates us in them with no hope of calling out to our fellows. That constitutes a caughtness just as pro-nounced as whatever bondage we slipped at conversion.

---

* One contemporary American Fundamentalist, Dr. Tim LaHaye, got so swept up in an ancient thought-world that he actually published a book recommend-ing the temperament-system of the ancient physician Galen as preferable to pre-sent-day psychology.

The author of the Epistle to the Hebrews complained,

> Therefore let us go on toward perfection, leaving behind the
> basic teaching about Christ, and not laying again the founda-
> tion: repentance from dead works and faith toward God,
> instruction about baptisms, laying on of hands, resurrection
> of the dead, and eternal judgment. (Hebrews 6:1–2)

He then proceeds to list some of the tedious fundamentals that he
was personally bored with. Yet at Charismatic conferences offering teaching to people who have "walked in the Spirit" for years,
seminars on the elementary topics are always the most crowded.
You have the sense that people are hoping to return to the beginning to repair a faulty foundation, hoping that a fresh beginning
will make it feel good again. The underlying impulse seems to be
anxiety of some sort.

To cross the aisle, it is common to find little tolerance for
wealth—its acquisition, its possession, its management, or its
enjoyment—among social activist Christians. I am talking about
admirable people—people whose sacrificial courage produced
our nation's racial integration, briefly (in the late '60s) cut the
American poverty rate in half, and who compelled the federal government to stop sending our soldiers to get killed in a war it
refused to explain truthfully. Yet, for all their sacrificial dedica-
tion, an important part of their map is missing, a sacrifice to some
pressure of self-restriction. They can only see contemporary economic phenomena through the lenses of class struggle, only critique or enjoy art in connection with its political content.

The claustrophobic effects of religious bondage may account
for the sometimes-spectacular failure of prominent ministries.
Occasionally leaders of Charismatic conferences share "holy gossip" in private, lamenting those of our number who have fallen
into marital disruption, substance abuse, or some other destructive pattern. Their tones, to their credit, more often reflect concerned bewilderment than schadenfreude; I am not talking about
hypocrites here but spiritual siblings. Any psychologically astute
listener readily recognizes the burnout and the agitated depression these reports describe. The apparent catastrophes seem to
have offered the victims the hidden benefit of rescuing them from
some life-smothering trap their religious success had constituted.
In more than one collapse of a prominent public ministry at
which I was a bystander, it has seemed that the "villain" at some

level could see no other way out of some claustrophobic caughtness, that the deep purpose of the "fall" seemed to be another
chance at freedom on different terms. Happily, sometimes it
works.

Happy descriptions of renewed lives obscure the likelihood
that religious bondage occurs more commonly than we like to
think. The happy descriptions mislead listeners by virtue of not
remaining current. A dramatic spiritual breakthrough becomes a
story we can dine out on. It may take us a while—perhaps a fresh
crisis—to recognize that our molten, God-yielded state has hardened into habit, into dogmatism, into moralism, eventually into
imposture—a false self. We come to talk about prayer more than
we pray. We consult with ministers in the projects more than we
practice ministry in the projects. The wave function has collapsed
into a particle without notice or resistance.

Should it be necessary to suggest that all of this misses God's
intention? Was not the gospel supposed to rescue us from such
traps? How has the gospel itself become a trap? None of that
accords with the promises of Scripture—promises of internal freedom, of joy, of mental clarity—that awakened hope in so many of
us. Nor does it resemble the hope awakened in us by the presence
of those authentic saints with which our lives are graced.

The fact that we are missing the target does not require that
we abandon the hope itself. The resistance a reader may have to
the discussion so far no doubt resembles the sadness I feel in writing it: how can it all wind up so wrong when it began so right? The
gift of hope bears within itself the conviction of its own validity; to
abandon it is to give up the farm. Is there any way to get beyond
what is clearly inauthentic and poisonous in religious conversion
without throwing away the pearl of great price?

Yes, there is. The solution is neither retreat from spiritual conversions nor persistence in phony patterns of religious expression.
It is rather to allow the Holy Spirit a deeper penetration in order
to remain molten. It is to follow the Spirit off our canvasses, to go
outside our own frame. It is what systems theorists call "second
order change." Second order change disrupts and opens the system. For example, a squirrel spinning the wheel in its cage faster
(first order change) does not find freedom; opening the gate
(second order change) does. Closer to home, it is analogous to
turning loose our death-grip on the wrist of our dentist so she can

care for us. By letting the Spirit lead us, we can reoccupy the position we enjoyed momentarily while immersed in the Presence. We can appropriate the courage to melt again and again.

Deeper conversion, fresh melting, in itself can be dangerous. What is to prevent a deeper penetration from being the simple escalation of an unacknowledged mistake, like speaking louder and faster to an uncomprehending foreigner?

We can pursue a deeper conversion safely if we are careful at the beginning to view our caughtness from a somewhat unfamiliar angle. That is, to deepen our conversions, to allow the ground in our souls wherein the bondage is moored to be softened requires that we understand the principle in each of us that *seeks* bondage.

That may strike some as a curious notion. Who seeks bondage? Surely we all seek to escape it. Yet it is worth considering that any persistent pattern in your life stays put in obedience to your own unconscious invitation. Our chronic burdens are not in fact punishments; they are invited guests. Our bondage will make sense to us more readily if we stop regarding ourselves as its victim and toy with the thought that we actually perpetrate it.

That bondage-seeking principle in each of us is our response to the knowledge that we're going to die.

I have never met a person who, upon first hearing that principal, acknowledged, "Yes, that's me all right; absolutely terrified of death!" Quite to the contrary, most will maintain truthfully that they are not particularly aware of dreading death. Sort of scared of actually dying one day, maybe—but being dead is no special problem.

Yet the best insights of the Bible and of the scientific study of humanity support its truth.

Consider Hebrews 2:14–15:

> Since, therefore, the children share flesh and blood, he himself likewise shared the same things, so that through death he might destroy the one who has the power of death, that is, the devil, and free those who all their lives were *held in slavery by the fear of death.* [Emphasis added]

It's folly to dismiss that observation on the basis of its demonology. It connects with a profound motif running through the Bible. The fear-of-death motif begins with Genesis 3:19 in which death is first perceived as our enemy. From that point on, virtually every instance of human sin serves the purpose of assuring the sinner's survival of death in either literal or symbolic form. One murders to enhance or maintain one's prestige, which entitles one to extended life. One steals in order to prosper and to prove one's superiority over the robbed. One lies in order to survive and excel. One commits adultery to prove one's superiority to another man, hence one's superior viability—or to get for oneself preferred progeny who will carry on one's line. One commits idolatry to secure a stronger or more immediate celestial patron(ess). Apostasy may be a means to prolong life. Isaiah accuses the drunkards of Judah:

> Therefore hear the word of the LORD, you scoffers who rule this people in Jerusalem. Because you have said, "We have made a covenant with death, and with Sheol we have an agreement; when the overwhelming scourge passes through it will not come to us; for we have made lies our refuge, and in falsehood we have taken shelter." (Isaiah 28:14–15)

Throughout the Old Testament, humanity's wish to defeat death underlies all human mischief.

ERNEST BECKER AND THE FEAR OF DEATH

So far, I have tried to substantiate the point about the fear of death being the power of bondage by using only a few of many biblical examples. The same point occurs also in the best secular psychological and philosophical writings. Truth normally transcends its sources.

Ernest Becker's books—his Pulitzer Prize-winning *Denial of Death* and his posthumous *Escape from Evil*—provide a detailed exegesis of that truth.*

Ernest Becker was a cultural anthropologist who struggled, eventually successfully, with a difficulty that bedeviled the human sciences: there was no uniform theory of personality that an anthropologist or behavioral scientist could confidently employ across cultural and historical boundaries. Theorists sensed the

---

* Any reader who knows Becker's late books will discern my debt to him on every page. I can wish for no more fruitful outcome of this effort than that his books might receive the attention from Christian readers they so richly merit.

tantalizing reality of "human nature," but it proved impossible to define or even describe. They could describe an Aleut and a Vermont Yankee; but there was no agreed-upon standard of comparison between them. What does a northwestern Native American potlatch have in common with, say, the Gulf War? Sharp minds had discerned but not delineated the connection. Beyond crude measurements of the average stress imposed by cultures on their inhabitants, there was no common agreement about what people in general were up to with all their fascinating customs, rituals, and beliefs. Physiology applies across cultures; until recently psychology had not.

Becker forged a theory of personality based upon our conscious and unconscious strivings in the face of death. Determine the symbology of death in a given culture, he predicted, and people's behavior will begin to make sense.

Becker joined his colleagues in rejecting orthodox Freudianism as the key to understanding human personality. Freud described the personalities of educated Viennese at the turn of the century, people who had little in common with, say, Maasai herdsfolk. Becker sensed that if Freud were not the solution, he still might be the catalyst for the solution. His consequent exploration of the dissenters from Freud's circle led him to read—and understand!—Otto Rank, a humanist psychoanalyst who had abandoned a pure Freudian position early on. Rank's writings pointed Becker to Søren Kierkegaard (1813–1855), a passionately devout Christian theologian. The result of Becker's encounter with Kierkegaard has been one of the truly fertile intellectual and spiritual achievements of recent years: a transcultural theory of humanity scientifically arrived at, consciously influenced by the deepest modern presentation of the Christian faith. Becker offers the reader a unified personality and social theory much deeper and more rigorous than the McPsych junk food we normally consume. If his offhand challenges to the church—which he sees, with Kierkegaard, as having betrayed her charter—are sterner than any we normally consider, the encouragement of a view of humanity consistent with the deepest strata of Christian thought should point us to nobler efforts.

The reader who dares this material—which requires courage rather than cleverness—will come away understanding the idolatry of religiousness in its various forms with the precision and dispassion which mature science allows, understanding how and why we rush so urgently into that idolatry. The corruption lurking beneath that urgency, masquerading as authentic piety, will not deceive Becker's reader again. It is difficult to imagine how you can readily recognize and understand the various religious expressions of idolatry afflicting the converted without a confrontation with Becker's analysis or something very like it.

Becker was a writer of immense personal charm. During his last illness, he gave a lengthy interview to theologian-journalist Sam Keen:

> Keen: As a philosopher you have thought as hard about death as anybody I know. And now as it were you are doing your empirical research.
> Becker: It only hurts when I laugh.[*]

Discovering his incisive tough-mindedness, his wry wit, his excitement with truth, and a quality of moral courage and personal decency will feel a bit like your first encounters with C.S. Lewis.

Though his books are scientific works, they read like Old Testament *midrash* commentary, forming a detailed description of human psychology deeply congruent with the Bible. Becker saw our knowledge that we are going to die and our inability steadily to manage that knowledge as the energy beneath most behaviors.

Becker selects quotes from others with generous humility. Here Becker discusses and quotes Gregory Zilboorg:

> Zilboorg points out that this fear [of death] is actually an expression of the instinct of self-preservation, which functions as a constant drive to maintain life and to master the dangers that threaten life:
>
> *Such constant expenditure of psychological energy on the business of preserving life would be impossible if the fear of death were not as constant. The very term "self-preservation" implies an effort against some force of disintegration; the affective aspect of this is fear, fear of death.*
>
> In other words, the fear of death must be present behind all our normal functioning, in order for the organism to be armed toward self-preservation.[+]

---

[*] Sam Keen, *Voices and Visions,* (New York: Harper and Row, 1974), 191.

[+] Ernest Becker, *Denial of Death,* (New York: Free Press, 1973), 17. Cited hereafter in text as *DD.*

The human being is the only animal consciously aware of its own impending death. This knowledge has to be managed lest it overwhelm and paralyze us. So we repress the knowledge of our mortality into unconsciousness and live as though forever. Repressing the fear does not make it inactive. Beneath the surface of conscious awareness, it influences and often controls our behavior, thoughts, and feelings:

> But the fear of death cannot be present constantly in one's mental functioning; else the organism could not function. Zilboorg continues:
>
> *If this fear were as constantly conscious, we should be unable to function normally. It must be properly repressed to keep us living with any modicum of comfort. We know very well that to repress means more than to put away and forget that which was put away and the place where we put it. It means also to maintain a constant psychological effort to keep the lid on and inwardly never to relax our watchfulness.* (DD, 17)

Most of human life, said Becker, is spent in keeping the awareness of death at bay, thrusting it onto others, and bargaining for more life:

> We don't want to admit that we are fundamentally dishonest about reality, that we do not really control our own lives. We don't want to admit that we do not stand alone, that we always rely on something that transcends us, some system of ideas and powers in which we are embedded and which support us. This power is not always obvious. It need not be overtly a god or an openly stronger person, but it can be the power of an all-absorbing activity, a passion, a dedication to a game, a way of life, that like a comfortable web keeps a person buoyed up and ignorant of himself, of the fact that he does not rest on his own center. (DD, 55)

We spend enormous energies proving to ourselves if not to others that we are worthy of life: "The child's character, his style of life, is his way of using the power of others, the support of the things and the ideas of his culture, to banish from his awareness the actual fact of his natural impotence." (DD, 54)

Becker recast many of Freud's salient points about sexuality into his analysis of our fear of death. For example, the so-called Oedipus Complex becomes the Oedipal Project, the object of which is no longer sexual. In the latter, the child struggles to gain the countersexual parent in order to be able to regenerate itself, to become, in Spinoza's term, the *causa sui*, the cause of itself, able to postpone death by self-reconception.

All that business about potty training turns out to be serious as well. But its real meaning has little to do with sex; the child is learning not to be overwhelmed with the discovery that his body *leaks*:

> This is the paradox: he is out of nature and hopelessly in it; he is dual, up in the stars, yet housed in a heart-pumping, breath-gasping body that once belonged to a fish and still carries the gill-marks to prove it. His body is a material fleshy casing that is alien to him in many ways—the strangest and most repugnant way being that it aches and bleeds and will decay and die. Man is literally split in two: he has an awareness of his own splendid uniqueness in that he sticks out of nature with a towering majesty, and yet he goes back into the ground a few feet in order blindly and dumbly to rot and disappear forever. . . . And when [children] try to master the body, pretend it isn't there, act "like a little man," the body suddenly overwhelms them, submerges them in vomit or excrement—and the child breaks down in desperate tears over his melted pretense at being a purely symbolic animal. (*DD*, 26, 28)

Reflect on the fact that there is no issue of fluid from your body that can be viewed in social comfort, whether that be blood, waste, sweat, semen, the menses, spit, pus, vomitus, or tears. The effluent, of whatever kind, is a harbinger of death. Witnessing a small child reacting to his first blood-dripping cut is enough to remove all doubt on that score. Such crying assumes a panicked tone never previously heard.

The repressed fear of death energizes our behavior, particularly behavior that we adopt to earn our own admiration, to enhance our sense of entitlement. The repressed fear of death shows up lurking beneath a welter of actions and feelings not otherwise connected.

Being (seen as) heroic proves our worthiness of life, our entitlement to immortality—if only in human memory. Embarrassment about our bodies is natural to creatures sliding deathward, making us vulnerable to the specious claims of quacks, cosmetic salesfolk, and fashion designers. Love affairs—or simple flirting—prove to us that we can still retail our waning attractiveness to others in exchange for material or symbolic benefits. Religious ritual links us to a deathless realm while furnishing a hero-system, something else to get good at. Political affiliation links us with the flow of progress, membership among right-thinking people who will surely fare better than the mob—especially after we take over.

We could go on and on. Becker taught us to see such activities as ways of bargaining for life, either here or in the hereafter. Where Freud saw sex, Becker peered deeper—and saw death.

Does that really describe me? asks the reader. Yes, replies Becker. If we walked about conscious of that fact all day, we would never get anything done, so the mechanism of repression comes to our rescue. We walk around unconsciously burdened with it, but not consciously immobilized. But the fear is never very far from the surface—as our fascination with death, sex, violence, crime, and disease readily demonstrate.

Becker himself died over two decades ago. I would be interested to hear his comments today on recent mobs of howling parents outside schools which accept children with AIDS, despite virtually conclusive evidence that children living close to each other for years at a time do not spread the disease to each other. The crash of an airliner routinely crowds other stories off the front page for days, often stories of wider social consequence. We have to ascertain how such a thing was allowed to happen. We have to find out who was at fault.

That still seems to leave a paradox. Perhaps the fear of death indeed lies beneath much of our behavior. But surely any kind of bondage is akin to death. Why would a death-avoiding creature indenture itself to anyone or to anything? The answer is not far to seek, for all of its depth. The constant, if repressed, fear of death makes us cautious. Ironically, to live too fully is to risk dying prematurely.

> [W]e have achieved a remarkably faithful understanding of what really bothers the child, how life is really too much for him, how he has to avoid the death that rumbles behind and beneath every carefree activity, that looks over his shoulder as he plays. The result is that we now know that the human animal is characterized by two great fears that other animals are protected from: the fear of life and the fear of death. (*DD*, 53)

So we live in the shelter of various culture-sanctioned structures of more powerful people. We transfer personal authority to persons and institutions we perceive as more powerful than ourselves. Becker brings it down with a single rifle shot: "Today we understand the dynamics of this long history of self-abasement: men need transference in order to be able to stand life."*

---

* Ernest Becker, *Escape from Evil* (New York: Free Press, 1975), 148. Cited hereafter in text as *EE*.

This need rests on the fact that in its unedited entirety, life is just too much to take:

> Most of us—by the time we leave childhood—have repressed our vision of the primary miraculousness of creation. We have closed it off, changed it, and no longer perceive the world as it is to raw experience.... We change these heavily emotional perceptions precisely because we need to move about in the world with some kind of equanimity, some kind of strength and directness; we can't keep gaping with our heart in our mouth, greedily sucking up with our eyes everything great and powerful that strikes us. The great boon of repression is that it makes it possible to live decisively in an overwhelmingly miraculous and incomprehensible world, a world so full of beauty, majesty and terror that if animals perceived it all they would be paralyzed to act. (*DD*, 50)

One of Becker's well-developed examples of self-sought bondage is our fascination with the leader, whose strength promises protection and sanction. Another is the relief of sheltering our mortality within the ranks of an apparently or symbolically immortal multitude.

Our energies flag. We cannot be Promethean heroes around the clock. Absorption by others is not the only form in which we face annihilation. Isolation is just as deadly. If we cannot merit an individual Karsch portrait on our own, getting into the second row of a group photo may have to do as well. Sensing the impossibility of meriting eternity by individual effort, we settle for identifying some group or movement, which seems to contain life-giving power. Agreeing to its terms, we nestle down into it, hoping to enter the pearly gates on its activity bus. That this group will tell us how to dress and joke, what to eat and drink, what to think and how to vote—all that is little enough to concede in view of the hoped-for benefits. Our bondages do not result only from others having enslaved us, as Marxists and revolutionaries would have it. They also result from little acts of self-indenture. We give up life in order to gain life. That may all seem demeaning, but as Becker reminds us: In matters of eternity, you take what you can get.

DEATH FEAR AND RELIGIOUS BONDAGE

If the fear of death in however unconscious or symbolic a form is the core of our bondage, then we can ask a simple question about our Christian conversions: Has my faith in Christ bracketed itself around—absorbed and transformed—my fear of death? Has Christ got down beneath it? Can I mean it when I recite "He descended into Hell..." in the Creed? Or has the fear of death wrapped itself around my faith? Have I clutched religion in desperation, transforming the gospel rather than being transformed by it, making Christianity something else I have to get good at in order to justify my life? In other words, am I using the Christian faith—or some party within it—as a Marxist uses the state or a socialite uses her club? Has it become a system of heroics? In the Reformation, the Protestants rightly rejected the Roman *extra ecclesiam nulla salus* ("outside the church nobody is saved") position; but it has been reintroduced in any number of forms consciously and unconsciously ever since. Life is only possible if the Junior League thinks my wife worthy of membership.

"Aha! You are talking about 'works-righteousness'!" cries the dogmatician. "Coming back under the Law!" intones the Bible teacher antiphonally. But knowing a word for it may not be a sufficient amulet against it.

Consider what happens all too often when you are first converted—at least among Charismatics. A sinner stumbles up the church steps. Out rush the ushers to drag him inside. We hear his confession—if we are a group that believes in such—exorcise his demons, get him saved through the Blood, get his memories healed, baptize him in the Spirit. In a short time he has been through a Christian car wash. In the course of all that, a subtle message is delivered. "You can tell you are saved and holy because you resemble these saved and holy people. These people all speak, dress, behave, joke, and worship in a uniform way. You are most deeply 'in Christ,' hence saved, when you are doing what they are doing, pretty much the way they are doing it." Nobody teaches that overtly. Nobody has to. The Moonies go to too much trouble with all that sensory deprivation brainwashing they are said to do. People fall into that uniformity automatically and always will in order to gain the sense of safety it affords. As Becker points out, we repress and indenture ourselves; we carry unfreedom within us. And we will do so until we allow the Spirit of God to do something deeper in us than most of us permit.

Perhaps the reader will protest, "Oh come on! Every society does something like that. All groups develop common styles of humor, dress, and speech. Isn't the fact that we Charismatics (read also Evangelicals, Catholics, Jungians, etc.) have our own a *good* thing, a sign that we have been changed?" The necessary response is that such a protest rests on a superficial, indeed dangerously innocent, grasp of the *religious* purpose of style. Styles in any society are mechanisms of salvation, tribal garb proving our entitlement to protection, whether we are describing the Mao jacket of the Chinese, the absurdities that emerge each year from Paris and New York, or the Heritage U.S.A. makeover.

If this seems to be taking a frivolity too seriously, reflect on how you felt on occasions when you arrived at a party incorrectly dressed. Recall being a teenager who had not yet bought clothing of the right style and label. We are not talking about a triviality. We are describing totemic markings that identify us as meriting—or not meriting—the protection of the group from the forces of death, even if death takes the apparently harmless forms of gossip or exclusion, every bit as surely as do the tattoos of tribesfolk in the Amazonian rain forests.

Christian conversion promises freedom from bondage to sin and idolatry. Yet more than one reader will be able to identify episodes of such terror since conversion, even in church gatherings. And when you are being twisted by the effort to avoid the anxiety that can overwhelm you when you have overdressed for a casual party—or when you have inadvertently cussed at a prayer meeting—you are momentarily not enjoying the fruits of sanctification.

To understand more deeply our bondage to the fear of death and how it counterfeits real spiritual freedom we need to learn an unfamiliar distinction. To that we turn next.

CHAPTER TWO
_____

RELIGION VERSUS RIGHTEOUSNESS

F or all of our concentration on Ernest Becker and others, spiritual talk is not merely veiled psychological talk, though there are overlaps between the territory each investigates. The perception that spiritual matters possess their own categorical integrity distinct from other modes of knowing pervades the writings of many generations of thinkers from all traditions down to the present time.

Off and on we will examine what light some behavioral scientists can shed upon our understanding of spiritual matters. I am confident that spirituality does not shrink in that light. It grows.

ANTONYMS POSING AS SYNONYMS

Let us examine some resources within the framework of the Christian faith itself to gain handles on toxic religious enthusiasm, using spiritual terminology to discuss spiritual matters. Specifically, Christian vocabulary offers us two essential concepts shaped to help us understand spiritual matters. Imprecise use of those concepts blocks understanding.

I suggest an important distinction between *religion*—or frequently in this discussion "religiousness"—and *righteousness*. That distinction will help us apprehend the appetite for spiritual bondage that survives spiritual conversion.

Though the words—*religion* and *righteousness*—often occur together, they properly refer to different conditions. The difference between them has to do with the presence or absence of an overriding personal affection. That is, religiousness pertains to bargaining, getting in a position from which you can offer God something in order to incur divine gratitude. Righteousness, on the other hand, refers to a loving relationship.

"RELIGION"

The word religion is akin to the word "ligament." It comes from a Latin word, *ligare*, which refers to something binding an individual. In Latin literature outside the Bible the word has a connotation of fussiness, what would later be called "scrupulosity." Interestingly, Old Testament Hebrew offers no word for religion, so there is no OT entry for it in your concordance. There are a few references to religion in English versions of the New Testament; they translate a couple of unrelated terms that refer to strict adherence to rules of correct worship.

Ernest Becker alerted us to the anthropologists' understanding of religion: *religion* is a human-crafted technology to influence divinity with. It is whatever you and I do in order to get God to love us more than God would be spontaneously inclined to do— or, failing that, to dislike us a little less. Religious procedures have to be done just right—you do not want to give the gods an excuse not to heed you. Religious communities worry about their purity a lot because they think God worries about it. Just as Jonah's presence in the ship almost cost his shipmates their lives, so the presence of impure or immoral persons in the group may bring bad luck.*

As I shall be using the terms, religion refers to a relationship with God that ranges from commercial to manipulative. Even

---

* Numbers 16 makes that point, as do any number of other passages in the latter four books of the Pentateuch. Jesus seems to overturn it in Matthew 13:24-30, 36-50.

where affectionate language occurs in a religious relationship it serves the same purpose (and merits the same suspicion) as the suddenly affectionate talk of a canny child angling for favors from a lonely parent.

"RIGHTEOUSNESS"

The word righteousness cannot be so easily grasped by etymology. Its definition emerges as we study the contexts in the Old and New Testaments within which it occurs. E.R. Achtemeier, in her splendid article, "Righteousness in the Old Testament," explains righteousness thus:

> Righteousness as it is understood in the OT is a thoroughly Hebraic concept, foreign to the Western mind and at variance with the common understanding of the term. The failure to comprehend its meaning is perhaps most responsible for the view of OT religion as "legalistic" and as far removed from the graciousness of the NT . . . .
>
> The concept deserves some negative definitions. In the OT it is not behavior in accordance with an ethical, legal, psychological, religious, or spiritual norm. It is not conduct, which is dictated by either divine or human nature, no matter how undefiled. It is not action appropriate to the attainment of a specific goal. It is not an impartial ministry to one's fellow men. It is not equivalent to giving every man his just due.
>
> Rather, righteousness is in the OT the fulfillment of the demands of a relationship, whether that relationship be with men or with God. Each man is set within a multitude of relationships: king with people, judge with complainants, priests with worshippers, common man with family, tribesman with community, community with resident alien and poor, all with God. And each of these relationships brings with it specific demands, the fulfillment of which constitutes righteousness. The demands may differ from relationship to relationship; righteousness in one situation may be unrighteousness in another. Further, there is no norm of righteousness outside the relationship itself. When God or man fulfills the condition imposed upon him by a relationship, he is, in OT terms, righteous. [*]

---

[*] George Butterick, ed., *The Interpreter's Dictionary of the Bible*, vol. 4 (Nashville: Abington Press, 1962) 80.

Righteousness is the preferable relationship. It connotes a relationship characterized by mutual delight in one another, by loyalty, esteem, durability, and indissoluble commitment. Where religious language occurs in a setting of righteousness, it serves the same purpose as a husband carefully and secretly making arrangements for his wife's delight on their wedding anniversary. Right behavior is the currency of a righteous relationship. It is never its substance.

Most of us grew up linguistically thinking that religion and righteousness are closely associated, almost synonyms of each other. We grew up thinking that being religious was a good thing, something we ought to be even if we rarely felt like it. Righteousness was supposed to mean compliance with religion's requirements.

In actual fact, they are often antonyms; they are each other's opposites.

"What is the chief end of Man?" asked the *Shorter Westminster Catechism.* "To serve God and to enjoy Him forever." The note of *enjoying* God seems strange (particularly in a Puritan document). Is it really correct to expect actually to enjoy God? The risk of *lèse majesté* looms in many of our minds. Yet the enjoyment of God is a wonderfully ancient sensibility in the Judeo-Christian tradition. A couple of examples, selected from a host of others:

> O taste and see that the LORD is good; happy are those who take refuge in him. (Ps. 34:8)

> You show me the path of life. In your presence there is fullness of joy; in your right hand are pleasures forevermore. (Ps. 16:11)

Enjoyment of God is central and essential if we are to get past the bondages previously described.

LOVE AND PLEASURE

In his wonderful little book *Pleasure,* Alexander Lowen carefully distinguished authentic pleasure from hedonistic escapade. At one point, in a discussion of "love," he made a breathtaking observation. He described love as *the experience or anticipation of pleasure in a relationship.* Period. If it gets too remote from actual pleasure, he went on to say, any talk of love devolves into mere moralizing. And moralizing, he wryly observed, never really did anybody any good.*

The theological implications of Lowen's little description seem limitless. When I say, "I love God," the question, "Do I actually *enjoy* God?" confronts me. "If I actually enjoy God, how often do I do so? For how long a time?" When I assert, "God loves me," a life-changing question confronts me: "Do I dare suppose that God *enjoys* me?" Not "Does God put up with me?" Not "Does God forgive me?" No—"Does God enjoy me? Does God like me? Does God delight in me?" We are approaching a relationship with God that does not put us in bondage, that releases our courage, generosity, and merriness. Such a relationship gets past religion. It gets past reciprocity of favors, past commercialism. It contains some of the qualities of the encounter with the Presence described in the previous chapter. It is what the two Testaments mean by righteousness.

In a famous passage in his *Confessions*—famous because it occurs on the first page, before the reader has laid the book aside—St. Augustine reminded God and, presumably, his eavesdropping reader: "You have created us so that our hearts find no rest until they rest in You."

Augustine was saying that there is a "God-shaped hole" in each of us that God alone will fully fit. What he might have gone on to say, had he dared, was that there is in the very heart of God a "*you*-shaped hole." God's own joy will remain unfulfilled until you occupy your intended place in that fellowship. I enjoy thinking of that as a place on God's lap that my fundament alone will fit.

Without exception, all our abstract theological words—all the terms ending in -*tion*—if tracked back to their linguistic roots, suddenly spring to vivid life. They are vivid figures of speech, images and metaphors that suggest or retrieve the quality of otherwise ineffable experiences. They convey action, they correspond to palpable

---

* No doubt some readers will wish to argue with that strenuously. Love is vastly more than pleasure, we want to protest. But take care. As Lowen was well aware, a lot of love-talk describes relational horrors, which are vastly less than pleasure. In fact, that little description of love turns out to be deeply empowering. For a start, it reduces the scope of your Christmas card list—or it flushes out dubious motives if you send the cards anyway. More seriously, it empowers us to love difficult people, by inventing ways to make our reciprocal dealings pleasurable. A few experiments along those lines will produce delightful results.

things, and they point to real experiences of real people whose lives are really changed for good. They are anything but abstract. "Redemption" refers to buying something back from a pawnbroker's shelf—or manumitting a slave into freedom. "Salvation" means to make somebody *salvus*, which in our terms would be something like "healthy" or "okay." "Justification" suggests being restored to a state in which the police really *are* your friends. *Adoption* means you're not only suddenly a member of the family but you're in the will. These are bright pictures lurking beneath familiar abstractions.

On the wall of a Sunday school classroom in my parish there is a mural painted by an artist in the congregation. It depicts Jesus and the little children in Mark 10:13–16:

> People were bringing little children to him in order that he might touch them; and the disciples spoke sternly to them. But when Jesus saw this, he was indignant and said to them, "Let the little children come to me; do not stop them; for it is to such as these that the kingdom of God belongs. Truly I tell you, whoever does not receive the kingdom of God as a little child will never enter it." And he took them up in his arms, laid his hands on them, and blessed them.

Jesus is seated in a meadow and kids are climbing all over him. All races, sexes, and sizes mingle in the frolic. One child holds a dripping chocolate ice cream cone; it bedribbles and stains his white robe but has no effect on our Lord's wide grin. I asked the painter how that ice-cream cone had occurred to her. "Well, actually it was the *second* picture I saw," she replied. "The first was a kid with a runny nose!"

I often suggest to people who are working hard at being religious that they spend an hour or so in front of that mural until they recover the point of life in God.

An anecdote may reinforce the point about reciprocal enjoyment with God. I once underwent training in door-to-door evangelism—an activity I hesitate to recommend—through a well-renowned procedure involving the posing of two questions in the course of a fraudulent "survey of religious attitudes":

1. "If you were to die tonight, do you know for certain that you would go to heaven?"

Any reply other than an unqualified "yes" provokes an unsolicited rote presentation of "the Gospel." If the mark says, "Yes," you ask,

2. "If you were to die tonight and stand before God and he were to ask you, 'Why should I let you into my heaven?' how would you answer?"

Any reply involving personal merits, deserving, or hopes triggers a memorized spiel about the Substitutionary Atonement.

One hot night a college student, naked to the waist, beer in hand, answered an evangelism team's knock. To the first question, he blithely replied, "Hell, yes!" much to the puzzled consternation of the abstemious team.

"Well, er. . . . *Why* should he let you into heaven?" they blurted.

"Because it wouldn't be heaven without me!" he beamed.

Beneath the flippancy of that reply gleamed a kernel of splendid orthodoxy—though it was lost on the evangelists. A note of mutual enjoyment between God and humanity echoes in it.

You can have a theology; you can even cultivate your "spirituality" as a sort of personal refinement. But if your faith does not embrace, arise from, and in turn result in such images then your house is built on the sands of the narcissistic intellect, not on the rock of the God-impregnated heart.*

Our images properly suggest an affectionate relationship with God. You might imagine God in a state outside of space/time speaking forth the syllable which will call you into individual

---

* To stay with this point a bit longer, let's quit being embarrassed at the use of anthropomorphic imagery for God. To conceive of God in human terms is not intellectually unrefined, in supposed contrast to terms like "The Divine," "the Inner Light," or even "The Force." When we try to refine theological vocabularies past human metaphors for God we succeed only in reducing God's personhood. Human persons are surely not the largest objects in the universe, nor are we spatially central to it—but we are easily the most *complex* systems of which we have present knowledge. The simplest reader is a more wonderful arrangement of neural circuitry than the very solar system itself or any single object in it. To liken God to the highest developed thing we know—ourselves—is not an insult to God or to our intellectual capacities. Doubtless there is vastly more to God than resemblance to ourselves. But there is not any less to God than that resemblance.

I am fully sympathetic to the women's voices that speak for all of us about the impoverishing effect of exclusively masculine language for God. Spiritual exercises which reappropriate God's femininity are always fruitful—often in breathtaking ways. They cast reproach on our ill health when we flee such exercise. They invite healing at the hands of One who is maternal and nurturing. I also suggest that the real grammatical gender to be avoided in theological parlance is neither the masculine nor the feminine—it is the neuter. Either or both of the former are preferable to the latter.

being, the secret name that expresses your perfected identity, that beckons you into courageous development, that name which you will first know consciously when Jesus hands you a small white stone with that name upon it. (Rev. 2:17) You might conceive of God's joy—indeed God's glee—as God whispers your name eternally within the Godhead. Indeed, if God were to stop that whisper for an instant, you would cease utterly to be. Your very being at this moment is the fruit of God's delight. And your life's highest purpose and deepest joy is to experience and agree with that delight.

The urging that we find sensory metaphors for fellowship with God has an important object. It will help us peel the camouflage of theological abstraction off the central concept of Christian life. If metaphor does not convey you into God's presence, it is not working as advertised.*

Aldous Huxley once wrote:

> God isn't the son of memory: He's the Son of Immediate Experience. You can't worship a spirit in spirit unless you do it now. Wallowing in the past may be good literature. As wisdom it's hopeless. Time Regained is Paradise Lost, and Time Lost is Paradise Regained. Let the dead bury their dead.[+]

The experience is more important than the metaphors it generates. And experience is here and now. It may not matter that I got saved in 1957.

That concept that needs its theologically abstract metaphorical camouflage peeled off is righteousness. It is the very point of everything in our life towards God and in God's life towards us.

Righteousness is enjoying fellowship with God the First Person of the Trinitarian metaphor. The operant word is *enjoying*. Our images of the warm presence of God, of God's delight in having us there, of climbing safely into that lap—even with ice-cream cones dripping or noses running—will serve us now. Indeed they must serve us, because no amount of correct doctrine can exorcise the

---

* Later in the discussion we'll repeatedly warn ourselves against the tendency to literalize metaphors, to presume that they tell us more about reality than they intend to.

+ Aldus Huxley, *The Genius and the Goddess*, quoted in D.H.Fischer, *Historians' Fallacies: Toward a Logic of Historical Thought* (New York: Harper Torchbooks, 1970), 308.

associations the word righteousness normally conjures up. Do we not think of the adult equivalents of the hall monitors we despised as school children? Or the little girl Saki wrote about with the goodness medal who was "terribly good, indeed *horribly* good"? Do we not think of *self*-righteousness, of the smug self-satisfaction of one who has never felt our temptations with compelling force? Perhaps some are free of such notions. But we likely confuse righteousness with moralism.

A word study through both Testaments will help, should the reader consult a concordance and undertake it. Those who are unprepared will be startled by a passage in Genesis 38:1–26:

> Judah married Shua and went in to her. She conceived and bore a son; and he named him Er. Again she conceived and bore a son whom she named Onan. Yet again she bore a son, and she named him Shelah....
>
> Judah took a wife for Er his firstborn; her name was Tamar. But Er was wicked and the LORD put him to death. Then Judah said to Onan, "Go in to your brother's wife and perform the duty of a brother-in-law to her; raise up offspring for your brother." But Onan spilled his semen on the ground whenever he went in to his brother's wife, so that he would not give offspring to his brother. The LORD put him to death also. Then Judah said to Tamar, "Remain a widow until my son Shelah grows up" — for he feared that he too would die, like his brothers. When Tamar was told, "Your father-in-law is going up to Timnah to shear his sheep," she put on a veil and sat down on the road. She saw that Shelah was grown up, yet she had not been given to him in marriage. When Judah saw her, he thought her to be a prostitute, for she had covered her face. He went over to her and said, "Come, let me come in to you." She said, "What will you give me, that you may come in to me?" He answered, "I will send you a kid from the flock." And she said, "Only if you give me a pledge, until you send it." He said, "What pledge shall I give you?" She replied, "Your signet and your cord, and the staff that is in your hand." So he gave them to her, and went in to her, and she conceived by him. About three months later Judah was told, "Your daughter-in-law Tamar is pregnant as a result of whoredom." Judah said, "Let her be burned." She sent word to her father-in-law, "It was the owner of these who made me pregnant. Take note, please, whose these are, the signet and the cord and the staff." Then Judah acknowledged them and said, "She is more in the right[eous] than I, since I did not give her to my son Shelah." [Edited for brevity.]

That chapter is rarely read in church for reasons that may be apparent. The startling occurrence of the term shows that righteousness does not mean behavior that passes certain moral standards. It is rather a state of integrity, of *shalomah*, between persons that produces affectionate appropriate behavior. Righteousness is primarily a relational term; only by extension does it describe behavior.

Let a metaphor display that difference. I have received hospitality in several other cultures where the table manners differ widely from those I learned (and practice) in America. These exotic etiquettes have included:

- leaving both hands on the table at all times in central Europe;
- using the fork with my left hand in England;
- using chopsticks;
- spitting bone and gristle onto the tablecloth;
- audibly slurping soup to convey enjoyment;
- boisterously burping after the meal to express satisfaction;
- eating all manner of things with the bare right hand without recourse to a napkin.

In several of those settings, my ignorance and daintiness has made my "bad" table manners conspicuous to all. And yet deep delight with my hosts, hostesses, and table companions made it all somehow okay. In contrast to those meals there have been any number of formal dinners in my own country that I have attended at gunpoint, occasions at which no amount of pushing the soupspoon or grace with a finger bowl has disguised my boredom and discomfort. In the former instances, I was "righteous"—in table terms—because I was lovingly related to the company. In the latter instances I was merely "religious."

Righteousness, correctly understood as fellowship with God, is the chief object of human life. It is also God's loveliest gift to us. If you bring your ice-cream cone up on God's lap, you do so by invitation.

Some may protest, "But why don't you drop your ice-cream cone—or blow your nose—before crawling all over God?" And the reply is that if God must wait until my sensibilities are refined enough to prefer God's company to the taste of chocolate, that wait will be lengthy. That delay is a condition God can bear better than I can. So in charming mercy God breaks the stalemate, beckoning to me, dirty face and all.

That understanding of righteousness helps us see the uselessness—indeed the silliness—of many questions that get asked in a typical religious gathering. Questions like, "Have you been saved?" "Have you been Spirit-baptized?" and "Have you spoken in tongues?"* provide little useful information about one's present spiritual condition.

As a teenager, Karl Marx—a baptized Christian of Jewish descent—wrote an acceptable essay on "Salvation through Christ Alone," though it is bad manners to mention it to a Marxist. As a teenager Nietzsche wrote Christian poetry almost erotic in its warmth. Stalin was a divinity student for a time, thus belonging to a population whose salvation rate is sometimes presumed to exceed the average. Hitler was for a long time the darling of the German churches, Protestant and Catholic alike. Each of these souls, a couple of them monsters, at some point would have passed any test for being "saved" we would normally think to impose.

No, there is only one really revealing diagnostic question you can ask yourself to diagnose your spiritual condition: "Am I presently enjoying fellowship with God the Father?" Any answer other than an unqualified, "Yes, indeed," reveals that the Spirit has work to do in you to which it is your task to submit in as relaxed and trusting a manner as possible.

RIGHTEOUSNESS AND MYSTICISM

Another way to put that question is, "Does my relationship with God ever involve mystical states?"

The word mysticism conjures up many images and feelings. But simply put, *mysticism* centers on an experiential encounter with the Ultimate Reality that cannot express itself fully in language or images. All the great religious systems of the world produce some form of mysticism. The best mystics can do is to say, "It was sort of like...but not really." Or, "This too is Thou—yet this too

---

* I used to joke, "Have you 'groaned in the Spirit with groans too deep for utterance?'" (Rom. 8:26) When I went to my first Primal Scream workshop that quit being funny.

is *not* Thou." Or smile at us with infuriating blandness, knowing we have to go after our own experience. At the level of mysticism, virtually everything this book views critically evaporates. Mysticism replaces religion. Experiential encounter with the Presence is the substantial foundation of righteousness.

Karen Armstrong's *A History of God* lucidly discusses the mystical elements in the so-called "Religions of the Book," Judaism, Christianity, and Islam. The reports she cites display fascinating parallel elements with each other. Indeed, it is not always possible without her help to tell what tradition produced what experience, so close is their resemblance. The resemblances lead us to suspect that the same force is at work in each, a force that does not originate in the human mind. That force is both personal and deeply loving.

Common elements are also detectable in the mysticisms of various Asian religions. Hinduism, Buddhism, and Taoism come immediately to mind. Though the personal and loving elements are not always named as such, the sense of peace and serenity towards the universe and compassion towards others is always conspicuous.

In mysticism, the soul has immersed itself in the dread of God and come through that dread into a fresh, lovely state. Like many pains and fears, those that God produces—if embraced bravely— emerge more often as portals than as obstacles.

Yet mysticism is not a common element in the Main Street form of any religious system. It could be. It should be. In God's good time it shall be. But it is not so at present.

When religion remains submystical its primary purpose is control. It seeks to control God's response to us. It seeks to control the individual self, in order to gain reward or evade punishment. It seeks to govern the behavior of others to assure social harmony. Why else would the Las Vegas Chamber of Commerce boast that their city contains more churches than casinos?

By now some readers may be feeling uncomfortable, maybe even angry. A new understanding of righteousness goes against our previous understanding. Old notions die hard. We sense that there should be more to righteousness. Our aggrieved sense of fairness wants it to be harder. Those who labored from the first should earn eleven times the wages of those who appeared just before the factory whistle blew. That is, after all, why God made labor unions.

Yet consider the mischief that very sense has caused us. Wanting fairness pushes us perilously close to religiousness.

For example, during my door-to-door evangelism training, some aspects of our religious condition became clear to me for the first time. A Charismatic friend and I attended the course together. We were the only two Episcopalians among about a hundred conservative pastors, being trained twelve hours a day for a week. At the end of the first day, my friend and I both had headaches, though fatigue did not seem the cause. At the end of the second day, sour stomachs accompanied the headaches. Stress, surely; but what kind? In spite of background differences—or perhaps because of them—our hosts had received us with warm hospitality. We prayed together, asking God to show us the cause of our discomfort.

"You are lonely," God replied.

"Lonely?—in this warm gathering?"

"Yes," God answered, "you are lonely for *me*."

Then it hit us. Several times each day we would pause for "worship"—hymns, readings, brief prayers, maybe a short pep talk by a leader. In all the hymns about heaven none addressed God directly. For every ten hymns about "salvation" or "the Blood," maybe one concerned Jesus as a person rather than a hematological Gestalt; again, none addressed him directly. The song-texts focused on our own spiritual status—"washed in the Blood," "saved," "bound for Glory"—but made no reference to nor offered any participation in the presence or companionship of God amongst us at the moment. The unmistakable quality of the encounter with the Presence was nowhere apparent. Our intercessions summoned God's blessing upon inflexible plans of prayerless human contrivance. We were immersed in God's work but we were never in God's direct company either in silence or in vocal praise.

As hours in small groups allowed mutual trust to grow, the other pastors timorously and heartrendingly confessed their spiritual aridity. They complained of Bible pages grown opaque, of mechanical prayers that could penetrate no ceiling. And all through it, these dear fellows kept protesting, "Of course, I *know* I'm saved; I went forward in 1958 at the Crusade."

My friend and I attempted to represent Spirit-baptism as a resource, as it was and remains in our lives. Unhappily, our colleagues' doctrinal commitments permitted only polite disregard. In this case Dispensationalism was the commitment, a belief that God has stopped the sort of dealings with us that the New Testament describes.* But doctrinal adhesions from further left on the theological spectrum can produce similar effects.

At the time, the only point I took from the experience was that it is probably better to be a Charismatic than a conservative Evangelical, since my friend and I seemed in better shape than they were. But since that time I have found the same caughtness in Charismatic circles. I have found it among liberal exponents of the Higher Criticism. Indeed I have succumbed to it personally: the same anxiety, the same depression with spiritual as well as emotional roots, the same thrashing around trying to improve my inner state, eventually the same torpor.

Again, that condition should be called *religion*, using the word an anthropologist does: to refer to a human-crafted technology designed to furnish some control in dealings with divinity. Recall that religion basically has always meant the scrupulous performance of rites and actions by which you feel bound. In discussing religious ritual among primitive peoples Ernest Becker says:

> ....the universal human ambition [is] the achievement of prosperity—the good life. To satisfy this craving, only man could create that most powerful concept which has both made him heroic and brought him utter tragedy—the invention and practice of ritual, which is first and foremost a technique for promoting the good life and averting evil. Let us not rush over these words: ritual is *a technique for giving life*. The thing is momentous: throughout vast ages of prehistory mankind imagined that it could *control life!*. . . Man controls nature by whatever he can invent, and primitive man invented the ritual altar and the magical paraphernalia to make it work. (*EE*, 6,9)

---

* Dispensationalism is a way of interpreting the Bible which grew up among the Plymouth Brethren in the nineteenth century under John Nelson Darby (1800–1882), entered and influenced conservative Evangelicalism through the Scofield Bible (1909), and stimulated the foundation of the ultra-conservative Dallas Theological Seminary by L.S. Chafer from whence these brethren at the training conference likely took it in. "Classical" Dispensationalism divides God's dealings with the world into seven dispensations: Gen. 1:28 *Innocence*; Gen. 3:7 *Conscience or moral responsibility*; Gen. 8:15 *Human Government*; Gen. 12:1 *Promise*; Ex. 19:1 *Law*; Acts 2:1 *Church*; Rev. 20:4 *Kingdom*. Its appeal to present-day Fundamentalists is its insistence that Jesus and the Prophets before him performed authentic miracles, which can be uncritically believed today, without the disappointed expectation of that seventh dispensation. It lets them be Fundamentalist without going the distance to Pentecostalism.

RELIGION AND THE SIN OF PRIDE

Becker's tongue is in his cheek as he writes those words, know-ing as he does how little has changed in human nature and behav-ior through the ages. As Becker knew, he and the anthropologists offer us an anthropological description of what theologians call the Sin of Pride, the first and most deadly of the Seven.

By pride, theologians do not mean vanity or conceit. If conceit is all that is wrong with you, the solution is simply to wait.* No, real pride is deeper, more sinister. It is death-fear-driven self-reliance in opposition to trusting God. Pride—not doubt—is the opposite of faith. It impels us to rely upon self rather than upon God. Pride is something a person without faith—here understood as *reliance* on God rather than mere belief in God's existence—does with the fear of death. Our knowledge that we are headed for the grave compels us to do everything we can to look after ourselves, to get our needs met, to avoid danger, to prolong our ride on the merry-go-round. *That* franticness—not mere preening or boasting—is what pride is really all about. And although our condition of sep-arateness from God makes it all seem necessary, we still seek to implicate God in it. Only we now do so no longer as God's chil-dren, beloved members of God's household; we now see ourselves as clients and customers of God, maneuvering for the best deal in a religious free market without government oversight.

My family and I once lived in a remote African village among people who are, to our way of thinking, primitive. We would awak-en each day and go to sleep at night hearing drums. Each night, just before she pulled a screen woven out of sticks and briars across the doorway to her sleeping hut, a neighbor-woman poured a small bowl of milk and set it on the ground just outside. She thought the gods liked milk; they would come for it. Was it not gone in the morning? Their presence would keep away harm-ful spirits and animals. She put it outside because she had more sense than to want *any* spirits—bad or good—too close to the house, too close for comfort, disturbing sleep with nightmares.

Now let's have a good laugh at that. You and I, being smarter, know the gods' diet doesn't include milk. We know what the gods

---

* The writer was once thin, with a full head of hair. The passage of time solves the problem of vanity handily.

really like: people who do not go to R-rated or NC-17-rated movies, who do not cuss, who do not smoke or drink or dance or gamble or listen to rock'n'roll or go to Disneyworld. People who raise polite children, who do not divorce, who pray in tongues, who vote right (should we capitalize that?). People who hold sound views on the Atonement, who use gender-inclusive pronouns.

In my denomination, the Episcopal Church, we waged a far more bitter internecine war over a revision of the hoary Book of Common Prayer 1928 with which we worshiped, than we ever considered waging over something like, say, civil rights.* The Book of Common Prayer is a religious object for us. It is essential for keeping God at a convenient middle-distance, not so far away that God neglects us, nor so close as to overwhelm us. Decorously performing the same rituals inflexibly from week to week conveys to us a wan sense of entitlement to God's approval and a consequent hope of well-being. Anyone who thinks Episcopalians are not really religious should watch us when some hapless assistant-minister tampers with our accustomed order of worship during the parish pastor's vacation. Unbelievable rage can greet any unannounced departure from these rites or any humanly avoidable accident during their performance. The relative inflexibility of the rites protects us from any fresh expression of God's presence—or indeed of God's absence. In some gatherings with co-religionists, I have the notion that we grip our prayer books as kitchen potholders, shielding our hands against the fire of God.

There are *righteous* ways to use the Prayer Book or any such manual, uses which frame the affections of cold hearts in a God-ward posture. But what I have just described is every bit as religious, is indeed as pagan, as the animist woman with her milk bowl.

Groups that eschew set liturgies are in more jeopardy than are those groups that use them, since leadership and personal participation must be offered without the express permission to do so that a liturgy provides. The liturgyless Charismatic prayer-and-praise meeting quickly becomes as inflexible as solemn High Mass—to protect the leaders and members from invidious overexposure.

---

* At the time, many Episcopalians were sufficiently wealthy and educated that we didn't rub shoulders with minority groups much. Racial justice was not much of a religious issue in our denomination, since it provoked few questions about our social status, our entitlement to survival.

Often that inflexibility does not keep leaders as safe as formal ordination does. In either event, the underlying religious purpose—the pursuit of well-being—is much the same.

I often get to witness the tension felt when visitors from some other Charismatic group just as super-charged as our own begin to exercise their gifts within my congregation. The very hair stands up on the back of otherwise hospitable necks. On some occasions I think I hear an audible reptilian hiss. More than one dear soul will have to struggle with the temptation to correct the visitors in some way, to teach them proper order, or at least to find some reason to assure ourselves internally that their ways have less voltage than ours. At issue in this smiling mortal combat is the need to be assured that our controls work better than theirs do, that the gods will heed us more than them, that our spiritual technology is superior to theirs. What could be more helpful than offering ours to them?

I recall, for example, a visitor who dropped in on a seminar on the ministry of healing I was conducting. She explained in the most sisterly tones that in *their* fellowship they did not actually *touch* people when praying for them because people find it distracting. You could almost hear animal growls in the throats of my loyal parishioners as this interloper tried to teach *their* preacher. My own smile probably looked pretty plastic. Interestingly, we eventually came to agree with her—but it took a while.

Becker offers a chilling observation from Alan Harrington's *The Immortalist*:

> Cruelty can arise from the aesthetic outrage we sometimes feel in the presence of strange individuals who seem to be making out all right. . . . Have they found some secret passage to eternal life? It can't be. If those weird individuals with beards and funny hats are acceptable, then what about my claim to superiority? Can someone like that be my equal in God's eyes? Does he, that one, dare to hope to live forever too—and perhaps crowd me out? I don't like it. All I know is, if he's right I'm wrong. So different and funny looking. I think he's trying to fool the gods with his sly ways. Let's show him up. He's not very strong. For a start, see what he'll do when I poke him. (*EE*, 113)

People go through internal monologues like that in church, just as they do on the subway, at cocktail parties, or at football stadiums. In a worship gathering, to allow ourselves to be taught by a "strange" person is to confess the *need* for teaching, that our system is incomplete, perhaps leaky.

What a far cry that is from simply relaxing in God's lap. And how welcome that fellowship is in contrast to all our striving for control. We need to know God's presence simply for itself, for ourselves, for the enjoyment of the fellowship between us. Only in God's lap is there safety—even from other believers.

RELIGION AND THE DREAD OF GOD

There are obstacles between us and that Presence and those obstacles lie within ourselves. They find no place in God and surprisingly few are in the world. William Blake expressed this dilemma in *Songs of Innocence*:

> We are put on this earth for a little space
> That we may learn to bear the beams of Love.

Blake's insight suggests that the joy of righteousness, of fellowship with God, has to overcome some reluctance in us, a low tolerance for joy.

Mark Twain poked fun at the Christians of his day in *Letters From the Earth* by having the not-yet-fallen Lucifer write to Gabriel describing how Americans think of heaven. He says we think heaven is a perpetual worship service, yet we can scarcely endure more than one weekly hour of worship on earth. Men rarely sing on earth and attend concerts only at uxorious gunpoint, yet we imagine we shall spend twenty-four hours a day in heaven, singing the same chorus over and over—and enjoy it. We think we shall play upon harps, yet we never practice.

Mark Twain was, of course, joking, though we might get a bit more serious with the same question. If, as C.S. Lewis maintained, joy is the very serious work of heaven, why do we not cultivate a taste for it? Who of us seriously cultivates joy—*joy*, mind you, not mere escapade—right now? What is the longest stretch of uninterrupted joy you have endured recently, Reader, before you did something stupid to mess it up? It seems that the same principal within us that seeks bondage also seeks unhappiness, as though that were a more natural, more tolerable, condition. It is as though the condition of unhappiness conferred on us more safety, more control. NASA is said to fire rockets into the heavens deliberately off-course, since gross corrections in direction are easier to make accurately than more subtle corrections; it may be that in seeking unhappiness we seek a similar control.

Really, it bears thinking about. If heaven is not simply an eternal *absence* of certain things—such as tears, or adulterous, murderous, or thieving impulses—but is in fact a Presence of One whose company makes us fully joyful, should we not begin to build up tolerance for that company right now? Should we not cultivate comfort with the emotional state that it must produce?

Some readers will be missing the presence of Jesus in all this talk of the First Person and ourselves. In a later chapter our Lord indeed must and will be central. The present stress on the First Person of the Godhead is important, however, in view of all the many devout Christians who are not comfortable with that Person. We must recall again and again that the primary object of Jesus' work with us is to bring us into a restored relationship with the First Person.* As long as the First Person does not attract us, Jesus' work with us remains incomplete. The very terror or repulsion many feel for the First Person means that a human being is unlikely to have a tolerable relationship with God without the ministry and mediation of Jesus. Yet let us never forget that Jesus came to draw us to himself in order that he might deliver us safely to our Creator. The *First Person* is the final destination of our lives by the very decree of the Trinity.

Let us examine now our resistance to that destination, the obstacle to our tolerance for the Presence of the First Person.

---

* All classical Christian liturgies address the *First* Person, not the Second or Third, however much the latter's assistance is invoked.

CHAPTER THREE

THE DREAD OF GOD

A normal human being does not like God. The natural sub-mystical experience of divinity is not pleasant. Indeed it is sinister. Much loose talk over the centuries about "loving God" masks that truth, but the truth remains. The gap between what God is and what we are immobilizes us.

Religion is a technology for coercing God. Our best expressions of love do not tolerate coercion as an ingredient. So religion has little to do with loving God. The lack of love for God among religious people should not surprise us.

However fervently a Muslim obeys God—the word "Islam" means "obedience" —few observers discover recognizable love in the matter. It is more than their native decorum that prevents Muslims from strolling around humming "Have You Talked to the Man Upstairs?" or "He Walks With Me And He Talks With Me." They typically do not view Allah as friendly.*

T.E. Lawrence, who profoundly admired Muslims and their

---

* Knowing that helps us interpret the despair lurking behind the vehement gaze of the Ayatollah Khoumeni's photos. He served a god who required his obedience but did not love him—as far as he knew at the time.

faith, refers to this absence in *The Seven Pillars of Wisdom*.* He describes coming upon an old Arab by a watering place; the man was singing of his and Allah's love for each other. When Lawrence inquired about the man, it did not surprise him to learn that the man's neighbors thought him crazy. The normal Muslim, Lawrence remarked, does not include love among his religious affections.

Thomas Merton's *Asian Journals* record his meetings with the cream of Buddhism, whose meditations had penetrated very deeply into reality's structure. But the Buddhism practiced on the streets of Rangoon is a system for attracting good luck. An astrologer tells you at which of the thousands of shrines surrounding the Shwe Dagon Pagoda you should pour out your cups of water. Zen it ain't.

In *Christian Faith and Natural Science*, Karl Heim relates an event that occurred in Indonesia in the second decade of the twentieth century:

> On the island of Nias during the time of the first world war, an awakening, which is still remembered in Indonesia as the unforgettable "great repentance", was brought about when an entire primitive people, a savage tribe of head hunters, quite suddenly and in a manner which even today cannot be explained at all in terms of the psychology of religion, were filled with the idea which is expressed in this psalm [Psalm 139:7–12] so that the entire life of this tribal community was radically transformed. These simple people could express their new discovery only in spatial terms, by saying, "God is but a hand's breadth above me," that is to say, He is everywhere immediately and inescapably near. And yet, of course, they were still at the stage of the primitive space-picture, the stage at which there is still only this one observable three-dimensional space. And so, just like the Psalmist in his prayer, they could still only say: While we are in this observable space, there exists incomprehensibly a power which is entirely unobservable and which nevertheless, just like this three-dimensional space, surrounds us on all sides, "behind and before", and accompanies us wherever we may go. We cannot continue in the presence of this power if we do not order our whole life anew. Many of these naïve people were impelled by this profoundly disturbing idea to take refuge in the primeval forest, in the fond hope that in the dense woods they might escape from the power which everywhere, no matter where they walked or stood, was but a hand's breadth above them.

---

* T.E. Lawrence, *The Seven Pillars of Wisdom* (New York: Dell Publishing Co. Inc., 1962), 356–358.

But all in vain. There too they ran into the arms of this uncanny power. And so a good many of them hanged themselves in the forest, in the hope that perhaps in this way they would elude this invisible reality which seemed to be accompanying them wherever they might go.*

GOD-DREAD AMONG CHRISTIANS

That example may seem far-fetched and exotic, inapplicable to us. So consider a similar example that happened to a friend of mine here in the United States. As an undergraduate, he was walking alone one spring night across a broad lawn on campus. Without warning he found himself in "a pocket of the Presence of God," much as a cyclist might pedal into a patch of cool air. It stunned him. When he awoke, he found himself flat on the ground trying to bury his head in a bucket-sized hole he had clawed through the turf. He was weeping and shouting over and over, "I'm sorry, I'm sorry, I'm so sorry!"

"What had you *done*, man?" I asked when he told me the story a year later.

"Nothing," he replied, "it wasn't that kind of thing."

"Do you think it was, well, *Jesus* you bumped into?" I asked.

Without a trace of irreverence, he replied, "No, man, it was the damn *Father!*"

We could go on and on with illustrations of the natural antipathy other people feel towards God. What concerns us more is its presence in ourselves. Is that true of us, after so many centuries of the Christian proclamation? Of course it is. You and I know any number of Christian people who do not trust the affection God is supposed to have for them.+

So far this discussion has deliberately focused on the First Person of the Godhead, whom tradition calls "the Father," after Jesus' example. Is every reader comfortable with the Father? The feminist theologians have protested the masculinist distortion in confining

---

* Karl Heim, *Christian Faith and Natural Science* (New York: Harper Torchbooks, 1953), 166–167.

+ You can test your own comfort with God by asking yourself how comfortable you are asking God for personal favors, praying for yourself. Catalogue all the theological and moral objections that well up within to forestall such an attempt. Now ask yourself what that is really about.

the parenthood of God to the male progenitor. Christian feminist clinicians have alerted us to the horror we are likely to superimpose on the First Person if we project onto God the templates of our flawed human fathers.*

No pastor can number the devout counselees who, for all their energetic church-work, secretly dread God and do not think God likes them. In most of us, the work of the Son and the Spirit is incomplete, however conspicuous, because the First Person is neither real nor comfortable to us. This antipathy underlies and fortifies our religiousness—and thrusts away the righteousness God extends to us.

Judgment and the Loss of Identity

What is frightening about God is comparable to what is frightening about marriage: the fear of judgment. My wife loves, honors, and esteems me in more ways than I can count. The difficulty in being married to her is that those qualities of mine she loves, honors, and esteems do not necessarily coincide with the list of qualities I want her to admire—qualities which, as it happens, I do not possess to any noticeable extent. She arrived at her perception of me largely without my help, and she sometimes does not welcome my editing it. So to take her seriously and live on emotionally intimate terms with her costs me the self-image I try to craft. To live with her is to live with judgment. Deeply loving, generous, favorable, appreciative judgment, to be sure; but I remain largely helpless in the face of it. To pay attention to Jean is to risk a part of my identity—at least my notion of it.

We can confront no greater fear than the loss of the sense of self, of the accuracy and consistency of our identity. Insofar as the mind experiences any change as loss, that fear underlies the resistance to even an improved self-perception, as every counselor knows all too well. When the familiar contours of your self begin to shift, when you have to see yourself in an unaccustomed light—even if more favorable—you can experience physical nausea and faintness. You feel the emotions accompanying the onset of madness.

---

* I am in agreement with those warnings. That agreement, to my way of thinking, justifies the awkward language of these discussions, using "God" both as a proper name and as a pronoun in order to avoid constrictive gender specificity.

The threat of death is at work here. That is how powerfully a changed self-perception can operate.

Does that not partially account for the failure of the average marriage to rise above a low plateau of familiarity? The fear of madness blocks access to the higher road. Friendships and acquaintanceships contain distancing mechanisms that offer relief when we have come too close to one another. We get "too busy" after a period of identity-threatening intimacy. It takes a day or so to return phone calls and maybe a week or so to arrange lunch. But marriage does not allow us that elasticity. Marriage is rigged to drive us "mad," to compel us to that death-to-self that a changed self-perception always constitutes—and thus to drive us through madness into sainthood. We pay close attention to our mates at the risk of our lives as we understand them. That is why marriage is a sacramental metaphor for Christ's dealing with all of us. That is—John Calvin to the contrary*—its connection with the Cross.

Now in marriage you take your time. The changes Jean has wrought in my self-image have occurred over the course of three decades. In contrast, the in-breaking presence of God threatens to accomplish in an instant—or less—what marriage takes years to do. When God speaks my name, my "Who art Thou, Lord?" is a dodge, a delaying tactic. Not only do I know who it is—as did Saul of Tarsus, we suspect—but, worse, I know for the first time who I am.

Does God read fiction? I don't know. Shakespeare is likely in Heaven, but it may be that Hamlet, Othello, and Lear are not. They are not God's creatures; they are Shakespeare's. You cannot take it with you.

How does that affect us? Gravely, considering that each of our lives is self-contrived fiction. My personal history is largely fictitious, even though I do not consciously pad or otherwise falsify my résumé. My more-than-normally truthful family still has an official version of all sorts of events. There is an official version of why Auntie did not marry the salesman, why Sis' marriage really failed, what the real trouble is with young Herbie. Family gatherings normally include periods of intense rehearsal of clan lore. We need to make sure everybody has it straight so that nobody will put out a different version. I add to that official version all my own ego-serving distortions, everything I have exaggerated, repressed,

---

* Calvin demoted all formerly sacramental actions from their status if he could not detect in them a connection with the Cross. One wonders if he ever had supper with his wife.

and fabricated. Then God says my name. For a moment the fiction all falls away and I am no longer my own creature. I am someone altogether different, though appallingly recognizable. The mere thought chills the blood.

Brain-washers and torturers have known all this for years. They take away the prisoners' clothing, shave their heads and mustaches, place them in unfamiliar settings, shout intimate details of their lives at them. The prisoners become putty.*

That experience, appalling to contemplate, lies at the core of our dealings with God. Why do we experience God as sinister? We fear judgment. No wonder we fear God, dislike God, and coerce God with our pathetic religiousness. Make no mistake—God's presence is judgment. And how are we to know that God's severest judgment is friendlier to us than our own most lavish self-flattery?

PROTECTIVE COLORING

We can export a helpful schema from our kitchens for understanding this process, referring to the common practice of making cookies or biscuits. Think of the model of a cookie cutter pressed into rolled-out dough. The dough is amoeboid in form; in contrast the cutter has distinct contours. We might picture it thus:

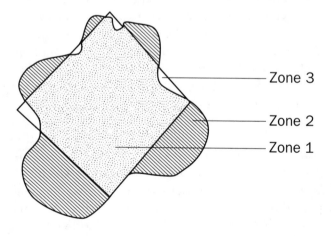

Zone 3

Zone 2

Zone 1

---

* One of modern literature's most chilling descriptions of such a collapse is the arrest of Major Innokenty in Soltzhenitzen's *The First Circle*.

Notice three zones in the diagram. Zone 1 (dotted) shows the unproblematic overlap of pattern and substance, of rolled dough to cutter. Zone 2 (striped) is the problematic substance that does not fit into the pattern, the dough outside the cutter. Zone 3 (blank) is also problematic: here the pattern imposes requirements, but the substance does not stretch into them; there is no dough where the cutter wants cookie to be.

Think of the dough as the person with her complete created inventory. The pattern is the "Law": good manners, family expectations, cultural norms, whatever those around us agree we have to be. Some part of every person does, in fact, correspond to the pattern. The culture, for example, sometimes punishes overt adultery and insists that people refrain from it. If your mate is more charming than the competition, you will find that law both easy to keep and a helpful protection against those who chose mates less wisely. If the culture insists that you enjoy learning, and you happen to be a bookworm, you will enjoy that norm.

Zone 2, the parts of us outside the pattern, is more difficult. For example, what do we do with those aspects of our sexual awareness stimulated outside our marriages? It may not even be agreeable for us to admit that we ever feel such things. What is an accountant to do with rage at a client? What is a soldier to do with a love for opera? Typically we hide and perhaps repress those aspects of our creation that do not fit within the pattern.

Zone 3 hurts too. Our surroundings impose requirements we cannot meet. What does a resident of Pittsburgh do if he finds football unintelligible? How shall a *nouvelle-riche* behave in the *raffiné* social setting into which her crisp new money propels her? Normally you find ways to fake it, to compensate, to camouflage the lack. We must not think of this as unnecessary. It feels as though our very lives depend upon the ruse, upon making our amoeboid selves fit the form.* Because each of our identities inevitably include zones 2 and 3, we live with a sense of imposture, in constant fear of exposure.

---

* Dr. Walter Brueggemann once told me that he noticed a pattern in his Old Testament students. Those who were at home with a view of themselves that contained contradictions, tensions, undeveloped capacities, experienced no difficulty studying the Bible critically, exploring its seams and internal tensions. Those who insisted on seeing themselves as fully worked out and self-consistent find modern critical approaches to the Bible intolerable.

Becker suggested that we handle such tensions by "repression"; we may not be able to live decisively if we are constantly aware of such fears, so we contrive not to stay conscious of them. An authentic relationship with God must entail "unrepression," as Becker again suggested. Exposure of the lies we retail to ourselves and others is a preliminary operation of God's judgment.

The problem of a dangerously imperfect identity and the dread of getting insight into it—the terror of unrepression—hit me forcibly years ago in the setting of Human Relations Training in T-Groups.* There used to be an exercise in T-groups called "The Lifeboat Exercise." Twelve people must imagine themselves crowded into a 10-seat lifeboat, uncertain of rescue. They must arrive at solutions to the problems posed by the situation. They would most frequently settle on the equivalent of human sacrifice, voluntary or involuntary. People would "go overboard," based on various criteria of personal worth or the lack of it. Eventually T-group trainers everywhere quit the game owing to the difficulty they met getting the players unstuck from their roles. Participants routinely displayed strong reactions of rage, guilt, and depression, occasionally at psychotic levels. The latter sometimes resulted in trips to the emergency room.

Why should a mere training exercise exert such power? It is a close metaphor for actual human life, that's why. One can get much insight into one's repressed personality structure—into the core of one's religiousness—by asking, "What am I doing to keep the others from throwing me out of the lifeboat?" Some of us keep beautiful (or at least cute), so the others would miss us too much to part with us. Some of us stay mousy and inconsequential, so that the others, looking for victims, won't even notice us. Some of us learn to manipulate the rest, getting the group to victimize

---

* T-group training is a method for learning to read the unexpressed dynamics of small groups by spending many hours in a "laboratory" group. A T-group possesses no designated leaders, no declared behavioral standards, and no manifest agenda, all to allow members to watch—and feel—how they emerge. As the group thrashes around to fill those vacuums, trained (sadistic?) observers called "trainers" lob gnomic observations into the circle, challenging the members to take stock of what they're doing and what effects their behavior produces. Laboratory training in human relations is a very difficult means indeed for gaining essential insights and skills. T-groups tend to be quite tense.

others. Some of us are too mean to mess with.* Others are so visibly troubled, in pain all the time over something or other, that the rest of us would just hate to add to it. Identify your own strategies—but, bless your heart!—stay in the boat.

That exercise as a metaphor exposes our religiousness because it shows us what we are doing to coerce Fate, to keep control of our lives, to keep death at bay. Extending the discussion back to its beginning, what is wrong with most of what passes for Christian spirituality, including any hyphenated variety such as Charismatic- or Evangelical- or Jungian- or Liberation- spirituality, is that, no matter how joyfully it begins, it devolves into another way of staying in the boat.

Whatever spirituality we embrace becomes something else to get good at, to become better at it than one's fellows. The joy of learning parts of the Bible by heart becomes pride in knowing more than the others. The joy of engagement and solidarity with the oppressed becomes a means of favorable self-comparison with others who're doubtless more callous or chicken-hearted. The thrill of learning to read the Bible critically devolves into a needle with which to burst the balloons of others. The fear of being tossed from the boat has reappeared in subtler guise right here in church. We do not venture to discover that we can, in Christ's company, walk on the water into which the others would cast us.

Beneath many a Christian grin lies a death's head; that smile is a rictus. It masks the anxious knowledge that being "spiritual" is a competitive blood sport. Spirituality gets exercised either by striving for individual excellence or by melting within a superior community that extends the promise of life.

The bitterness we feel towards those who leave our gatherings, abandoning our teachings and procedures in favor of some other, should show us that a matter of life and death is at issue. "If she leaves, am I a chump for remaining? Does he know something that I don't? Surely there is something the matter with them. I always did feel sort of funny around both of them, now that I think about it. Let 'em go."

Our fear of death then, in all its symbolic forms, has formed brackets around our conversions—even our Spirit-baptisms. At

---

* The writer is a warm and loving priest; the others would be far too grateful to throw me overboard. Believe me. Please.

moments when the fear of death has bracketed our dealings with God, a mystical connection is not available. So we struggle hard, making sure of our religious styles and antipathies, of what books to read, of which opinions to eschew. And we struggle to evade our sense that all is not right. In effect we avoid our mounting cognitive dissonance. We feel so little actual righteousness, so little joyful fellowship with the First Person. At the moment that one is worrying about all that, one is far from God's lap. And yet, the very thought of God's presence makes such trains of thought momentarily shameful, then hilarious in the next instant as God hugs us to the divine breast.

For God looms above all as its judge. God is the enemy of our paganism, our inner Canaanite, precisely because God is our friend. In the best of his Unspoken Sermons, entitled "The Consuming Fire," George MacDonald describes the rebellious people of the Exodus in the following terms:

> While men take part *with* their sins, while they feel as if, separated from their sins, they would no longer be themselves, how can they understand that the lightening word is a Saviour—that word which pierces to the dividing between the man and the evil, which will slay the sin and give life to the sinner? Can it be any comfort to them to be told that God loves them so that he will burn them clean? Can the cleansing of the fire appear to them anything beyond what it must always, more or less, be—a process of torture? They do not want to be clean and they cannot bear to be tortured. Can they do other, or can we desire that they should do other, than fear God, even with the fear of the wicked, until they learn to love him with the love of the holy? To them Mt. Sinai is crowned with the sign of vengeance. And is not God ready to do unto them even as they fear, though with a feeling and a different end from any which they are capable of supposing? He is against sin: in so far as, and while, they and sin are one, he is against them—against their desires, their aims, their fears and their hopes; and thus he is altogether and always *for them.*[*]

If you and I take any of that religiousness into ourselves, if we identify ourselves with it, if we say of any of it, "This is me," then God must to that extent seem our personal enemy.

That is why people do not like God very much. We cannot have God's presence without God's judgment because God is

---

[*] George MacDonald, "The Consuming Fire," in Rolland Hein, ed., *George MacDonald: Creation in Christ* (Wheaton, Illinois: Harold Shaw Publishers, 1976), 72.

truth itself. And we do not yet know the kindness, the friendliness, or the necessity of God's judgment.

Should not Jesus make that clear to us? Indeed he should and shall. But corruptions in our apprehensions of Jesus slow his work in us. And we need to discuss two additional matters before approaching the person and work of Jesus.

The first matter focuses on overcoming our difficulty in taking development over time into account in our thinking. We absolutize various metaphors, doctrines, and customs religiously, indeed idolatrously, because we do not understand them as periodic markers in the process of spiritual growth. From that discussion we need to take a hard look at how we use the Bible. Typical use of the Bible in recent centuries has made it into a religious object *par excellence*, as close to absolute as anything under heaven can be allowed to be. And, as we shall see, our absolutizing of the Bible is not a response to any quality it manifests, indeed it blinds us to its best characteristics. Before we use the Bible to fund our views of Jesus, we need to clean up our use of it. Then we can more safely explore what the Bible says about him.

CHAPTER FOUR

GROWING VERSUS GROWN

A German psychologist, Dietrich Dörner, got interested in why people's normal thought processes serve them so poorly when they are operating complex, dynamic systems—in effect, why things go wrong. One of his important conclusions had to do with our trouble visualizing time:

> We often overlook time configurations and treat successive steps in temporal development as individual events.... Even when we think in terms of time configurations, our intuition is very limited. In particular, our ability to guess at missing pieces... is much less than for space configurations.[*]

In another place, Dörner states it succinctly: We must learn to recognize "shapes" in time.[+]

In Matthew 5:48 we read, "Be *perfect*, therefore, as your heavenly Father is perfect." In recent years that verse has provoked discussion among scholars stemming from interpreters' inability to fit such a clear "counsel of perfection" into the framework of our Lord's

---

[*] Dietrich Dörner, *The Logic Of Failure* (New York: Henry Holt and Company, Metropolitan Books, 1996), 109.

[+] Ibid., 198.

teaching. Luke's Gospel (6:36) offers a clearly related passage: "Be *merciful,* just as your Father is merciful."

Notice the similarity. If you read what surrounds each verse in its respective Gospel, you will see even more similarity.

Our word "perfect" clearly comes from *perfectus* in Latin, a term that means "completely made; susceptible to no further process." Perfection is static, not dynamic. It's a freeze-frame, not part of the on-going film. So that's what we tend to think Jesus said and meant when we only read Matthew's version. Many commentators favor Luke's version and use it to interpret Matthew's. That preference is more than simply choosing what you like and rejecting what you don't. It's rather an attempt to resolve the tension in a direction more congruent with Jesus' other sayings. One can develop more mercy over time. Perfection, on the other hand, isn't developmental.

RESISTANCE TO DEVELOPMENT

So far, we've explored the way our repressed fear of death leads us to prefer "religion" to "righteousness," to seek a commercial, manipulative relationship with the God whose favor we cannot live without nor whose proximity can we tolerate. That dismal arrangement makes us controlling and perfectionistic. It suppresses the development of our real selves. When we are being commercial and manipulative, we're acting out of a false self. It's pretty far removed from any mystical sense of the Presence.

People who need to be in control, who need to appear perfect, aren't in a particularly fluid state. In all senses of the word, they lack grace. They greet change—even growth—with suspicion. Authentic selfhood grows, it evolves. Roles—false selves—do not evolve as readily. For the false self, change is more often experienced as decline. Edgar Bergan, the ventriloquist, probably grew and matured; it would have meant Bergen was getting better. Bergen's dummy, Charlie McCarthy, the one the world saw, did not change. If he did, he clearly needed repair. The false selves we retail to God and to others are similarly inert, resistant to change and growth.

As we've seen, we form institutions to help us resist death. All institutions, all governments, all corporations, all schools, all representative sports teams—and all churches—are liable to idolatry.

Each promises more life, or superior life, better life than its rivals can offer. At least some of those claims to offer or extend life are spurious. The life offered has little palpable substance.

Religious institutions don't gain adherents by changing their minds frequently as new insights flow in, developing from stage to stage by periodic dramatic breakthroughs. Religious leaders don't garner admiration and esteem by candidly admitting the limits of human knowledge and of our powers to express the ineffable. That makes death-fearing members nervous. No, they gain adherents by claiming to have reality all wrapped up in a packet, invulnerable to correction. Nor does their institutional life remain harmonious by encouraging members to cultivate their personal uniqueness. "Growth" in the typical religious organization means learning to restrict our perceptions to those featured by the group's dominant model.

A spiritual leader's own level of maturity forms an effective ceiling beyond which the system won't permit individual members to grow. Few leaders want their people to outgrow them. That results in subtle pressures from the leadership down to the membership not to develop. Learning to agree with your leaders and teachers is not always growth.

A consequence of these unspoken pressures is a deep tension. On the one hand is our very real and Spirit-impelled desire for spiritual development. On the other is our fear-driven tendency to deny needing further development when we feel threatened by it. We want to look good. Denying that we need to develop much further gets us caught up in relatively inflexible institutions, institutions that traffic in comforting "absolutes."

To be sure, the tension in our thinking between absolute states and developmental processes has roots other than the disparity of word choice in parallel passages in the First and Third Gospels. But thinking that Jesus requires us to be "perfect" through the centuries has hardly helped.

And that tension isn't going away anytime soon. We'll continue to grow and develop because God's voice calls us to do so—and such is our own deepest and truest wish. Furthermore, we'll continue to participate in institutions, however static. For all their idolatrous claims, institutions remain necessary for cooperative life. The emperor may not be wearing any clothes, but he's still the boss. Humans are gregarious. And, at points in our development, participating in institutions "anyway," loving their members and taking part in their procedures "anyway," is necessary for building spiritual muscle.*

Wanting to look perfect, wanting to display identities that entitle us to life, makes us resist candid realism about the selves we really are. Fact and fiction will war on within each of us. And it's not always possible to recall that God prefers fact, however untidy.

Given the tension between needing to develop further and the yearning to appear already fully developed, in this chapter I intend to add some weight to the developmental side of the seesaw. That side needs all the help it can get, as Dietrich Dörner pointed out. We think in snapshot images, not videos, but real life is not like that. In the Introduction, I spoke of my frustration that conservative co-religionists so often needlessly hobble themselves intellectually when they absolutize things that are best seen as fluid. Under pressure, we all think in terms of fixed positions we're prepared to defend to the death—rather than trajectories of growth. Any amount of effort to weaken that bad habit is worth it. But I don't just have conservatives in mind. More centrist and liberal groups also exhibit symptoms of paralysis, which an appreciation of developmental aspects of spirituality could alleviate as well. Dörner points out that though humans have uncanny ability at recognizing spatial configurations (we can recognize a familiar person from virtually any angle, at most distances) we're virtually blind to temporal configurations—it's next to impossible for us to imagine how things, people, and situations metamorphose through time. It's difficult to look at a $100 bill and multiply it by six percent over ten years; it's easier to see another couple of Wagner CDs with maybe a bottle of single-malt from the change. As a result, most of our solutions to problems address a freeze-frame rather than the whole film—and go awry. If we cannot think in developmental terms, the primary source of our problems will be previous solutions.

Against the temptation to retail ourselves as complete, whole, and perfect, there are weighty considerations that dignify growth

---

* Anybody can experience the Presence of God in the cool stillness of an empty, shadowy, quiet church sanctuary. Rubbing hearts with the same Presence while surrounded by coughing and sneezing, by squirming children and bellowing infants, by perfumes and after-shave lotions rivaling tear-gas, by voices singing off-key—now *that* takes effort and maturity. It is good for us.

and change—which it will not harm any of us to contemplate. To emphasize the need for constant development is hardly a sell-out to relativism. If the following discussion succeeds, there should be a happy outcome. We'll more readily think in developmental terms in all circumstances—and life will make more sense. We'll critique our own frozen certainties with the happy thought, "...and yet, there is still more—I wonder what lies beyond this?" We'll put up with antagonists more patiently, knowing that they won't always occupy the position they now loudly defend any more than we'll occupy ours. I'm trying to describe a deeper trust in God the Creator: the Creator here and now and in the future, a Creator no longer doctrinally confined to the past.

VARIOUS DEVELOPMENTAL MAPS

People have always known that personhood develops—it does not burst onto the stage fully formed.

The Sphinx posed a riddle to Oedipus, with life or death at stake in his correct answer: "What creature walks on four legs at dawn, on two legs at noon, and on three legs at dusk?" Oedipus gave the correct answer—man—because he could think developmentally, he could see his fellows as processes rather than static objects. One way to measuring human maturity, in other words, is to count legs.

In *The Symposium*, Plato depicts a dinner party during which Socrates described how his own teacher opened to him the path of the soul's development in love. Love begins with men's attraction to women in order to conceive children, he explained. Then one outgrows women in preference for the superior love of young men in order to conceive souls. The love for men leads the soul to the love of art and poetry, thence to social order, thence to the love of Beauty and Goodness. You could (or at least Socrates could) gauge a person's maturity by watching what he loves.

The Greek dramatists included wonderful speeches about the phases through which human beings can develop. Shakespeare picked them up and gave them a new twist, suggesting that not all movement from phase to phase can be called progress. For example Jaques' classic speech from Act II, scene 7, in *As You Like It* suggests no ideal:

...One man in his time plays many parts,
His acts being seven ages. At first the infant,
Mewling and puking in the nurse's arms.
And then the whining school-boy, with his satchel
And shining morning face, creeping like snail
Unwillingly to school. And then the lover,
Sighing like furnace, with a woeful ballad
Made to his mistress' eyebrow. Then a soldier,
Full of strange oaths and bearded like the pard,
Jealous in honour, sudden and quick in quarrel,
Seeking the bubble reputation
Even in the cannon's mouth. And then the justice,
In fair round belly with good capon lined,
With eyes severe and beard of formal cut,
Full of wise saws and modern instances;
And so he plays his part. The sixth age shifts
Into the lean and slipper'd pantaloon,
With spectacles on nose and pouch on side,
His youthful hose, well saved, a world too wide
For his shrunk shank; and his big manly voice,
Turning again toward childish treble, pipes
And whistles in his sound. Last scene of all,
That ends this strange eventful history,
Is second childishness and mere oblivion,
Sans teeth, sans eyes, sans taste, sans everything.

Rembrandt's paintings and sketches reveal an interest in physical and physiognomic development wonderfully metaphoric of spiritual development. Various collections of his works present self-portraits at various stages of his long life. We sense his growth in wisdom even as his bodily strength and eyesight decline. Though dim, his eyes seem to see so deeply into *us*. His wrinkles reflect hardship and personal tragedy. I've never seen all the self-portraits displayed in a chronological row, but I'd love to; I think the experience might encourage me to embrace my own aging.

Subsequent philosophical and theological sources through the centuries offer us any number of schemata for plotting our developmental progress. Bernard of Clairvaux, for one example, offered some especially nice arrangements that still rank among my personal favorites. He described the soul coming to Christ:

- first kissing Christ's *feet* as a surrendering suppliant;
- then kissing Christ's *hands* as a servant;
- then kissing Christ's *face* as a friend and lover.

Charming. Bernard also described the soul's progress from the Purgative, through the Illuminative, to the Unitive stages of life with God, an understanding of abiding value to spiritually serious people.

There is a famous episode recounted by the Curé D'Ars in the nineteenth century. He used to find an old man sitting in his church building all day just staring forward. Possibly nervous that the old man might pilfer the poor box, the Curé approached him and asked, "Hien! What do you do in here all day?" And the old man replied, "I look at Him. He looks at me. We're happy." Spiritual directors use that story to illustrate the Unitive Way that Bernard described.

In our century psychologists have taken over the task of identifying developmental stages from poets, philosophers, and theologians. They offer us the advantages of scientific rigor in addition to inspired intuitions, allowing us to enjoy both. Freud's identification of stages of childhood psychosexual development—oral, anal, genital—still informs the cocktail party talk of college-educated tipplers and may indeed still find some application among actual psychotherapists here and there. Jean Piaget, Eric Erikson, Lawrence Kohlberg, and Daniel Levinson (whose work was popularized by Gail Sheehy in *Passages*), and James Fowler (whom we shall shortly consider in detail) all offered us schemata of human development in use to this day.

Before we consider a developmental scheme in detail, there are a couple of questions to address. First, is development inevitable? Not the kind we're interested in. A man could go from youth to age without cultivating the wisdom hidden behind the aged Rembrandt's eyes—and many do. And is all movement from stage to stage desirable? The answer to that is more complicated. A tentative, cautious answer might be: not if the movement were premature. Real wisdom is earned, not copied or inherited. Yet though the overlap between second order change and desirable development is not total—death or disablement, for instance, are second order changes—development as we are using the term usually makes a desirable difference. My own rule of thumb is that I start trusting that a particular change is really development if there is some noticeable struggle connected with it, a struggle that scares me and wakes me up.

Another difficulty germane to this discussion more nearly is keeping development in mind at times when it's quite necessary to keep it in mind. When I'm in an argument, it feels like bad tactics

to concede, "Of course, what I'm saying is my present understanding—no doubt future growth will modify it considerably,
perhaps even in the course of what you're saying to me." I'd much
rather bellow, "Thus saith the LORD!" I can't remember if I have
ever answered a question saying, "I am not sufficiently developed
to address that." Have you? That's real hard to keep in mind.

Developmental thinking is surprisingly difficult to employ in
some circumstances where you would expect it to fit helpfully. For
example, you would imagine developmental thinking would be
useful to religious educators. It is not easy to select Sunday school
materials. Some curricula are much more useful than others and
appearances can deceive. You'd think it would be clear to anybody
who ever tried to teach table manners to toddlers that small children cannot assimilate moralizing precepts. But a rapid survey of
the field indicates that such awareness is far from obvious to all
curriculum designers. Likewise, teaching Bible stories to young
people and adults, stressing their literal details, seems like the
height of good sense to some, if the plethora of such materials is
any indication—though if you afflict your Sunday school class
with them, your students will drop out in droves. Evidently all the
advances in our understanding of how children, young people,
and adults develop don't always outweigh non-developmental
dogmatism. Yet I suspect many dogmatic curriculum designers
could dilate with conviction and at length about the importance
of respecting the users' growth stages. In a crunch, under pressure, we tend not to.

A small child who asks whether the dinosaurs missed Noah's
Ark is right on schedule. An adult who asks the same question is
far behind schedule and has some catching up to do.

Any cleric accustomed to hearing sacramental confessions
knows that she must weigh what she hears in relation to the spiritual development of the one confessing. An advanced soul who
confesses gossip, a sin pattern mature spirits have typically outgrown, is opening a serious matter indeed, one that the confessor
should explore respectfully. Yet the cleric would expect such a
confession from anyone early on in his spiritual life; indeed its
absence would arouse suspicion. Either requires a different
response. A cleric who is herself not really growing in the
ordained ministry may be more prone to say, "Sin is sin."

When we are pressing our religion into the service of death-denial, making a hero system of it, striving to gain the gratitude and admiration of the gods, we're not patient with our own developmental requirements or those of others. Indeed when we're feeling threatened we're least likely even to take those developmental requirements into account. At such moments we're too busy constructing and maintaining an imposture, trying to appear firmly established, tougher than death. At such points we benefit from constant reminders that reality—especially divine reality—keeps expanding as our appreciative capacities increase. As we pretend less and less, as we embrace the friendliness of what is, we want to grow and stretch in order to take more in.

Some of the stuck-points I discussed earlier—like Sam's inability to appreciate his dad, George, or the tendency of recent converts to ape the mannerisms of those in the cults they join— are characteristic of particular stages. That's another good reason to understand ourselves in developmental terms. If we view problematic ideas or practices against a moving, developing background we will exercise more understanding towards those who hold them while feeling less tempted to get stuck in them ourselves.

Just as a teenager knows he can accelerate his muscle growth and coordination with physical exercise and wise dietary choices, being aware of how real faith develops offers us decisions to make, habits to cultivate, new questions to ask, and old judgments to abandon, all of which accelerate our developing tolerance for God's presence.

FOWLER'S SIX STAGES OF FAITH DEVELOPMENT

PRELIMINARIES

Reading James Fowler's *Stages of Faith* will benefit anyone who's serious about spiritual growth.* Fowler shares Tillich's realism about what faith is. Faith is not necessarily the creed—or the doubt—you profess. Faith is more process than content. In the Fourth Gospel faith is always a verb—never a noun. Faith is "ultimate concern." If that sounds too abstract, consider the kind of questions you'd ask yourself to determine your real faith:

---

* James W. Fowler, *The Stages of Faith* (New York: HarperCollins, 1981). Hereafter cited in the text as *SF*.

- What are you spending and being spent for? What commands and receives your best time, your best energy?
- What causes, dreams, goals, or institutions are you pouring out your life for?
- As you live your life, what power or powers do you fear or dread?
- What power or powers do you rely on and trust?
- To what or whom are you committed to in life? In death?
- With whom or with what groups do you share your most sacred and private hopes for your life and for the lives of those you love?
- What are the most sacred hopes, the most compelling goals and purposes in your life?
  (*SF*, 3)

Your ultimate concerns will emerge from ruminating on such questions. Someone who knows all that about you knows your real faith a whole lot better than your preacher does.

Fowler is also clear that *faith* is not identical with *religion* or *belief.* Belief is holding certain ideas and opinions. Those ideas may or may not pertain to ultimate concern. Religion is a cultural institutional setting within which we enact some of our beliefs—the "spiritual" ones, although politics is often not far off. These distinctions give us additional settings within which to grasp the religion vs. righteousness distinction of a previous chapter. Faith for Fowler is much the same as "righteousness" in that discussion. Belief is the stuff of "religion" as we were considering it. Fowler uses "religion" somewhat more neutrally than I do, but his understanding of it leaves considerable room for the corruption we have discussed.

Fowler quotes from William Cantwell Smith's *The Meaning and End of Religion* for the description of faith that governs his own discussion:

> Faith, then, is a quality of human living. At its best it has taken the form of serenity and courage and loyalty and service: a quiet confidence and joy which enable one to feel at home in the universe, and to find meaning in the world and in one's own life, a meaning that is profound and ultimate, and is stable no matter what may happen to oneself at the level of immediate event. Men and women of this kind of faith face catastrophe and confusion, affluence and sorrow, unperturbed; face opportunity with conviction and drive; and face others with cheerful charity. (*SF*, 11)

Critics of Fowler raise fruitful questions to be borne in mind as you read him. Did Fowler have a broad enough database? Is it really a good idea to separate the contents of faith from the process of faith? Is Fowler always scrupulous with that distinction? Does he think you have to be real smart to achieve the higher stages? Important questions. Still those same critics read him attentively and gratefully. I think his categories are well worth our attention in this discussion.

Fowler offers an appreciative summary of Smith's etymological studies of the words our ancestors and we use for faith. The Greek "*pisteuo*" in its biblical contexts always meant to rely on someone, to trust them; it was a personal word, not part of a catalogue of opinions. "*Credo*" comes from a combination of two Latin words meaning "to give [my] heart." And our present day word "believe" comes from an older English word meaning "to hold dear, to love." Again, personal trust and relatedness is the thrust of the original word. Smith summarizes the relevance of the etymological shift:

> There was a time when "I believe" as a ceremonial declaration of faith meant and was heard as meaning: "Given the reality of God, as a fact of the universe, I hereby proclaim that I align my life accordingly, pledging love and loyalty." A statement about a person's believing has now come to mean, rather, something of this sort: "Given the uncertainty of God, as a fact of modern life, so-and-so reports that the idea of God is part of the furniture of his mind." (*SF*, 13)

"Righteousness versus. religion" again.

Fowler goes on to borrow three terms from the field of Comparative Religion to characterize different types of faith. The first two are clearly idolatrous, commitments to finite concerns as though they were ultimate.

The first is "*polytheism*":

> Some years ago a *New Yorker* cartoon showed one blue-jeaned coed talking with another. The subject was the latest male object of her enthusiasm. Describing him she gushed, "He's into scuba diving, motorcycle scrambling, bluegrass banjo picking, pottery making, Haiku poetry, and Gupta Yoga! He's a real Renaissance Man!" Whatever else he may be or become, I'll wager her boyfriend is a *polytheist*. Here I use this anthropological term to characterize a pattern of faith and identity that lacks any one center of value and power of sufficient transcendence to focus and order one's life. For the polytheist not

> even the *self*—one's myth of one's own worth and destiny—
> can lay a compelling enough claim to unify one's hopes and
> strivings. (*SF*, 19)

The second is *"henotheism,"* the worship of one particular god
among various others.

> I…use the term *henotheistic* to characterize a pattern of faith
> and identity in which one invests deeply in a transcending
> center of value and power, finding in it a focal unity of per-
> sonality and outlook, but this center is inappropriate, false,
> not something of ultimate concern. The henotheistic god is
> finally an idol. (*SF*, 20)

Fowler's third borrowed term is *"radical monotheism."*

> In keeping with our use of the two previous terms I want to
> broaden our understanding of monotheism. By it I shall mean
> a type of faith-identity relation in which a person or group
> focuses its supreme trust and loyalty in a transcendent source
> of value and power, that is neither a conscious or unconscious
> extension of personal or group ego nor a finite cause or insti-
> tution. Rather, this type of monotheism implies loyalty to the
> *principle of being* and to the *source and center of all value and
> power.* (*SF*, 23)

Fowler proceeds to discuss faith as a form of imagination:
since the ultimate "source and center of all value and power" is
vastly superior to anything our senses can directly apprehend, we
have to construct images, metaphors, and symbols which direct us
toward and stand guard over our periodic encounters with God.

This is an important element in Fowler's discussion. We need
all the help we can get to hang onto the metaphoric character of
all religious language—otherwise we all too readily absolutize it,
freeze it, "thingify" it. As we shall see in Chapter 7, much of our
religious stuckness in the United States is reinforced by
metaphors for Jesus' work in our lives that we literalize, trying to
believe we inhabit a world run by a God who really requires somebody to die whenever there is sin evident. Literalizing Atonement
metaphors, imagining that's the way the world really is, highlights
our fear and our sadism, as history amply demonstrates. Few
forces in history have proved as toxic as reified religious
metaphors. We kill in their name.

Religions, at least the ones that survive time, are made up of
images, metaphors, and symbols that have proved themselves
"true" through the centuries by reliably leading men and women

into the Presence. Some symbols and metaphors clearly work better than others. Changes in culture produce changes in live symbols and metaphors. Moribund symbols and metaphors have to be enforced by external authority; live symbols require no external enforcement.

And as cultures change, their members' experiences necessarily change apace—resulting in new ways of speaking. An example: We think of mirrors as reflecting a clear, memorable image. We consequently use mirrors as metaphors of clarity and accuracy. However, New Testament authors had only mirrors of poorly burnished metal. So two New Testament references to mirrors (1 Col. 13:12 and Jas. 1:23–24) highlight mirroring as fuzzy and evanescent in ways that confuse us today.

It is easy to trace the path by which breathtaking reports of encounters with God employed similes and metaphors: "It was like being a slave and having somebody you love find you in servitude, buy you, set you free—then once you're free asks you to marry him!" The metaphors in turn became abstract technical terms: "Redemption." Finally they became the parroted jargon of a religious ghetto, difficult to paraphrase because people no longer grasp them experientially.

So the experiential funding for a traditional metaphor can evaporate—sometimes rapidly. In both the history of a religion and the history of an individual it is necessary to progress from obsolete, ineffective or indeed harmful apprehensions to those that convey us to the Presence. Fowler analyzes this progress as a series of stages:

> I believe that we can identify reasonably predictable developmental turning points in the *ways* faith imagines and in the ways faith's images interplay with communal modes of expression. Less predictable are those more momentous changes in the life of faith when one's image of the ultimate environment undergoes a shift of center. When one of our deeply invested henotheistic "gods" fails us or collapses, it results in dislocation, pain, and despair. When we are grasped by the vision of a center of value and power more luminous, more inclusive and truer than that to which we are devoted, we initially experience the new as the enemy or the slayer—which destroys our "god." Alfred North Whitehead wrote, "Religion [here used non-pejoratively] is the transition from God the Void to God the Enemy, and from God the Enemy to God the Companion." Only with the death of our previous image can a new and more adequate one arise. Thus "substantive doubt" is a part of the life of faith. (*SF*, 31)

The latter quote ought to remove any question about the necessity of thinking of our faith in developmental terms. Tillich had said, "The courage to be is rooted and grounded in the God who appears when God has disappeared in the anxiety of doubt." The path of spiritual growth leads in a predictable direction. The only (minor) question is what increments we use—and how we name them—to measure distance along it.

That quote—and Tillich's observation—may also illuminate our stubborn, terrified, and bellicose resistance to development, either in ourselves or—more enragingly—in others. I was once embroiled in a controversy that could not honorably be ducked, one that pitted old friends implacably against each other, severing relationships we had all thought bombproof. I understood why well-meaning people would take a position contrary to the one I espoused; after all, I had formerly shared (and noisily advocated) their view. But why should lengthy friendships dissolve over the dispute? A thoughtful college student resolved my confusion when she sent an enlightening note on hearing about the struggle. She wrote, "To someone in Stage 3, anyone in Stages 4, 5, or even 6, must appear evil." That observation led to one repaired friendship, at least. It also made understanding how we develop spiritually all the more urgent.

Skipping much of interest and importance in *Stages of Faith,* let's consider the stages themselves. There are six.

STAGE ONE

The first, which Fowler calls the *Intuitive-Projective Stage,* is normally found among children between the ages of four and eight. It is the birth of imagination, heavily influenced by older people in the child's world.

STAGE TWO

The second is the *Mythic-Literal Stage.* We see it among those between the ages of seven and, say, twelve years. The child is aware of taking on the identity of the community to which she belongs, and she swallows the rules and norms, the stories, the values, pretty much whole. Stories and narratives mediate how things are and how things can be.

STAGE THREE

The third is the *Synthetic-Conventional* Stage. Think of this stage as utterly conventional. Discussions with people in this stage may be quite interesting, provided they are talking about something they have a real investment in; but religious discussions at this level tend to tedious banality. Beginning in the early teen years, it may last all of one's life. Faith is now one distinct part of life, one of a growing number of departments into which life is divided. Presumably faith helps the person negotiate between the competing demands of the other departments. Stage 3 faith is fairly conformist, as the person either cannot yet or does not yet see much need to practice independent critical thinking. A person's beliefs at this stage will be what sociologists of knowledge call "reified," i.e. regarded as so automatically true that it's not questionable.* Indeed you may not even be aware of holding a particular belief, it seems so obvious. Don't believe me? Well, there was a time when common sense dictated that the world is flat.

At this stage, any circumstance that wakes us up, which makes us question inherited beliefs and identity, turns into a crisis. Recall that the Chinese word for "crisis" is a combination of the pictograms for "danger" and "opportunity." The opportunity, of course, is to begin thinking through deep matters for oneself. The danger is descent into cynicism and distrust—or madness.

STAGE FOUR

Stage 4 is the *Individuative-Reflective Stage.* It's important to understand a couple of aspects of this stage quite well.

One enters Stage 4 by the sort of processes that we earlier saw as both desirable and problematic: conversion or self-commitment. Stage 4 is a clear gain over Stage 3. A person is now thinking actively about faith. Conversion and self-commitment are admirable processes in themselves. Fowler himself and those who

---

* Reified—"thing-ified"—thought pattern used to be called "false consciousness" among students of social processes. It is what happens when we talk too long without paying attention to what we are saying, when our words undetectably slip loose from our actual lives. French sociologists and critics came to call it *mauvais foi*—bad faith. Notice that all this happens outside our conscious awareness. Wittgenstein once remarked that if any language contained a verb meaning "to believe falsely," it would possess no first person of the present active indicative.

refer to him in their own work clearly admire people in this stage, maybe in reaction to the tedious torpor felt in adults in Stage 3. This stage is, to my way of thinking, the first interesting stage in faith development. Discussions of faith with people at this stage may be querulous or inspiring—but rarely dull.

A danger is that on entering Stage 4, we may admire ourselves. Self-admiration serves the death denial project. Even sadder, it seals us off from additional wonder. If we land in an attractive group as a result of conversion or self-commitment, we're likely to embrace its idolatrous pretensions along with its other attractions. The result is that people in Stage 4 define their beliefs and communities in energetically adversarial terms. Phrases like "We are not..." and "We do not believe..." and "We never..." come up repeatedly in the self-descriptions of people in Stage 4.

In effect, people in Stage 4 are a curious combination of being molten and being rigid. The heat of the encounter with God has melted them, put them in a state where they can no longer live conventional lives. Yet they are rigidifying. Likely they will join some highly defined group whose profession resembles their own convictions closely enough to qualify as being "right." That means that groups or persons who take another approach are "wrong." The rigidity shows up in their intolerance for ambiguity, for disorder, eventually for complexity.

Groups of any stripe whose internal life is specified by people in Stage 4 radiate an attractive persuasiveness. Becker borrows a phrase from a social psychologist to describe their leaders: the "infectiousness of the unconflicted personality." People whose dearly won convictions make them one with their message attract us—sometimes they immobilize us as though we were deer staring into approaching headlights. When they speak in public or private they don't lick their lips, rub their noses, or cut their eyes sideways. They betray no inner voice whispering, "on the other hand...."

And yet, they have to manage cognitive dissonance just like the rest of us, and its attendant tensions require polarization. By polarization I mean the social equivalent of what we call "projection" when individuals do it. In projection I place my own unassimilated characteristics on others and either hate or adore them. In polarizing, a group projects the dark side of some tension between darkness and light onto some other group with which it then contrasts itself favorably.

Such groups define themselves in adversarial terms. I wonder if the much-vaunted Jesus Seminar would manifest anything like its present energy in the absence of all the TV-evangelists with their triumphalist Fundamentalism? Whom would conservative Evangelicals deplore if all the "liberals" packed up and left? American *Kulturkampfen* following the collapse of the Soviet "Evil Empire" give us some sense of what awaits energetic parties of opinion who lack a clear enemy. Below a certain level of maturity, groups that lack an external enemy turn on themselves. When we do so in the name of Jesus Christ, the outcome is invariably grotesque.*

The author of the Ephesian Epistle warned us that our struggle is not against our fellow mortals—it is against spiritual principalities and other nexuses of power that we moderns no longer focus clearly. Our struggle isn't with "conservatives" or "liberals" or with any other philosophic tribe. Our struggle most often is a collision at Stage 4 between faith systems that people enter by conversion. Don't you have lots of delightful friends whose views you don't share? Yet you thoroughly enjoy being with them, your conversations enriched rather than embittered by differences. Differences aren't the problem. The impulse to polarize, the impulse to define one's position by its adversaries—*that's* the problem.⁺ The breadth of the American religious spectrum is intrinsically no more problematic than the variety of instrumental timbres in an orchestra. But if the violinists are making heavy weather of accompanying the brass section, and if they shake off their difficulties by disparaging trumpet players and trumpets altogether, the orchestra is in trouble. So's the audience. And the audience for the religious symphony orchestra is neither the media nor the population they lull—the audience is God.

Fowler's own description of Stage 4 is gentler. Nevertheless, he describes its occupants facing unavoidable tensions, e.g.:

---

* I think I will always lean towards some expression of the Charismatic Movement for one simple reason: at the weeklong conference at which I was finally converted, not one speaker at any time disparaged any other group or party of opinion. Their energy was "towards" God—not "against" antagonists. I saw there that it could be done. *O si sic omnes!*

⁺ When advocating aspects of the Charismatic Movement, I am used to hearing people say, "But that movement is so *divisive!*" I customarily reply, "No movement is divisive per se—*people* are."

> Stage 4's ascendant strength has to do with its capacity for critical reflection on identity (self) and outlook (ideology). Its dangers inhere in its strengths: an excessive confidence in the conscious mind and in critical thought and a kind of second narcissism in which the now clearly bounded reflective self over-assimilates "reality" and the perspectives of others into its own world view. (*SF*, 182–183)

Ernest Becker had addressed "the nexus of unfreedom," our yen to engage in "transference" onto individuals and institutions which promise more life than we can summon on our own. That is what Fowler is talking about here.

Relief in the form of transition to Stage 5 may comes as....

> Disillusionment with one's compromises and recognition that life is more complex than Stage 4's logic of clear distinctions and abstract concepts can comprehend press one toward a more dialectical and multileveled approach to life truth. (*SF*, 183)

STAGE FIVE

Stage 5 is called *Conjunctive Faith.* At this stage people are beyond resolving tensions by choosing sides, because tensions now feel like a necessary fruitful part of the landscape. Nor do people in Stage 5 describe or locate themselves in adversarial terms. A Stage 5 Methodist no longer disparages Roman Catholics.

In Stage 5, the ambiguity-rejecting rigidity of Stage 4 has yielded to a sense of wonder, grounded in an experienced confidence in the friendliness of the universe, in the ultimate competence of God. Stage 5 people are both clearer and gentler. Their faith is becoming more exploratory than explanatory.

Carl Jung had observed that real spirituality has to await our entry into mid-life. Jung saw little spirituality worth the name before age forty. Though I wonder what he would have made of Theresa of Lisieux or of Anne Frank, he at least had a statistical point. My wife, a psychotherapist in private practice, observes that her clients below age forty seek and clutch answers; those beyond forty seek and clutch questions.*

With Stage 5, we notice a sort of cosmic "disorder tolerance" replacing the anguished struggle with cognitive dissonance. People

---

* Another bumper sticker seen in Atlanta: "Jesus Is The Question To All Your Answers."

in Stage 5 are patient—indeed they are curious—in the face of paradox and ambiguity. If the truth be known, they somewhat distrust any presentation in which those qualities are entirely absent.

Look at Fowler's observation:

> The new strength of this stage comes in the rise of the ironic imagination—a capacity to see and be in one's or one's group's most powerful meanings, while simultaneously recognizing that they are relative, partial and inevitably distorting apprehensions of transcendent reality. Its danger lies in the direction of a paralyzing passivity or inaction, giving rise to complacency or cynical withdrawal, due to its paradoxical understanding of truth. (*SF*, 198)

Such people know that you're unlikely to be able to point to the box God came in. Boxes can't hold God.

A helpful theological ideology ought to serve us as an instrument of expanding perception. It needn't be and indeed mustn't be a compendium of all truth. In Christian theology at least there can never be a "T.O.E."—a "theory of everything." Though it confines our gaze in order to focus it, the vision of Glory should ultimately outweigh the confinement. Which end of the funnel are we looking through? Downward into the wide opening in order to see very little—at the risk of believing what we're seeing is everything? Or outward through the narrow hole so that view widens? In Stage 5 Fowler is describing individuals who've succeeded in using the resources of their faith community to promote expansive growth rather than submitting to institutionally mandated constrictedness.

Stage 5 people manifest an unsupercilious recognition that a symbol is precisely and only that—a symbol. A lens is neither a star nor a paramecium, nor is a windowpane a vista. Symbols and metaphors are not the thing itself. Yet they focus a Presence not otherwise accessible.

> Stage 5 can appreciate symbols, myths and rituals (its own and others') because it has been grasped, in some measure, by the depths of reality to which they refer. It also sees the divisions of the human family vividly because it has been apprehended by the possibility (and imperative) of an inclusive community of being.
>
> But this stage remains divided. It lives and acts between an untransformed world and a transforming vision and loyalties. In some few cases this division yields to the call of the radical actualization we call Stage 6. (*SF*, 198)

In other words, there's just no getting around the importance of actual contact with God—not just belief that there is a "god," not just holding orthodox opinions—but actually sitting on God's lap. Do justice, indeed; love mercy, by all means; but that all follows from walking humbly with your God.

Is Stage 5 another name for liberal? The answer is no—for two reasons. People convert to being liberal and that conversion produces the same polarizations and divisive behavior we'd expect from any religious system. Though tolerance of philosophic differences is an ingredient of many liberals' creed, it takes a while to work its way into the heart, into the reflexes, into the brain stem and medulla oblongata. Until our openness to others becomes faith rather than mere belief, (we) liberals will resolve tensions with polarization at about the same clip as the so-called Christian Coalition or Moral Majority. I do like to think we're wittier about it, but I could be wrong.

Second, all of us treasure friendships with theologically conservative Stage 5s. A point I offer about the Ark of the Covenant in Chapter 8 came straight from a country Baptist preacher; it is his perception, not mine, and it flows from his intimate and superior friendship with God. And if you were to try to draft a list of the Stage 6 people you can think of, at least two would be conspicuous conservatives: Mother Theresa of Calcutta and Billy Graham. I would add a third: the great apostle of Pentecostalism, the South African Dr. David DuPlessis. Those latter are just some of the famous ones.

STAGE SIX

Stage 6 is *Universalizing Faith*. It is bracing to read about people in that stage. Fowler is our source again:

> Persons best described by Stage 6 typically exhibit qualities that shake our usual criteria of normalcy. Their heedlessness to self-preservation and the vividness of their taste and feel for transcendent moral and religious actuality give their actions and words an extraordinary and often unpredictable quality.
>
> Stage 6 is exceedingly rare. The persons best described by it have generated faith compositions in which their felt sense of an ultimate environment is inclusive of all being. They have become incarnators and actualizers of the spirit of an inclusive and fulfilled human community.
>
> They are "contagious" in the sense that they create zones of liberation from the social, political, economic and ideological

> shackles we place and endure on human futurity. Living with felt participation in a power that unifies and transforms the world, Universalizers are often experienced as subversive of the structures (including religious structures) by which we sustain our individual and corporate survival, security and significance. Many persons in this stage die at the hands of those whom they hope to change. (*SF*, 200–201)

Again, consider that as our personal lists of individuals in Stage 6 grow, at least half are drawn from outside whatever our theological party happens to be. Conservatives must reckon with the godly charm as well as prophetic courage of Dietrich Bonnhoeffer, Martin Niemöller, Desmond Tutu, Nelson Mandela, John XXIII, or Krister Stendahl. Liberals must reckon with John Paul II and Metropolitan Anthony Bloom. Nobody knows where or how to catalogue Will Campbell of Tennessee. Converting opponents to our own point of view is "first order change"—as futile as mopping floors in a building that is afire. "Second order change" requires the sort of spiritual maturity the descriptions of the latter two stages point to: confronting our own cognitive dissonance, welcoming the "other," and discovering God's sturdy energy and towering delight as we make those efforts. No conflict is ever really resolved at the level of experience where it was waged. Tugs of war and arm-wrestling settle nothing for long. Conflicts get resolved and healed in acts of transcendence in which we ascend to the next experiential level and, shoulder to shoulder with former antagonists, look down at what we were doing and resolve to be siblings. Such acts are the very quintessence of "spirit."

Stage 6 people do that as a reflex. With prayerful disciplined effort, so might we.

GOOD HABITS, PURE THOUGHTS

As we noticed when we started, when we're using religion as a hero-project to deny or forestall death, we're most prone to the defects we see in the various stages. The active fear of death paralyses us in any position that feels safe. It makes us prone to swat perceived conflicts between our belief-systems with authoritative swatters.* It makes us appeal to spiritual leaders whose job is to

---

* I cannot shake the image of a shower mat stapled to a two-by-four coming down on a fly.

keep it all plausible for us at the cost of our freedom to grow. Bad habits, all. Impure thinking.

Seeing our lives on a developmental spectrum, experiencing ourselves and others as being attracted through time into Glory permits relaxation, patience, and humor that are absent when we try to retail ourselves as finished projects. It's wise to prefer Luke 6:36 to Matthew 5:48. Merciful people are merrier than perfect people, more supple in God's hands too, I suspect. A good habit, all in all, purer thinking.

The defects within each stage happily impel us to higher development—if we embrace them bravely. Ironically, a self-critical posture keeps us moving along a temporal trajectory; posturing spiritual heroics paralyses us individually and polarizes us communally. At first we resist, denying that we experience cognitive dissonance as we perceive discontinuities in our selves, our beliefs, our institutions. But then, following where the discontinuities lead us, exercising non-resistance rather than resistance, we so frequently arrive at a firmer footing than before. There is no habit more helpful to spiritual growth than this: *pay attention to your cognitive dissonance.* Embrace and nurture your doubt. Doubt only threatens the spurious permanence of a *stage* of faith—not faith itself. Doubt carves space for more faith. Learn that and you've achieved spiritual escape velocity; you can voyage to the stars. Refuse to learn that and you'll remain in the tedious orbit of idolatrous notions and customs which pretend that God's permanence requires their own.

As suggested above, add to that embrace the willingness to expose yourself to the persuasive tug of your enemy's perspective. When you run that perspective through your own circuits, you come away wiser and more godly. That doesn't mean you have to change jerseys. You're only expected to add sportsmanship.

In the 1950s Gregory Bateson suggested a theory for the origins of schizophrenia which psychiatrists briefly took seriously—the "double bind" theory. According to Bateson, ambivalent mothers produce schizophrenic children by speaking love with their words, but enacting rejection with their body-language, facial expressions, and tones of voice. The child goes crazy in the face of the cognitive dissonance. Happily, most psychiatrists no longer believe that, to the great relief of mothers everywhere. But they believed it for a time because they knew that suppressing cognitive dissonance is bad for you.

To get through the struggle with whether to deny our discontinuities or to embrace them we have to develop a tolerance for
disorder, an ability to face into the discomfort of uncertainty. This
feels like a crisis the first number of times we have to undergo it.
But there comes a point in a maturing marriage when the onset
of an argument is welcome—as an invitation to know and trust
each other better and as the promise of an energetic reconcilia-
tion. So it eventually becomes in our faith crises. The struggle to
resist cognitive dissonance is an attempt to postpone a needed
faith crisis. Faith crises are good for us.

Both Sam, the nineteen-year-old boy, and George, his recov-
ering father, mentioned in the first two chapters were already at
Stage 4. Each was ahead of many of us. Yet they were not getting
along with each other. Each belonged to a dynamic spiritual community that used other groups as straw men. They missed recognizing that there are further stages of development in which a cig-
arette-smoking, coarse-mouthed dad and an ultra-devout, desper-
ately differentiating son can delight in each other, can recognize
each other as kin, sheep of different flocks sharing a common
shepherd. Choices were there for each to make that might have
jump-started their mutual delight—if they'd had wiser counsel.
Better resolutions lay at hand for them than battering each other
vocally, seeking to get the other to change.

◆ ◆ ◆ ◆ ◆

A closing anecdote: Anyone who attempts to reflect on human
life *sub specie aeternitatis*—as clergy are supposed to—will periodically be aware of the untidiness of it, of how hard it is to construct
a model of the universe with no embarrassing facts left over. Crises
ensue, predictably. On one occasion a nasty tragedy in the congregation and some pretty confrontational reading about church
history by a non-propagandist combined to mess up my theological model of things. That can be awkward if it lasts over six days
and you're a preacher—do the math. So it was a great relief when
after about three weeks of inner struggle, I felt a surging breakthrough into the Presence of God again, this time in a theological
arrangement that made much more room than before for disorder and the inexplicable. The vision was inexpressibly beautiful
and vastly more complex than any I'd enjoyed up to that moment.

I recall praying something like this: "O God, right now I'm having to stretch all my understanding and all my courage farther than I ever did before just to take some of this in, and I'll probably miss most of it. I'm fairly bright, but what you're showing me points way beyond my abilities to track. What happens to people whose capacities don't even reach this far?"

And God's utterly graceful reply?

"I am equally present at all levels of complexity."

That truth is the real fuel for all spiritual growth.

CHAPTER FIVE

THE DESTABLILIZING BIBLE

So far we've seen that people often harden into false religious selves after a conversion meltdown. When we harden, we collude with the cultural customs of some group or other in the hopes of coping with death. We've noticed the Bible's preference of righteousness (an integral, authentic relationship with God) over religion (a behavior system for securing God's favor). We've seen how easy it is to revert to our old antipathy towards God as our judge, forgetting our brief conversion-based sense that divine judgment expresses God's favor and understanding, not the threat of annihilation. We've seen that a period of being critical of other people's approaches can either be a single point on a trajectory of spiritual growth or a stuck-place from which we never escape. Our relative inability to see "shapes in time" is akin to our inability to honor alternatives to our own positions, to see our own positions and those of our antagonists as linked elements of a larger design. At all points we see the same tug-of-war between religious bondage and righteous suppleness. At all points we actually *seek* the bondage rather than having it thrust upon us by others; we're perpetrators, not victims. Righteous suppleness scares us—though it is clearly God's wish and gift.

THE BIBLE AND RELIGIOUS BONDAGE

Though all of these observations can be substantiated from the Bible—and indeed some rise directly from the Bible—it can't be said that reading the Bible automatically produces freedom from religious bondage. Our use of the Bible is a prime example of the human tendency to take the resources God extends to us and embed them right into the problem itself.

Years ago, I read a biography of Jonathan Swift. Though I can't remember the name of the writer or the book, one observation from the introduction has stayed with me to this day: "Jonathan Swift forged the deadliest arrow ever forged and shot it straight at the heart of man; man caught it—and turned it into a plaything for children." That greatest of social satires, *Gulliver's Travels* had been successfully dodged by using it for a different purpose than the purpose its author intended. Something very much like that has been the Bible's fate.

A deliberately diverse collection of scrolls has been edited and bound into a single volume, its diversity ignored if not indeed cloaked.

People take that vast panorama of unresolved arguments and pretend it's a rulebook for *settling* arguments. People take that broad record of evolving moral understanding and pretend it's a monument to an *unchanging* eternal moral system. People take that record of transformed lives and act as though *it*—rather than God's Holy Spirit—were the agent of transformation.

Though the editors of the Bible deliberately went to little discernible trouble to square conflicting details or viewpoints with each other, you can find a vast literature dedicated to helping us pretend that the Bible is unitary and univocal. Though the Bible constantly stresses the deep incomprehensibility of God, we hear people insisting that it contains everything about God—including every significant divine thought—which we can, should, or might want to know. Though the Bible stresses God's favor towards the underprivileged throughout both testaments, people have regularly used it to protect the privileged: male over female, wealthy over the poor, owners over slaves, bosses over employees, whites over blacks, married people over single.

More to the point of the present discussion, the Bible is used to prevent spiritual growth rather than to enhance it, to confirm rather than challenge—to keep people in religious bondage.

All of that takes place using reading strategies, i.e., an approach that we use to make our way through the Bible's vastness, trying to form patterns of understanding. When we don't admit that we employ such strategies and don't declare how we're using them, we pretend to voice the Bible's intent even while favoring one set of passages over all others.* We probably won't declare our own stakes in the interpretations we retail as God's own. For example, very few biblical-theological arguments against women's ordination ever concluded with statements like, "Of course, I who write this am an ordained male."

It is difficult to imagine how a deliberate campaign to subvert the Bible could achieve more mischief than we've managed on our own inadvertently. It almost makes you believe in the devil.

If the liberating Word of God written is used for undeclared privilege maintenance, if it's used to protect people from the very doubts and crises the Bible was given to express and provoke—doubts and crises which are, after all, the necessary preconditions for spiritual maturing—then those who want to grow up and go on with God will swiftly discover themselves low on resources. Or, as the Arab proverb puts it so succinctly, "If water sticks in your throat, what will you wash it down with?"

That we normally use the Bible to confirm what we already believe is so simply demonstrated that it's almost bad sportsmanship to point out instances of contradictory practices—e.g., that most Bible readers own interest-bearing bank accounts and pensions; or that congregations which pretend to emulate the "New Testament Church" do not veil their women (1 Cor. 11:10). Yet the Bible's most easily demonstrable power is to *disconfirm*, to challenge, to destabilize even the most sacred pieties.

THE BIBLE AS ENZYME

Indeed in the latter regard the Bible is unique among the sacred literatures of the world religions. Virtually all the others produce stability when they are read, pondered, and taught. Continual

---

* A clergyman with high name-recognition recently insisted, "Others interpret the Bible; I proclaim it." He's mistaken. All proclamation is interpretive, including his own, because the Bible is multivalent. We can't escape that fact if we read the Bible at all. What we *can* do is try to be honest about our presuppositions and interpretive strategies.

iterations of the Q'ran produce predictable pressures for Sharia law—stability, in effect. Thousands of years of iterations of the Hindu Vedas have simply reinforced the caste system, despite its being outlawed periodically in modern India. But repeated iterations of the Bible have overthrown slavery (at least twice), political and economic feudalism, the suppression of women, and the legitimacy of armed conflict. The Bible is at work in our day countering the suppression of ethnic and sexual minorities. The Iron Curtain recently fell to it; most of the liberation movements in the former Soviet block were grounded in churches. Iterations of other classical religious scriptures produce stability; repeated iterations of the Bible generate novelty. The Bible—free of the interpreter's voice—precipitates change.

Most of us would benefit from personal change, especially change from religiousness to righteousness, from bondage to suppleness to the will of God. It's terribly important, therefore, that we allow the veil to fall from our eyes when we dare to open the Bible. (2 Cor. 3:12–16) We need to loosen our restrictive interpretive grip on the Bible so the Spirit can use it with us again to foment godly novelty. Until we dare do so, no matter how much we protest that we're "biblical Christians," "Bible-believers," we have not permitted the Bible an independent voice distinguishable from our own.

They used to chain Bibles to church lecterns so they wouldn't be stolen. An apter symbol than a chain today would be a leash and muzzle. Jesus turned water into wine. We have turned the Water of Life into embalming fluid.

WHAT THE BIBLE IS FOR

Everyone knows how much easier it is to criticize what's wrong than to lift up what is right. Though we'll return to fruitful and faithful uses of the Bible late in this chapter, let's get fortified right now with excitement at some of the Bible's authentic purposes.

The Bible exists in order to aim our hearts and minds toward God. The New Testament of the Christian Bibles* makes that aim even more specific. It aims our hearts and minds toward Jesus

---

* I use the plural of the word Bible here because within Christianity alone there are various Bibles whose contents and internal arrangements do not coincide with each other. At a minimum, these include the Roman Catholic, Anglican Protestant, and Eastern Orthodox Bibles.

Christ so that the Spirit might convey us into trusting, adoring fellowship with the First Person.

Consider that nearly every word in the Bible was originally written to be read, sung, discussed, and applied aloud to groups of people. When I, as a congregational preacher, pore over the upcoming readings for next Sunday, grasping at sermon ideas, I am not using the Bible as it was originally intended to be used. Indeed when I stand before the congregation, raised high above contradiction, declaring the purposes of God from the Bible to an attentive (I dearly hope) gathering, I am—"biblically" speaking—performing an unnatural act. The Bible was not given to preachers to use on congregations. It was given to congregations to be read in groups.

When Milton wrote in "Lycidas," "The hungry Sheep look up, and are not fed...." he was criticizing the (non-Puritan) clergy of his day. But the reason the sheep weren't being fed had little to do with what flavor church they attended. It was that they looked up towards a preacher—rather than down at their Bibles and across the circle to one another.

Properly used, the Bible is a launching pad into the Presence. When a group prayerfully invites the Spirit to lead its reflections on a passage, it discovers that the "Word of God" is not so much the specific words in India ink on India paper pages as they are the very here-and-now speech of God. The Bible catalyzes the living Word of God among us. How thrilling it is when the Spirit is able to coax us away from discussions of "What *it* (the Bible; the particular passage) means" and introduce us to the more attentive question, "What is *God* saying to us right now?"

My richest experiences of the Presence of God in community with others present have been occasions when groups of us were being attentive—and God did what God does. Those experiences have occurred in a variety of denominational settings. Liberals and conservatives engage such a project with equal tremors, with equal energy, with equal fruit. And recollections of these moments keep my hopes from flagging.

GETTING REAL WITH THE BIBLE

When we get attentive to God with the Bible in the company of others, we no longer need assert things about the Bible that anybody can tell are not accurate. We no longer experience the weight of cognitive dissonance that burdened us when we thought it was in some modern sense "infallible"* or that it is absolutely self-consistent. We quit defending it. God can now use it to change us. When we get real with the Bible, we no longer have to pretend things about it, which are so strenuous to maintain. The Bible's reality is superior to our notions or wishes.

To begin with, when we get real with the Bible we do not have to defend its statements in twenty-first century terms—because it wasn't written in twenty-first century terms. For example, there are people who go to great trouble to insist that Genesis 1–2:3 offers us an accurate scientific account of the origin of things. It's so much more relaxed—and unsettling—to see that glorious passage for what it was and is: a seven-day Hebrew liturgical ceremony of thanksgiving for the Creation.

Likewise the account of the Flood and Noah's ark was not written to supply scientific or historical information. In context with everything that follows right up to the account of the Tower of Babel, it's an alternative, and fuller, account of the "fall of humanity," a narrative structure that allows us to focus aspects of why being human feels like it does. These accounts are also Hebrew retellings of much older Canaanite and Babylonian accounts, some of which, like *The Epic of Gilgamesh,* we have on hand for comparison. The work of the inspiring Spirit becomes quite evident when you compare the job the Hebrew editors did with their pagan originals.

Anyone who brings to the Bible the literary-critical tools they'd use in front of an airport book rack, selecting the sort of literature they want to take aloft, can readily discern much of that without even relying on the vast scholarly literature. Most of us can distinguish prose from poetry, fiction from non-fiction, or science fiction from historical romance. Something like that skill works pretty well with the different biblical genres.

Resistance to that kind of grown-up Bible reading has been with us since the late Middle Ages. People resist it out of the fear of a "domino effect" in which, if we "concede" that the story of Noah's ark isn't literal history, the whole Bible will unzip to where we lose the historicity of the Resurrection—hence our salvation by God in Christ.

---

* Something that our biblical and pre-Reformation ancestors didn't worry much about.

But two truthful considerations serve to relax us on that score. First, mature scholarship has not dispelled the Resurrection; rather it has helped us to see more deeply into what the biblical writers want us to understand about it.

Second, the truth of the Resurrection—and of our salvation— doesn't derive directly or exclusively from the New Testament. Rather our faith in the risen Jesus Christ and the New Testament itself derive from a common source: his current presence among his worshiping people by the power of the Holy Spirit.* If you want to test that, simply find a group that really wants to worship and see what you discover.

Now relaxing with the Bible, letting it say what it says the way it really says it, relieves us of cognitive dissonance. The Bible contains a number of passages that, were we to find them in any other literature, we'd unhesitatingly recognize as conflicting, as fanciful, sometimes as folkloric, occasionally as mistaken. When we drop the pretense that they are otherwise just because they're in the Bible, we find our trust growing, not shrinking, in the face of truths that overflow their narrative containers, truths that are greater than we are, truths that flourish and transform us under our own terms.+

I insist that such readings are not disrespectful or unfaithful. To the contrary, I challenge those who dissent to tell us how it's really respectful to read poetry as though it were prose, to read perpetually fertile mythologies as though they were journalistic history. That seems disrespectful of the very Spirit who chose those genres as the media for parts of the Bible. Our faith is in God, not the literary categories of sacred literature. To rely otherwise is idolatry, even if the idol is an expensive book, bound in real calfskin, engraved with your name and a gold cross.

When we get real with the Bible, we no longer have to pretend that the Bible is either the sole source or the full compendium of the Christian faith. It is, of course, neither.

Virtually all orthodox Christians subscribe to the doctrines of the Holy Trinity and of the two natures of Christ. Both of those

---

* That faith produced the New Testament; it wasn't the other way around.

+ When New Testament theologians refer to parts of the Bible as "myth," this is what they mean: a truth that overflows its container, that remains generative. To call something a myth is not necessarily to falsify its claims to historicity. Many events are both historical and mythological: e.g., Valley Forge.

doctrines were partially undergirded by the New Testament and each can be discerned in embryonic form in it as well. But both doctrines are post-biblical in origin, as any cursory survey of church history will readily show. And each owes almost as much to the thought-forms of Hellenistic philosophy as to the biblical witness or thought-forms. Indeed, that latter point is one of the standard critiques of those doctrines in their traditional inherited forms. When you read, for example, the Chalcedonian Formula (Book of Common Prayer 1979, 864), no particular Bible passages spring readily to mind. That's a defect in the formula.

We can't repeat often enough that the Bible is not the source of the Christian faith. Rather the Bible and the faith have a common source and a common theme. The source of our faith is what God has done for us in Christ as the Holy Spirit has interpreted it to the worshiping and praying church. The theme of the faith and the theme of the New Testament are identical: the Spirit's work in redeeming human lives in and through Jesus Christ. Both the Bible and the faith are products of the same force.

If the Bible is not the source or the compendium of the faith, neither is it the source or ordinal for the Christian church. Again, the Bible and the church are common products of the same work: the Spirit mediating the grace of God in Christ to worshipers.

Settling into that obvious truth is surprisingly relaxing. It relieves us of all the need to pretend that what we're doing is "biblical." Those of us who don't dare try to force our womenfolk back into veils or who don't want to take our congregational funds out of the stock market can settle back in comfort. Roman Catholics get to keep calling their clergy "Father" if that feels good. The rest of us get to keep ordaining women. We can all keep praying for our armed forces. We can wear two fabrics at once—even in church—though the Old Testament thinks that's abominable. Preachers inveighing about what's "natural" and what's "unnatural" can even do so wearing polyester suits and vinyl belts without fear of criticism. I can obey my bishop, even though his (or her!) ministry evolved over long centuries after the last New Testament document was drafted. With all the extra energy that abandoning the struggle with cognitive dissonance releases for our use, we can pay some attention to God and to the world God gave Jesus to live and die for.

Though it feels scarier, when we relax and recognize that the Bible is not the exclusive source for, nor the full compendium of, our moral behavior, we make more room for the Spirit's work in our characters. Again, that's scary. We know our personal propensities for mischief all too well, how readily we play games with ourselves, how we rationalize destructive behavior. We discern similar mischief in others, if anything more clearly in them than in ourselves. So is it really safe to temporize with "biblical morality"?

Yet a close, fresh reading of the Old and New Testaments shows us things we had not seen before nestled in and amongst the familiar elements. What's familiar is the fact that moral behavior is the currency of our righteous relationship with God and others. Moral behavior is a central component to God's covenant contract with us. Our behavior matters to God; it is consequential in our dealings with neighbors; it is a primary way we express our love and respect for both. Moral inattentiveness cannot ever go on the negotiating table for those of us who embrace the biblical revelations.

What's likely to emerge as a surprise when we look closely at the old familiar texts, however, is the fluidity of the reasoning underlying various biblical moral codes. Morality is the substance of an on-going conversation between God and the People of God rather than a once-and-for-all announcement from heaven. Morality is an emergent phenomenon.

The Old Testament permits divorce. The New Testament doesn't. In the various New Testament divorce discussions, no two phrasings are exactly the same. Each occurrence is slanted towards local conditions—not to evade the prohibition but to apply its rationale more precisely. For example, Matthew has Jesus address the prohibition to men alone—since he was writing in a largely Hebraic setting in which women did not have the option to initiate it. Mark on the other hand, writing in Rome where women *could* initiate divorce, prohibits it to women as well.

Sometimes the rationale itself changes—so the outward form of the commandment remains the same but the inward meaning is altogether different. In Exodus's version of the Decalogue, the Sabbath commandment is to commemorate the Creation. In Deuteronomy's version, it is to commemorate Israel's deliverance from slavery, commanding that slaves themselves be allowed restorative rest. By the time of the New Testament, Hebrews were going to great lengths to respect the Sabbath commandment. Yet Jesus swept some of them aside, toying with their moralistic discomfort as he did so.

By the time of the New Testament, Hebrews were taking the Old Testament dietary laws and the traditions based on them equally seriously. Yet it was the very voice of God that swept them out of Peter's life in Acts 10.

An attentive reading of the Old Testament prohibitions of adultery indicates that the underlying rationale was to soothe the husband's worries about the legitimacy of his children—as well as his personal dignity. Similarly, the prohibition against unmarried daughters expressing themselves sexually rested upon the same fear on the part of their eventual grooms, with the consequent loss of the bride-price paid to the young woman's father. A prohibition of adultery appears in the New Testament, yet the rationale is both different from and maturer than the Old Testament worries: this time they have to do with honoring Christ in our bodies. Today we base our opposition to adultery on the concept of its creating a virtually irreparable breach of intimate trust between married partners. Oddly, we do not find that motive in the Bible, though most of us would agree that it's God's own thought.

So a careful and respectful reading of the Bible passages that come up in our moral discussions shows us that we can neither dismiss the moral concerns found there out of hand, nor can we apply them uncritically as they are presented. Either reaction is "unbiblical." As William Countryman said, "The Bible is not God's last word on anything; it is God's first word on everything." It launches the discussion: a discussion in which the Risen Jesus Christ enjoys seat, voice, vote, veto, and presidency.

It's quite important to grasp that the Bible itself models for us a more subtle process than do our present debates. Listening to television evangelists or their occasional opponents in the public media, it's easy to decide that there are only two alternatives before us. We can throw out the charts of "traditional biblical morality" and launch our lives out onto uncharted libidinous seas. Or we can stringently insist on the rigid enforcement of "traditional biblical morality," by legislation if necessary. A grown-up reading of the Bible demonstrates that there is no such thing as "traditional biblical morality." What we discover is an on-going set of conversations, conducted by people eager to glorify God in their moral dealings, striving to improve on what they have received from the past, to correct injustices as they emerge, to discover new applications for new circumstances. The very word "tradition" means that you and I at this moment are part of that conversation as, pray God, shall our children be. As a lady once said, "Tradition is not wearing your grandmother's hat—it's having a baby."

There is one more surprise awaiting a reader seeking a fresh apprehension of the Bible's reality. That is, for all its thickness, the Bible's actual transformative passages are surprisingly few. That is, if you want to reconstruct your inner life—or if you want God to reconstruct it—there are much more compact resources available within the Christian tradition than the Bible.

Not that transformative passages are altogether absent. There are psalms that change us when we pray them—Psalms 51 and 139, just to pick two outstanding examples. There are songs of praise in the New Testament and the Apocrypha that nourish the soul when we offer them to God ourselves.* And any regular Bible reader—even those of us who resist memorizing—can report instances where just the right phrase, just the right verse, popped into our conscious minds during a crisis. The passages in question do not always come from otherwise emotionally thrilling sections.

Martin Luther underwent a profound conversion—one whose impact reverberates to this very day—when he encountered a single verse—"Now it is evident that no one is justified before God by the law; for 'the one who is righteous will live by faith.'" (Gal. 3:11)—in which Paul quotes from Habbakkuk. Yet Paul wrote Galatians and Romans to help Jewish and Gentile converts to get along with each other, not to induce personal conversions. Paul assumed his readers were already molten converts. When I need a chisel and only have a screwdriver, I may rejoice to get the job done with the tool at hand; when I need a screwdriver and have only a kitchen-knife, I may still get the job done, but that's not what those implements are primarily for.

What most of the Bible seems designed for is the transformation not of individuals but of communities. That's certainly what Paul's writings were about. If you read all the letters that scholars

---

* Look at Luke 1:47–55, 68–79; the first three chapters of Ephesians; all the songs in Revelation. If your Bible has an Apocrypha attached (or if it's a Roman Catholic version) read the Song of the Three Jews.

assure us are from Paul's dictation* you come away aware that Paul's primary interest and emphasis was not "justification by faith" (or, more accurately, "justification by grace through faith") but all the communal implications of being "in Christ."

Again, if I want to use passages from Paul to shore up my flagging sense of being righteous before God, there is certainly nothing to stop me doing so. But if I teach my congregation that such was Paul's primary purpose, then Paul needs an attorney in the room.

In fact, the Bible-nourished Christian church has produced many thousands of rich transformative resources. There are one or two small matters I regret about Augustine's impact on history— but when my radio drifts off God's station, I often retune it by dipping into *The Confessions*. Lady Julian of Norwich's *Revelations of Divine Love* will do for you what the hippies said dope would do— with longer-lasting positive effects. Same with Bernard of Clairvaux. Or Francis de Sales. Or Ignatius Loyola's *Spiritual Exercises*. Or the writings of C.S. Lewis or Charles Williams. Oswald Chambers' writings will open your soul right up. Alcoholics Anonymous rightly avoids any sectarian endorsements, but "The Twelve Steps" are a jewel of Christian ascetical theology made practical.

THE BIBLE AND THE WORD OF GOD

Most of this becomes readily apparent to steady readers of the Bible who are willing to allow nagging objections to come into the forefront of their minds as they read. Such nagging objections are as often the voice of the Spirit as of the devil. The naggings are friendly. They call our attention to cognitive dissonance, to the fact that we're trying not to see what we see, feel what we feel, think what we think, know what we know. Not that our own sight, emotion, thought, or knowledge is always or even usually accurate. But we ignore them at our peril, and suppressing them is self-abusive.

---

* That list is generally thought to include: 1 and 2 Thessalonians, Galatians, Philippians, 1 and 2 Corinthians, Romans, and Philemon. Opinion is divided about Colossians. A significant minority argues for the Pauline authorship of Ephesians. One and 2 Timothy and Titus are generally thought to come from disciples of Paul, based on their content, style, and vocabulary. There is virtually no claim at all today for Hebrews as part of the Pauline canon. Can you imagine Paul's writing that long a letter about Jesus without once mentioning the Resurrection?

If we could pay prayerful attention to what we see when reading the Bible, I think we would come away loving it more.

In a court of law, do not tell the judge that you stole your neighbor's lawnmower as an expression of the "inalienable right" that your Creator endowed you with to "life, liberty, and the pursuit of happiness." She will reply that those phrases come from the Declaration of Independence, not the legal code or the Constitution. The Declaration, for all of its importance to us, has no weight in a court of law. She will point out sections of the local criminal statutes that you violated and the sections of the Constitution that allow her to deprive you of your liberty and your pursuit of happiness as your punishment. And yet, try to imagine our Constitution or our law courts if the Declaration of Independence were not loved and revered as the cornerstone of our Republic.

The place of the Bible in the church is analogous to the Declaration's place in America. It is essential and indispensable to any discussion of anything. Yet there is always more to be said.

In this chapter I am pleading for an embrace of the Bible that neither distorts its nature and purpose nor hardens our religious frozenness in the ice-trays our faith communities pour us into. I seek an alliance with the reader's years-long sense that, "When *I* read it, it doesn't seem to say what it did in church." We may move more quickly into trusting the Spirit's guidance of such thoughts if we take time to understand how the Bible came to occupy its present isolated position as the putative supreme authority within Christianity.

That God "speaks" is evident all over the Bible. Yet the Bible seems unselfconscious as the "Word of God." When that phrase occurs, it usually refers more to an act of self-disclosure on God's part than to any document. Indeed, when we view the Scriptures, as we have them today, with fresh eyes we are struck—perhaps startled—with how casually various parts of the Bible regard other parts. Relatively little of the Bible claims to be oracular; very little of its text gets introduced by "Thus says the LORD . . . ." One biblical writer seems to feel free to alter what another has written with impunity.* Generations of editors allowed readily correctable

---

* Witness the famous contrast between 2 Samuel 24:1f. and the account of the same episode in 1 Chronicles 21:1f. The Chronicler feels no compunctions about correcting the theology of his predecessor, nor did the editing rabbis feel compunction about offering us both texts.

conflicts of fact to stand, rightly adjudging them impertinent to the thrust of the message.* For many centuries nobody worried about that sort of thing.

St. Paul made surprisingly little use of the Old Testament in the writings that survive.+ He appeared to have no worked-out interpretive method for the Old Testament Scriptures, no systematic "hermeneutics" as theologians call it. We search Paul's writings in vain for any discussion of the doctrinal or moral importance of the Scriptures *per se*, though he clearly valued the doctrine and morality God revealed to him. (Paul carefully distinguished between thoughts he knew God gave him as opposed to his own thinking, though he relied on the latter.) His primary source for God's truth was the Presence itself. His letters grow much more from his prayer than from his study of scrolls.

Only one record of our Lord using a biblical text as the point of departure for any of his teachings has reached us, the Nazareth synagogue sermon of Luke 4. His interpretation of it did not accord with the gathering's understanding, as their reaction attested. We do know that various texts from what we know as the Old Testament greatly enriched his inner life—for example, from his use of Deuteronomy against the devil's temptations in the Wilderness. But Jesus did not tell us specifically how to use the Scriptures. Jesus used Old Testament passages as much for contrast with his own teachings as for corroboration. He weighted one passage against another unhesitantly without telling us how he chose as he did:

> Some Pharisees came, and to test him they asked, "Is it lawful for a man to divorce his wife?" He answered them, "What did Moses command you?" They said, "Moses allowed a man to write a certificate of dismissal and to divorce her." But Jesus said to them, "Because of your hardness of heart he wrote this commandment for you. But from the beginning of creation

---

* E.g., Who was the Priest when David ate the Showbread—Abimelech (1 Sam. 21:1-3)? or Abiathar (Mk. 2:25-26)? Did a fish eat Jonah (Jo. 1:17) or a sea monster/whale (Mt. 12:40)?

+ And I do not know of evidence that he used the Hebrew Scriptures in his Christian ministry—his Old Testament references seemed based on a Greek version (LXX?) rather than any Hebrew version or Aramaic targums.

> [i.e. the book of Genesis], 'God made them male and female. For this reason a man shall leave his father and mother and be joined to his wife, and the two shall become one flesh.' So they are no longer two, but one flesh. Therefore what God has joined together, let no one separate." (Mk. 10:2–9)

What little he said about the permanence of the Torah—"For truly I tell you, until heaven and earth pass away, not one letter, not one stroke of a letter, will pass from the law until all is accomplished." (Mt. 5:18)—occurred in the context of his critique of what would become Talmudic expansions of the Torah, a process to which he was implacably opposed. Notice that Matthew has him proceed to say:

> Therefore, whoever breaks one of the least of these commandments, and teaches others to do the same, will be called least in the kingdom of heaven; but whoever does them and teaches them will be called great in the kingdom of heaven. For I tell you, unless your righteousness exceeds that of the scribes and Pharisees, you will never enter the kingdom of heaven. (Mt. 5:19–20)

His citations of various passages are usually part of some argument, almost playful demonstrations of the Old Testament's multivalence.*

> You have heard that it was said to those of ancient times, "You shall not murder"; and "Whoever murders shall be liable to judgment." But I say to you that if you are angry with a brother or sister, you will be liable to judgment; and if you insult a brother or sister, you will be liable to the council; and if you say, "You fool," you will be liable to the hell of fire. (Mt. 5:21–22)

> You have heard that it was said, "You shall not commit adultery." But I say to you that everyone who looks at a woman with lust has already committed adultery with her in his heart. (Mt. 5:27–28)

---

* My talk of the "Old Testament" here is anachronistic. At Jesus' time, the Hebrew Scriptures had not yet been "canonized" by the Rabbis at Jabneh. But in his day the Torah was already regarded as a discrete authoritative unit. Other than assuring us of its invulnerability to the passage of time, Jesus gave us no instructions or models of how to use the Torah. Certainly his own use of it was sometimes whimsical: e.g., his play on Deuteronomy 15:11 in Matthew 26:11.

No liberal or conservative modern seminary would allow him to ignore the context in Deuteronomy 15:11 and expect a passing grade:

> Since there will never cease to be some in need on the earth, I therefore command you, "Open your hand to the poor and needy neighbor in your land."

... from which Jesus drew his famous, "The poor you have with you always."

> But when the disciples saw it, they were angry and said, "Why this waste? For this ointment could have been sold for a large sum, and the money given to the poor." But Jesus, aware of this, said to them, "Why do you trouble the woman? She has performed a good service for me. For you always have the poor with you, but you will not always have me."

Jesus played more casually with original contexts than a modern preacher of any stripe would dare. We have no teachings of our Lord's demanding that we use Scriptures the way Christians routinely attempt to do today. This is a shaky guess, but I think Jesus, like Paul, preferred prayer to Bible study, though he might not have separated them altogether.

Here is a text that will occur to readers who want to dispute what I have been saying:

> All Scripture is inspired by God and is useful for teaching, for reproof, for correction, and for training in righteousness, so that everyone who belongs to God may be proficient, equipped for every good work. (2 Tim. 3:16–17)

People cite those two verses relentlessly to substantiate all sorts of things about the Bible that the verses neither declare nor support. People often assume these verses refer to the whole Bible. That is by no means clear and unlikely on the face of it—at the time those verses were written, there was no such thing as a "Bible" in our sense.[*] Clearly those verses are true as written, so far as they go—biblical texts are indeed useful for the functions mentioned and it is no great difficulty to regard favorite texts as "Spirit-breathed" if we can resist literalizing that metaphor. What's equally important is what they do *not* say—especially in the present climate. Not a word do we

---

[*] Indeed, if those verses were applied to the whole Bible, it would be an instance of paradoxical self-reference, a "strange loop," like the famous "All generalizations are false," or "Every word I say is a lie."

find about "inerrancy," about final infallible or indefectible
authority, about the Bible as the complete source and all-inclusive
compendium of the faith.* But we hear those verses quoted as
though such were exactly their denotation, as though they war-
ranted a Q'ranic use of the Bible. If the Bible were indeed such
an authority as the misinterpretation of those verses claims, would
not so casual a disregard of their actual meaning be impious?

Modern biblical interpreters of all parties properly discourage
what is called "eisegesis"—to read your own meaning into a passage that clearly meant something else. It is proper to do "exegesis"—to present what the passage meant in a manner faithful to
the intent of the original writer. That strikes all of us—liberals and
conservatives alike—as a helpful scruple. So it's awkward that virtually all of the New Testament citations of the Old Testament are
openly eisegetical rather than exegetical. We might gather they
did not think exegesis was very important. So what *was* important,
if exegesis was not? The obvious answer is a faithful account of
what God was doing and saying to them right then as they prayed,
knowing themselves to be the on-going expression of God's work
with a select people in history. To that end they unblushingly
employed any Old Testament passage that the Spirit brought to
mind to highlight God's present action—eisegesis, in effect. Off
hand, I cannot think of a single instance of pure biblical exegesis
in the New Testament. But the New Testament thrills us in every
paragraph with the experience our spiritual ancestors enjoyed of
the actual Presence of God in the context of their conscious identity as God's people.+

It is important to consider that the gospel message took shape
in a setting that did not include a "Bible" in the sense that we
mean the term, either as an absolute authority or as a single volume. The parts are far older than the whole. In fact, the gospel

---

* Notice that we are not talking about "literalism." Liberals, usually unfamiliar
with the actual discussions of conservatives, typically target literalism as their
strawman. That assumption is mistaken and undiscerning. Literalism requires so
much energy to keep inflated that those who attempt it don't have the breath to
cause much trouble. The actual Fundamentalist and Inerrantist postures are
necessarily more nuanced. The mistake I am identifying is that of elevating the
Bible as a discrete unit to full and ultimate authority—not literalism.

+ Reading an endorsement of biblical inerrancy into 2 Timothy 3:16 f. would be
a prize-winning specimen of "eisegesis."

message—the good news of our membership in God's Kingdom in Christ—preceded "the Bible" by centuries and resulted from the same historical forces as produced the Bible. When later Christian authors—the "Fathers"—wrote their invaluable materials, they cited Old and New Testament passages copiously to corroborate various points they were stressing—but they rarely appealed to them to establish a point authoritatively. Their reason for not doing so is well worth our consideration: the heretics were quoting and citing the Bible to telling effect!

The Fathers found that heresy could not successfully be refuted by use of the Bible alone, as though it were the only authority for belief or practice. Augustine reported that he believed the Gospels because the Catholic Church told him to—not vice versa. I know of no place in the patristic literature in which a writer stresses the Bible as authoritative for belief or practice, nor any in which the writer presents the Bible as God's *primary* means of revelation. They had discovered it was too multivalent, too vulnerable to multiple interpretations. The Fathers were more likely to stress the Spirit's witness within the church, "Apostolic Tradition," or even the person or office of the bishop. We misunderstand the Fathers unless we recognize that they viewed all of those along with the pre-Bible scrolls—often even including illustrative pagan sources, such as the Greek Sybils—as a seamless witness of God's Spirit to humanity. They were more confident than we that God is always generously addressing us.

We must recognize that the Bible was not in any sense a *book*—a single work—until, at the very earliest, late in the second century C.E. Yet our ancestors of that period displayed no sense of lacking God's guidance.* Prior to the emergence of the codexes—and for long afterward—the word "bible" meant *biblia*: books (plural), a list of approved scrolls any combination of which a local group might possess, secure in the knowledge that believers elsewhere

---

* The history of how the codex arrangement that we still use replaced separate scrolls is fun to study. Competition for wealth and prestige between the libraries in Alexandria (Egypt) and Pergamum (Asia Minor) led the Egyptians to restrict the export of papyrus, causing the scroll-keepers of Pergamum to develop parchment from animal hides. Papyrus curls up readily into scrolls; parchment tends to lie flat. So the codex was developed as an (eventually more practical) alternative to scrolls.

found them worth treasuring.* Likely the first biblical codices were not complete collections. The first Christian list of books regarded as "scripture" coinciding with a Bible that we would recognize only occurs in 367 C.E. in a letter of Athanatius. Indeed, the Bible—what many today are calling the "canon" and viewing as a unitary work—was never officially pronounced closed or complete by any universal council competent so to pronounce.⁺ The result of all that is delightful: the *Bible is a stable but open system.* That makes it an enduring enzyme all through subsequent history, constantly catalyzing change, precipitating judgment on all present arrangements.

Since he knew that the canon was not officially closed as of his own day, Martin Luther did not hesitate to place the Epistle of James last in his New Testament and to omit the Revelation altogether. Luther felt a freedom with the Bible that his followers—and the followers of the other reformers—abdicated. Other reformers decided to ignore those portions of the Old Testament which did not correspond to the Hebrew texts—the so-called Apocrypha, since Roman Catholics were defending some of their objectionable practices (like prayers for the dead) using apocryphal materials.◆ The Protestants simply sawed it off. Clearly they felt free to do so with impunity.

The Anabaptists rejected the Old Testament for all sorts of reasons, some of them good ones. Indeed, it has been strongly

---

* There seem to have been several criteria for selecting books to be included. The church borrowed the OT list from Jewish decisions. The "NT" books were included if there was reason to connect them to the Apostles; if in worship, prayer, and group study they comported with the felt Presence of God; and if believers, when commanded to surrender them to Roman police, chose death instead. Think of those criteria while holding a Bible—the volume will make your hand tingle.

⁺ Various sub-universal councils have closed it here and there for their own groups, but those clotures do not bind the Church Universal. By the same token, denominational groups have no permission to add or subtract from the present open list of books until some competent council of the Church Universal allows it. That will not happen anytime soon, if present indications are reliable.

◆ The Apocrypha is a collection of materials found in the Greek version of the Old Testament called the Septuagint (LXX) but not in the extant Hebrew texts. Roman Catholics regard apocryphal material as integral to the OT; Protestant editions of the Bible omit it altogether; Anglican Bibles collect it and print it between the Testaments. When you mention the "Bible" don't be surprised to be asked which of at least five arrangements you mean.

suggested that Luther, Zwingli, and Calvin retained the Old Testament chiefly to warrant their habit of calling in the police and soldiers against those who disagreed with them—a habit they'd have had trouble warranting from the New Testament.

THE BIBLE'S CATASTROPHIC PROMOTION

Until the Reformation, the authority of the Bible wasn't a major concern for Christians. The *whole* of God's self-disclosure was authoritative, but the primary arbitrating authority tended to be the church herself as represented by the pope and his appointees. The Bible was an integral part of God's self-disclosure and faith-funding, but to remove it from the whole pattern of God's self-revelation and exalt it above the other elements wouldn't have occurred to anybody. Obviously no pope ever felt the need to.

In recent centuries the Bible has undergone a status upgrade that places it beyond what most previous Christian generations would recognize or recommend. Protestants have pulled the Bible out of the whole pattern of God's self-revelation and made it the single arbiter of all the rest. Historians who track this innovation locate it during and following the Protestant Reformation in Europe during the sixteenth century.

The Protestant elevation of the Bible was an understandable reaction to the centuries-long self-elevation of the church as the primary authority, but the nozzle had begun to confuse itself occasionally with the water tank. As long as the church's authority was acknowledged and her prestige unstained, things were relatively stable. But the authority and prestige of the Roman Church, which had heroically held Europe together in all ways for so many centuries, began unraveling seriously a couple of centuries before Martin Luther.

The collapse of the Roman Church's authority in Europe was accelerated by a few specific developments. First came the Black Death, an epidemic of the bubonic plague that killed between a quarter and a third of Europe's population in slightly more than a decade, a horror against which all the church's sacramental and ritual armamentarium proved impotent. Europe realized that the church could not say, "Rise up and walk!" with any confidence.

Nor could the church any longer claim, "Silver and gold have I none," as a medieval cardinal pointed out to a pope. The power and wealth which previous churchfolk had generated by their virtue attracted less devout ministers into the church's hierarchy.* These officials dissipated the prestige of the church by abusing its taxation privileges for private indulgence. In the century prior to the Reformation, there were rival papacies backed by rival parties.+ At one point four different claimants to the papal tiara were excommunicating each other and each other's followers. That sorely taxed the patience of the laity and undermined trust in the church's reliability.

The fifteenth century invention of printing with movable type—ironically the inspiration of a devout Catholic, Johannes Gutenberg—made the Protestant Reformation technologically possible. It broke the church's virtual monopoly on literacy. Bibles sprouted all over the place and information spread more quickly and more accurately than ever before.

Luther's initially inadvertent defiance of the Roman Church's hegemony is so familiar that we need not recapitulate it here. Local kings and princes saw in his rebellion a theologically justifiable means for withholding monies from Italy; they embraced the Reformation with that blend of piety and economic self-interest that stains Protestantism to this day. Much of Europe was stretching into the resulting freedom under the umbrella of local rulers. Where that umbrella of aristocratic support was absent, the Protestant struggle usually failed—a fine reason to clutch the Old Testament, so much friendlier to kings and nobles and rulers. By the time the erstwhile monk was a middle-aged husband and father the church in Europe could no longer claim unity.

The Reformation was a heady period. Fifty years or so ago, Dietrich Bonnhoeffer wrote from prison about "humanity come of age." It must have felt that way to be a Protestant during the early Reformation. Certainly the writings of the reformers still breathe a freshness that excites and challenges us today. Finally

---

* A notoriously corrupt pope—Leo X, if memory serves—remarked to his brother upon acceding to Peter's Throne, "Since it hath pleased Almighty God to bestow the papacy upon us, let us enjoy it!" It is difficult to imagine such a quip from, say, Gregory the Great, or even Innocent III.

+ The wines named Chateau-Neuf du Pape—"the Pope's new castle"—reflect the "Babylonian Exile" period, in which the papacy was hostage to the French throne and involuntarily quartered outside Avignon.

out from under the pope with a whole religion to recover and redefine—what an adventure. Europe burgeoned with socio-religious experiments, restructurings, doctrinal formulations, and liturgical revisions. As in any stochastic process, some of them proved adaptive and sank roots. With papal authority disavowed, much of Europe was "home alone."

Eventually being "home alone" got old. Freedom is as threatening as it is beckoning. (Don't forget Becker—ever.) A discredited church hierarchy could no longer slake the death-fear-driven lust for trustworthy umpires. Over against the rejected authority of the papacy and curia, Protestants now elevated a new authority that had never been used in such a manner before: the Bible.* Rapidly the Bible took the place of the pope and clergy as the arbiter of certainty in matters of belief, morals, church order, eventually of historical and scientific fact. The phrase *sola scriptura*—the Bible alone—became a sort of theological mantra, as much a source of self-consolation as of self-approval.

PROBLEMS FOLLOWING THE PROMOTION

The idea itself of elevating the Bible as the sole authority was reasonable and honest. The problem was its incongruity with the Bible itself. At its new prominence, previously unrecognized problems came into unavoidable focus.+ Pretending those problems were not there was neither reasonable nor honest. The emergent difficulties formed ticking time bombs, potentially able to blow up the entire novel arrangement of authority crouching behind the Bible. Much effort would eventually be needed to prevent such an explosion.

---

* Though I regret much of the outcome of that choice, its rationale makes deep sense. The Roman hierarchy could always be suspected of self-interest even as it spoke for God. The Bible, on the other hand, was not copyright in any group's interest. It appeared to be an objective, God-given standard to which all could apply and be held accountable. Clearly and unmistakably its early applications prompted spiritually fruitful discoveries. The fact that subjectivity did not reside in the authority itself—as it did in the Vatican—concealed the subjectivity resident in each interpreter. But it was a fully understandable mistake.

+ Many an averagely moral judge has come to regret the close scrutiny that attends consideration for the Supreme Court; before he was prominent nobody much knew or cared whether he had smoked dope or had hired babysitters without green cards. In something like that process, the Bible came in for a scrutiny it could not long sustain.

The Old Testament was a problematic case in point. Up until the Reformation nobody had had to worry much about how Christians should read the Old Testament. The Fathers and early theologians had strip-mined it at will for examples for their teachings, finding wonderful allegories substantiating points they had previously arrived at by other means. In fact, the great bulk of Christian usage of the Old Testament was either allegorical or typological, some of it quite ingenious, coloring our understanding to this day.*

Now there are no rules against one religious group using the revered documents of another in such a manner—in fact that may be the safest means to withstand their native appeal. Until the nineteenth century, it is virtually impossible to find any prominent Christian writing on the Old Testament that takes a passage seriously for its own sake that exhibits any regard for the intention of the original writer. Christians had shown no interest whatever in what the Old Testament writers thought they were writing about. The tendency of Protestants, whether Lutheran, Reformed, Anabaptist, or Anglican, was to value Old Testament passages only to the extent they could be used either to make a (proleptic) point about Jesus or to shore up whatever moral teaching one happened to favor.†

In other words, the first three quarters of the inspired, now inerrant, Bible had no *intrinsic* worth of its own. The Old Testament's value was *extrinsic*, serving as a sort of reserve battery to energize the New Testament to which it was attached. History furnishes

---

* For example, much present day baptismal theology still echoes typological interpretations of Noah's Flood, the Parting of the Sea of Reeds and of the Jordan. Eucharistic theology still echoes typological interpretations of post-sacrificial fellowship meals. Though our appreciation of the original texts has broadened to include what they actually meant in their own contexts, we would only part with inherited interpretations with reluctance.

† "VII. Of the Old Testament.
The Old Testament is not contrary to the New: for both in the Old and New Testament everlasting life is offered to Mankind by Christ, who is the only Mediator between God and Man, being both God and Man. Wherefore they are not to be heard, which feign that the old Fathers did look only for transitory promises. Although the Law given from God by Moses, as touching Ceremonies and Rites, do not bind Christian men, nor the Civil precepts thereof ought of necessity to be received in any commonwealth; yet notwithstanding, no Christian man whatsoever is free from the obedience of the Commandments which are called Moral." ("Historical Documents," The Book of Common Prayer, 869)

no parallel to a literature so consistently, lengthily, blandly, and authoritatively misused.

That arrangement would eventually have to explode. It only awaited a time when people would read the Old Testament and pay attention to what it actually says. Then the scramble would have to begin in earnest.

Another ticking bomb: *church order.* Before the Reformation, no one had ever claimed that church doctrine or governing order derived or should derive from the Bible. Both derived from the Spirit's witness, as did the Scriptures themselves, within the post-Apostolic church. The threefold ministry of bishops, priests, and deacons fell along a biblical trajectory. And, although ordained ministry could be seen as a coherent outgrowth of patterns already discernible in the New Testament, the church had never required its membership to view it as a "biblical ministry." But once that the Scriptures became enmeshed with church governance, they had to be seen as the source of doctrine and order.* In *The Churches the Apostles Left Behind,* Raymond E. Brown, a prominent Roman Catholic scholar, has identified no fewer than seven distinct, sometimes disparate, ecclesiologies (systems of church order) in the New Testament. Once you've seen them distinguished, it's difficult to forget or pretend not to have seen them—and it becomes difficult to listen with complete confidence to one who insists that "the New Testament Church" used to do this or that. On such matters, the Bible's multivalence makes life complicated. Baptists, Episcopalians, Presbyterians, and Quakers have equal claim to being "biblical"—though who could confuse them or (on bad days) think them connected to the same movement?+

I do not intend this as mockery. I mean this example to point out the unavoidable complexity of matters of "biblical authority" when it comes to church order.

---

* That led to one of the (mercifully few) truly silly statements in the Anglican Book of Common Prayer: "It is evident to all men diligently reading Holy Scripture and ancient authors, that from the Apostles' time there have been these orders of Ministers in Christ's church,—Bishops, Priests, and Deacons." Rubric, BCP, 1928, 529.

+ Indeed, in some American cities there are intersections three of whose four corners are occupied by easily distinguishable churches, each able to demonstrate from selected biblical texts that it is the current best expression of the "New Testament Church."

It was in the course of debates with English Puritans about church order—whether the Bible set forth a single authoritative pattern of organizational arrangement for the church—that Richard Hooker, the greatest of the "Anglican Divines," was to spell out an abidingly useful approach to authority in the church. Unfortunately Hooker's thoughts had little impact across the Channel or north of the Roman Wall. So church order persisted as a test of the Bible's authoritative adequacy.

In the post-apostolic epoch, elaborate systems for institutional governance, practice, and belief had evolved. They are referred to as Canon Law. Canon Law went the way of the pope for most Protestants, leaving only the Bible and local preference in its place. Both proved more volatile than Canon Law had ever been, as the bewildering proliferation of different Protestant groups attests.

Doctrine was another ticking bomb. Most Protestants would agree that the Jehovah's Witnesses and the Unitarians have departed from the Christian consensus with their respective rejections of the doctrines of the Holy Trinity and of the two natures of Christ, divine and human. Yet it's notoriously difficult to convince Jehovah's Witnesses or Unitarians of their errors using the Bible. If they're studied up, they can read the Bible back at you to support their positions. What divides us are post-biblical doctrines.

Various evangelical groups offer training sessions in which participants learn to witness (in order to convert) and reply (in order to resist being converted) to a host of irregular Bible interpretations, i.e., the interpretations of Mormons, Jehovah's Witnesses, Roman Catholics (!), and Darwinists. These evangelical efforts do not usually make significant inroads into the targeted groups (though the occasional convert from one of those groups can dine out forever on his conversion among conservative Christians). And, to be sure, converting others is not really the point. The training sessions rather serve to assure us of the abiding superior plausibility of our own beliefs.* In other words, such efforts are for *our* sake, not for theirs. They minister to our need for certainty—or at least for confidence; they help us stave off the cognitive dissonance that a cognitive rival provokes willy-nilly just by entering the room.

---

* For a discussion of such functions see Peter Berger, *The Sacred Canopy* (Garden City: Doubleday & Company, Inc., 1969).

Internal conflicts were another bomb ticking between the book covers. Until the Reformation began elevating the Bible past papal altitudes, the manifold conflicting reports and perspectives in the Bible had never really been a problem. After that elevation, these conflicts and disparities became so many little hand grenades with loose pins, awaiting any careful reader with an average attention span. Job's counselors derived their preachments from the Psalms and Proverbs, as anyone reading through the Old Testament sequentially will see—yet God repudiated them in the last chapter. Was God repudiating Psalm 1 or 37? Deuteronomy did not allow Moabites in the Assembly of Israel up to the tenth generation; yet King David's grandmother Ruth was a Moabite. Jerusalem had thought itself proof against the Babylonians based on traditions like this one:

> Your house and your kingdom shall be made sure forever before me; your throne shall be established forever. (2 Sam. 7:16)

Unhappily, they had paid no attention to *this* tradition:

> Now therefore, if you obey my voice and keep my covenant, you shall be my treasured possession out of all the peoples. (Ex. 19:5)

The latter was the biggest "if" in Israel's history. Both traditions were equally "biblical." Jerusalem bet her life on one of them, the wrong one, as it turned out in 586 B.C.E. when the Babylonians finally conquered the city.

Culling out conflicting biblical passages and brandishing them in front of anxious conservatives is a soul-corrosive exercise, demonstrating bad taste, and unworthy of any spiritual grownup. It is also an utterly modern exercise, not more than two centuries old. Until the Bible became the primary authority for many Protestants, few were drawn into such hassles. But inflated claims for the Bible will always generate that sort of scrutiny—not all of it sniggling or supercilious.

A friend of mine was once thrust into such a contest, pitted against a Fundamentalist minister at a Rotary luncheon. For every contradiction in the Bible he pointed out, his antagonist had a plausible rejoinder. Finally my friend played his trump: "In the following passage, 'Then he made the molten sea; it was round, ten cubits from rim to rim, and five cubits high. A line of thirty cubits would encircle it completely,' (2 Chr. 4:2) what was the value of pi?"

His antagonist muttered, "We have a committee working on that!"

I doubt the debate improved the spiritual condition—or the digestion—of any of the spectators or either of the participants.

People encounter such internal clashes regularly. Therefore, a large literature exists to help anxious Bible readers manage them. For example, readers made anxious by the previous anecdote can take relief from a detail I found in such a book: The value of pi remains 3.14 if you assume that the diameter was measured from the inside edge and the circumference around the outside edge. The walls of the bowl seem to have been six inches thick.* Such plausible explanations are important for consumers, because the admission of error or disparity becomes a slippery slope, resulting in a domino effect, depriving us, many believe, of our primary contact with the mind of God. I have heard people say, "If we lose the literal historicity of Noah's ark, we'll lose the Resurrection!" Anyone (including myself) who mocks that anxiety or the heroic belief-projects it fuels, silly as various examples may strike us, is at that moment being a cad. Fear is not funny. It hurts, and it makes us hurtful to others. Death scares me too; I too yearn for inerrant certainty.

The leader of a parish Bible study group once asked me to sit in with them because a frequent visitor from another denomination was gradually taking them over in ways the leader felt unhelpful. When the visitor saw that the preacher was there she let me have both barrels. Brandishing her Bible aloft, she proclaimed, "*Jesus* is the Word of God; *this Book* is the Word of God; *this Book is God!*" I forget exactly how I reacted—this was years ago—but the reader can by now imagine. I recall saying something about nothing on earth, not even God's direct gifts, being perfect by the time they reach us, going on to mention various disparate passages to rattle her.+ She cried, "It's people like you that cost my brother his faith. Somebody like *you* started showing him so-called contradictions in the Bible, and now he doesn't believe in anything!" Ungallantly I replied, "Lady, it's people like *you* that cost your brother his faith. You taught him that the Bible's authority

---

* Harold Lindsell, *The Battle for the Bible* (Grand Rapids: Zondervan Publishing House, 1976), 165–167.

+ A cad, I confess it. One learns with time.

depends on its freedom from error. So once he thought he saw a defect he was free of its authority."

As you may guess, the exchange was less than fruitful. Such issues require pastoral intervention; they are not matters to quarrel over. We can only be effectively pastoral if we understand the fears that underlie them and how they entered the church's experience. We need to know that there are godly, historically integral alternatives not only to what we call Fundamentalism but also to Biblicism itself. "Errors" and "contradictions" in the Bible are a pseudo-problem. But—Lord have mercy!—look at the time wasted on it.

"BIBLICAL AUTHORITY" = LOCAL READING STRATEGY

The history I have just skimmed leaves us today in parlous straits. Once the Bible got thrust into the position it holds in many sectors of many denominations,* interpretive scaffolding rose up around it as rigid as the papacy had ever been. In effect, what was canonical was not so much the Bible itself in all its complexity, but the interpreter's personal sense of what it ought to mean. The instabilities listed so far required that great care be taken with the Bible's reading and interpretation. It had to be read in particular ways and not in others. Given the expansive nature of the Bible, the alternative might be chaos.

But let's be clear about the implication of all this: When any of us, myself included, talk of "what the Bible says," you are hearing reading strategies masquerading as the Bible's single voice—as though the Bible had only a single voice.† The Bible works through many voices, not a single one. If our post-biblical understanding of God as Holy Trinity tells us that God's very being is dialectic, conversational, how should the Bible be otherwise? As listener, you always deserve to know the speaker's reading strategy, the prior doctrinal commitments that impel him to select one passage over

---

* Including my own denomination, the Episcopal Church, which debates "biblical authority" whenever we get anxious about sex.

† I suggest that readers cultivate reflexive caution whenever you hear someone use the word "biblical" as an endorsement for anything, especially if the speaker appears to be saying something he approves of himself for saying. Arguments about what is biblical and what is unbiblical nearly always camouflage undeclared reading strategies. At least require that the speaker expose his strategy to public scrutiny and tell you where he got it.

another. For example, "And the one who has no sword must sell his cloak and buy one," (Lk. 22:36b) in preference to "Put away your sword" (Mt. 26:52).

Reichsmarschall Hermann Göring once remarked, "Whenever I hear the word *Kultur*, I reach for my gun!" A bad reaction from a bad man to a good word. But we should cultivate a reflex of caution whenever we hear the adjective "biblical" used as an endorsement of something the speaker favors. The use of the word begs a huge question—it assumes that the Bible is univocal. The Q'ran is univocal. The Bible is not.

All proclamation is interpretive, because the Bible is multivalent. We can't escape that fact if we read the Bible at all. What we *can* do is try to be honest about our presuppositions and interpretive strategies. God uses the Bible in manifold wonderful ways. But I can't recall any instance when God has used it satisfactorily to resolve the tension we feel when confronted with groups whose opinions differ from our own. This kind of demon "cometh not out but by prayer and fasting," as the Savior said—not by Bible reading alone.

A clerical colleague and I were once on opposing sides in a matter of considerable controversy. It caused him, as he insisted, to doubt my Christianity. I replied that I had arrived at my present position through lengthy attentive prayer and requested that before we converse further he pray about the matter himself. He reacted as if stunned, eyes and nostrils wide with momentary confusion. Raw prayer clearly scared him. (No reason it shouldn't; it scares me.) After a brief delay, a sudden insight popped up to his rescue. He smiled with triumphant relief and replied, "I don't *need* to pray about that; I already possess God's inerrant decree on that matter—in the Bible!" He then cited a couple of verses which he thought covered the matter, sedulously refusing all subsequent invitations and challenges to approach the Throne on the scary matter in question. He had hit upon a way to avoid the Presence of God in a manner that seemed actually to honor God, which allowed him to maintain his self-approval. That is an example of using the Bible to anesthetize pains we really ought to feel, to unstring potentially fruitful tensions.*

---

* I still feel pain reflecting on that episode—and any number like it. I hate what happens between people in such quarrels. Take that pain into account as you read this chapter. It colors my perceptions, shapes my reading strategy.

Ironically, since being elevated to papal heights, the Bible has nearly ceased to be the catalytic enzyme God generously allowed us to scrape together across so many eons and cultures and languages, at such heroic cost to those who wrote its parts, wove it together, edited it, revised it, treasured it, protected it, and died for it. Should liberals alone regret that loss?

THE ELEVATED BIBLE AND THE FEAR OF DEATH

The Bible got elevated to the status of sole guide, compendium, and arbiter because people during the Reformation were as scared of death as we are and have been ever since. The particular expression of death-fear at play in the resistance to anything other than a submissive reading of the Bible is *our longing for certainty*. This is no new reaction. The Gospels constantly contrast personal trust in Jesus with people's fear-driven insistence that they see signs and wonders.

The Bible was not given us in order to provide certainty. It was given to point us towards God—whose personal Presence is the closest thing to certainty we've got. Insisting that it's inerrant or even self-consistent presses it into services for which it wasn't designed.

Ironically, the Bible has regained its destabilizing voice in the last two centuries at the hands of scholars and interpreters who have from the very first been stigmatized as its enemies.* Modern biblical scholarship on the model of the other inductive sciences has been one of humanity's most fruitful intellectual and spiritual adventures. It has read the Bible painstakingly, seeking to identify authorship, provenance, purpose, cultural setting, social power dynamics, literary structures, narrative frameworks and rhetorical devices, archaeological considerations, and connections with other available documentary sources. It has more often than not pursued those studies within church-owned universities, publications, and conferences. More often than not the sponsoring churches have summoned up faith in the truth's ultimate

---

* The stigma is an undeserved slander. The so-called Higher Critics regularly get accused of trying to water the Bible down, temporize with it, and evade its authority. The antagonists to critical scholarship appear to think that scholarship can only derive legitimacy from its apologetic thrust—that is, faithful scholarship must only seek to preserve, not to explore.

friendliness and the truth's power to prevail over error. For the most part they have been good sports about the anxieties involved in hosting such explorations. Things really have gotten somewhat better since Galileo's day.

Not all of these scholars have been Stage 6 saints. You could match their egos against those of any discipline without losing money. Deliberate falsifications occur in biblical and historical scholarship at about the same rate as in physics, biology, medical research, or chemistry—though somewhat less than in the humanities—and for the same unseemly motives. Yet rigorous methodology usually evens things out. As in any science, the "free market of ideas" works as a corrective.

Nor do all scholars share complete agreement on theology, method, conventions, or terminology. As in any rigorous discipline, there are surging parties of opinion battling each other. Again, that is how public thinking takes place. It's a strength, not a weakness.

As a professional consumer of the insights of modern biblical scholarship, as a parish priest, as a director of souls, as one who loves and fears the struggle of prayer with an open Bible on my knees, I'm tempted to wax rhapsodic about what God offers us through and around such scholarship, dull as it usually is to read. Perhaps somebody needs to wax rhapsodic about it. From its very beginning, modern biblical investigation has been attacked as though it were a trick of the devil by those who oppose its threat to their favored reading strategies. (I'm a bad sport for hours after something I read overturns a favorite interpretation of my own, no reason they shouldn't be.) And gallery-players like the over-publicized Jesus Seminar, which bypasses scholarly peer-review by going to the press, openly display the silliest distortions of modern scholarship.* But just as it took the force of a Luther, a Calvin, a Zwingli to wrest loose the pope's grip on much of Europe, so only the plodding, patient, methodical work of many thousands of scholars who help us pay attention to what we are reading could rescue the Bible from its dogmatic confinement.

The reaction against scientific Bible scholarship from conservatives has obscured several things about it. It has left the average

---

* Any who find the Jesus Seminar troubling—or too promising—should consult Luke Timothy Johnson's *The Real Jesus.*

person thinking that there are only two approaches to be taken to the Bible. The first approach would be to view the Bible as Muslims view the Q'ran, to exalt it, history notwithstanding, as the sole or primary source of Christian belief and practice, refusing anyone permission to read it critically. So widespread is this notion that even those who do not hold it sometimes feel a sort of guilt because they don't, as though they were spiritually deviant.

The alternative approach the average person would seem to be left with is what opponents to scholarship call "liberal."* By "liberal" they tend to mean flippant skepticism fueled by moral mischief, accepting only what one already wishes to believe, finding disingenuous ways to evade anything inconvenient. Others would phrase the alternative less abrasively: to declare the Bible outmoded, a way station on the race's evolution into spiritual and intellectual maturity.

The latter caricatures survive scrutiny no better than the Q'ranic. Both are fear-based.

Since it is not difficult to show that neither proposition is plausible as stated, antagonists to inductive scholarship often insist on their points by shrillness, by non-attendance at gatherings where such matters are rigorously discussed, and by trying not to think about the problems very much.† The reaction against scientific biblical scholarship has failed on academic professional terms. It simply hasn't proved persuasive. That it persists so prominently suggests that it taps into fears we all feel.

Let's look at those fears again. They have at least two roots. The first root is the sense of exposure to death we feel in the face of uncertainty. If my maps aren't accurate, maybe I'll drive over a precipice. Making the Bible "authoritative," using it to reinforce my own sense of how things are, pretending that it's "inerrant," "indefectible," "infallible," won't make it any more accurate than it is already—but if I *feel* like it is, that can look like a gain. If fear is bad, relief—even spurious—feels good.

---

* The movement within Protestant theology which actually called itself Liberalism did not survive the First World War, so it is not always clear what is meant when "liberal" is used as a reproach nowadays. The word is often used pejoratively rather than specifically denotatively.

†It reminds me of the marginal notes found on the preacher's sermon manuscript: "Point weak—SHOUT!"

The second root of that fear is a wish for social control, a reaction against the threat of other people's badness. I'm aware that I harbor potentially mischievous impulses, which, if enacted, would discomfit others and lead them to harm me in retributive vengeance. And if I'm this bad, you're likely worse. It's tempting to use any tool that lies at hand to scare myself into being good and to see that you stay good too. A Q'ranic use of the Bible feels helpful. Whatever blunts that weapon serves chaos. The need to get others to behave themselves is a recrudescence of the fear of death in yet another form.*

The cost of using the Bible that way is not being able to read it very exactly, because the Bible is not so clear about morality as we'd like to think. Calvin was surprised that the New Testament says so little about confining sex to marriage. (He knew Greek, and knew that *porneia* is not exactly "fornication.") We pay little attention to moral teachings we'd like to disregard; numberless neglected prohibitions of usury come to mind. And where our moral present-day sensibilities seem to coincide with biblical law, the underlying rationales are often quite divergent—as mentioned earlier, we no longer reject adultery out of fear for the off-spring's legitimacy, nor do we ask our daughters to refrain from sex in order to maintain the commercial value of their bride-prices.

There is a deeper, more corrupt element in this second root of our fear. That is, from at least the time of the Emperor Constantine the authority of the church has been used not to defend the powerless (as many passages in the Bible attempt to do) but to protect privilege. It was used all over the Roman Empire to defend wealthy landowners against the protests of the landless— until God brought in the Muslims to institute the very land reform the Old Testament identified as a divine mandate. The church's authority, and subsequently the Bible's, has been used to defend slavery, defending, in effect, the privilege of slave owners. It has been used to suppress merchants at the behest of the indebted but prodigal nobility, protecting their aristocratic privilege. It has been used to protect male privilege from anything female in every sector of life, including marriage and church leadership. During our lifetimes, the Bible has been used on two continents to

---

* Something like that superstition clearly grips the United States Congress, which recently refused to consider gun control in the wake of several high school massacres, but thought it effective to post the Ten Commandments in classrooms.

protect the privilege of whites over blacks. It is currently being used to protect the privileges of the married over the single or divorced, of the heterosexual over the homosexual. The rhetoric in each instance has been amazingly uniform, the stretch of centuries and the difference in privileges notwithstanding.

The latter use of the Bible inclines some of us to ask for a power analysis from any speaker who uses the phrase, "The Bible teaches...." We want to ask, "Whom does that teaching empower? Whom does it disfranchise? Why did you reject all the balancing or even countervailing passages? Who's paying you to say that?"

When "liberals" look nervous when Bibles appear, consider that it may not be God's authority we're scared of. The dismal history of its human, Bible-based counterfeits scares us: witch hunts, slavery justification, justifications of warfare and economic exploitation, oppression of racial and sexual minorities—the list is as heartbreaking as it is endless.

When you and I are in the grips of the fear of death and the loss of our sense of privilege, we're not inclined to be either ethical or intellectually precise. So whatever scruples might normally restrain our lashing out with our Bibles and every other weapon we can muster are likely pretty weak. At such times, we do not primarily need Bible verses any more than we need assurance of the validity of our sacramental status—though both point towards the One we need. We need the personal Presence of God, just as a frightened child needs his mama. Nothing short of mama will do, however much it points to mama. It's mama we need. It's God alone. And as we're safe with God, pray God we become safe for others to be around.

Neither the Bible nor Christian doctrine brings us into the Presence of God. They helpfully focus the Presence, call our attention and concentration on particular aspects of God and God's dealing with us. They attune our hearts, point them Godward. But it is the here-and-now Spirit of God who carries us to God's merciful, bounteous lap. It is, as we shall discuss, Jesus of Nazareth—one and the same with the Risen Christ—who beckons us to hope that God's lap has a vacancy with our name on it. It is Jesus who both teaches and models the attitudes and behavior that alone can survive the effulgence of God's goodness. It is Jesus' life of merry insouciance that extends to us the courage to risk our wealth, respectability, country club membership, and property on behalf of the despised. It is Jesus' self-offering on the Cross that both breaks the power of evil over the universe—and us—and displays what God determines to go through in order to have us for God's own. It is Jesus' Resurrection which assures us that we are not fools to hope in God's powerful mercy in the face of all tragedy, all conflict, all contradiction. It is Jesus' Ascension to the place of honor with God that assures us that we have a friend in the very control center of all reality. It's the coming of the Holy Spirit with her extraordinary gentle, utterly natural, superhuman endowments that tells us that God is every bit for us.

ENGAGEMENT WITH THE BIBLE

Why stress all this? Why worry about the importance of the Bible while disputing some of the claims made on its behalf? Four hopes underlie the foregoing discussion.

First, I want to highlight the case for not using the Bible as a tension-reducing authority. Embracing uncertainty will allow us to remain molten in our sense of the Presence as we grow through the stages of faith. The tension our uncertainty exposes us to can be welcomed as a gift. God can and does approach us in that struggle and is equally present to us at all points of it—provided only we don't succumb to dishonesty. The Cross, among its many meanings, signifies that God knows all about our fear, our struggle, and our uncertainty. "*Eli, Eli, lema sabachthani?*" Embracing the tensions God wants us to share with Jesus gets us more rapidly out of Stage 4 into Stage 5. To put it simplistically, if God had wanted to allay our tensions with the Bible, the Bible would be a whole lot clearer, more systematic, less ambiguous, and easier to read. It would be more like the *Dharmapada*, the *Tao Te Ching*, the Q'ran, or like any number of subsequent Christian devotional classics—all of which are more internally consistent than the Bible. Any of them will help you improve yourself if you read and heed. But they won't change your community like the Bible will.

The attempt to resolve life's ambiguities by using the Bible thrusts you into an unfruitful struggle with cognitive dissonance in which you are told to feel furthest from God just when you are becoming personally the most honest and authentic. If we safely slip through that temptation we can proceed from Fowler's third to fifth stages in faith development without getting snared in the polarizations and arguments that occur so naturally in Stage 4.

Second, I want to urge readers to experiment with the thought that the modern period is as friendly to faith as any period of history. Critical scholarship of the Bible—along with other secular disciplines—has made it impossible to reverse the clock, lodging us firmly within the present day. We can no more pretend to a premodern mentality when we read the Bible than (to borrow a sardonic image from C.S. Lewis) a divorcée can pretend to be a virgin. This is a gift. Rigorous critical scholarship has in no way disproved, invalidated, or falsified the Bible. To the contrary it has given us a more precise understanding of how God has always self-disclosed to people and how they have struggled with that self-disclosure. It has restored the Old Testament to us. The only things it has really disrupted have been impertinent claims for the Bible mounted by our fellow fear-victims, seeking to lodge their own reading strategies above the high-water line of critical intelligence.

Just as the Reformers in Europe left people "home alone" when they overthrew their papal parent, so modern scholarship leaves us once again "home alone" with the Bible removed from the parental pedestal upon which the anxious seek to set it. "Home alone" is a scary condition. Yet Christians have frequently found it necessary for discovering that we are never alone—that God is our home, here and now. Oddly, relinquishing superstitious misapplications of the Bible encourages us to go the distance into real mysticism, into a personal relationship with God. Bible reading—and more often, arguing in favor of the Bible— takes up the place in our lives that actual time spent in God's presence could more fruitfully occupy. As we enter that relationship, we discover that God continues to apply the Bible to us quite merrily and specifically. "Whoever attempts to save his 'psyche' [that is what the Greek text says] will lose it. But she who loses her psyche for Jesus' sake will gain it." Whoever attempts to save his psyche with his Bible will lose both.

Third, the reader can gather something of my own reading strategy from the foregoing discussion. My blindspots and prejudices show openly. In the ensuing chapters I shall make copious use of the Bible. The reader deserves to have some notion of what I think I'm doing. My reading method is simple and obvious—and doubtless flawed. Under normal circumstances, what can be known of the provenance, authorship, likely purpose, and literary form of a passage governs my interpretation and sets understandable limits on how the passage can be applied today. Yet so long as we say what we're doing, any of background work can be suspended instantly when the Holy Spirit uses a passage to call attention to something we had never considered—regardless of critical, hermeneutic considerations. There is little harm in allowing the Spirit to use a passage on us like a Rorschach Test, inducing us to project onto it whatever internal process we need to bring to the surface. The only harm springs from refusing to acknowledge that's what we're doing.

That leaves God—our ultimate and authentic authority—plenty of scope to do anything at all with us when we are reading the Bible.

Fourth, I wish there were more grass roots conversation between biblicist and non-biblicist Christians. Experience indicates that no one presently embracing biblicism will be persuaded to open up by these considerations. Yet I want these considerations to serve as a kind of invitation to civil discussion. A conservative biblicist who wants to engage non-biblicists in conversation deserves to know that many of them are as theistic as himself; as prayerful and as submitted to God as himself; love the Bible and read it as faithfully as himself. It need not be a quarrel. Imagine the richness of the exchange if those who have received grace through the medium of an "inerrant," authoritative Bible could share that *grace* (rather than condemnation) with those who have received grace through a reason-based seeking after the whole counsel of God? Imagine if the latter could share that *grace* (rather than scorn) with those who embrace the Bible as primary? Simply imagining such a discussion makes it worth a try.

Clearly I believe that elevating the Bible to the position of primary authority introduces problems more troublesome than the ones it seeks to solve. In fact, the solution is more trouble than the problem. Arguing that publicly, however accurate it may be, is still a soul-corrosive exercise for writer as well as reader, as it pits us as antagonists against fellow believers. So here are some suggestions about how we might benefit mutually from the Bible's authentic authority.

Late in the sixteenth century Richard Hooker struggled successfully with the issues we have considered and, in his *Laws of Ecclesiastical Polity*, outlined how God actually communicates with us. He offered a three-fold process comprising Scripture, Tradition, and Reason working in harmony. By Scripture he (like Luther) meant the "matter of Scripture," faith in God's self-disclosure in Jesus Christ. By Tradition, he meant the historic Creeds and major doctrines hammered out in the post-NT period.* By Reason, he meant something like the contemporary testimony of the Holy Spirit to the prayerful conscience.† Those were not three rival authorities. We do not pick the one that gives us the answer we like, rejecting the others. Rather, they work as a gunsight. When Scripture, Tradition, and Reason line up together on any matter, you can take it to the bank.

To this day what remains so exciting about that understanding is that it allows us to use the Bible and the Tradition full force—simply by being candid about how we use them. That means, by always showing open-handedly how we are using Reason in the process. Prayerful, God-submitted opponents in a theological debate can disclose their governing assumptions and presuppositions, share the biblical passages and narratives that appear pertinent and their excitement with them, and their sense of how their positions square with the on-going life of the people of God. There is nothing whatever the matter with using reading strategies on the Bible and the traditional doctrines—indeed we cannot grasp them without reading strategies, since they both require lots of choices. The problem—the only real problem—occurs if we cloak the reading strategy or the fact that we have one from our interlocutors or from ourselves. In the latter case we might pretend that our opinions are identical with those of God. That pretense has killed a lot of people and suppressed many others.

When godly, humble, and eager servants of God discuss a matter prayerfully with open Bibles in their laps, they're in for an

---

* It is important to be honest when talking about "Tradition." Historical memory is usually politically selective, favoring one group over another. By "Tradition" Hooker was not referring to mere custom or habit. People who oppose the ordination of women call that a "traditional" position. To others it seems a matter not of Tradition but *custom*, out of line with deeper principles discernible in the NT and in early church doctrinal conversations.

† He did not mean mere logic, though he valued it; in that period, the word Reason referred to the spiritual capacity to register God's truth. Contrary to Luther and Calvin, but along with Aquinas, Hooker believed that even "fallen" humanity remains able to distinguish a crooked line from a straight one. The "Fall" did not twist our perceptions; it twisted our preference, so that we now like crooked lines better than straight ones. Reason, to use a modern metaphor, is what allows the prayerful mind to function as an antenna for God's voice.

adventure. At such moments they won't be troubled or derailed by questions of who was high priest when David ate the Show-bread; or by the value of pi in the Chronicle; or whether it was a fish or a whale that ate Jonah; or how Judas really died. Such considerations rarely come up in that setting. When we use the Bible in Hooker's suggested manner, those simply aren't problems. Staying abreast of God in the room with us is challenge enough.

Among my most treasured recollections are occasions when I (a relative liberal) have sat with deeply conservative friends, Bibles open, alert to God's presence, reading passages and offering to each other the new meanings that strike us. Partisanship vanishes in such settings except as fodder for appreciative humor. I covet that treasure for the whole church, across its entire political spectrum.

◆   ◆   ◆   ◆   ◆

Years ago I was in conversation with a devout friend whose interpretive methods differ dramatically from my own. He described going to a science exhibit and seeing a fossil from fifty million years ago. He reported crowing loudly to his wife, for the benefit of all present, "There *wasn't* any fifty million years ago!" He was referring, of course, to his acceptance of Bishop Ussher's famous dating of the Creation in 4004 B.C.E. I probably flinched and blurted out something tacky, because within seconds we were quarreling energetically. Our love for each other eventually prevailed in the fracas, though we never reached substantive agreement.

However, I found the episode so painful that I crept off to a private chapel, dragging my adrenal body, wounded heart, and soiled soul. Facing the altar, I sputtered at God, "Look, God—you gave me my brain, and you can have it back! You gave me an education; you want it back? Say so! You taught me to value critical thinking, even about the Bible, but I don't *have* to think that way. You want me to believe that a literal fish swallowed a literal Jonah and spit him out alive after three days? Just say so, and I'll manage to believe it. You want me to believe it just took six days to create everything? Say so; I'll work on it. Give me a frontal lobotomy while you're at it—I'll hold still...."

When my tirade was exhausted, I sensed that God was present, asking me a question: "Are you willing for me to teach, direct, encourage, and convict you with every passage in the Bible? Or are there sections you'd prefer that I not use?" The tone was whimsical, affectionate.

Subdued and cowed, I replied, "Lord, if you want to teach or correct me you can use anything you choose: the whole Bible—you can even use the Atlanta Phone Book."

"That's exactly where I want you," God replied.

Since then I've regretted not asking if the fish really swallowed the fellow and spat him out alive—while I had God on the phone, so to speak. At such times, stuff like that doesn't occur to you.

CHAPTER SIX

THE INCARNATION

At the conclusion of the discussion about the dread of God in Chapter 3, we were left hoping that something about Jesus would dissipate the dread that seals us up in religion to protect our unjudged false selves by closing off the likelihood of any experiential encounter with the God we fear. At this point, after reminding ourselves of the developmental aspects of any spirituality and of the temptation to misuse the Bible, it's time to investigate what Jesus can do for us—and what might block his impact on our lives. To do this, we need to get clear about Jesus. And to get clear about Jesus we need to scrub away centuries of ossified theory and get to the essential core of the meaning of the Incarnation and the Atonement.

We must approach Jesus with caution. Peanut shells aren't as tasty as peanuts, but they fool the eye. And if we prefer religion to righteousness we probably haven't embraced the most reliable notions of Christ. People who have permitted the non-historical distortion of the Bible's real purpose may find the same distortion has polluted our notions of Jesus' identity—based on the same fears, in the service of the same false selves. People who cloak or ignore their own incompleteness ought to suspect an element of rigidity in their Christology.

Happily, Christology is a place where the faithful reports of our ancestors to which the Scriptures witness make a great difference.

The New Testament says Jesus rose from the dead. Skeptics say he didn't. The argument can't be settled. It was a one-time event, not vulnerable to scientific or historical investigation.

What *is* quite open to scientific and historical investigation, though, is the record of lives turned inside out by encounters they reported with the resurrected Jesus Christ. We have the existence of the church as witness and its gentle capture of the hearts of the Roman Empire within decades of the event. That reality has merrily prevailed in the face of any amount of skepticism. Those people encountered something that changed them. Effects are seldom greater than causes. Those lives were transformed by an irresistible personal Presence. That same Presence in the vulnerable, pre-crucified Jesus provoked competent Roman jurists and Judean clerics to abandon their sworn principles. It scared them into trumping up charges against him in order to prevent his disruption of everything they took for granted. We know that impulse pretty well too.

Transformed lives recognized the one who transformed them in the accounts that eventually formed the Gospels. The Gospels, to be sure, aren't biographies in our sense. They're complex blends of historical memory and the sort of folklorish accretions that tell us as much about a person's style as journalistic accounts do—often more. The Gospels tell us of one whom it's possible to know and recognize—today even. The trick is to read the Gospels and the earlier epistolary writings with fresh eyes.

TWO PARTIAL APPREHENSIONS OF JESUS CHRIST

Ask somebody on the street what she thinks of Jesus and you'll probably be told that Jesus was a good human being whose primary mission was teaching people about loving each other or something. That response is, of course, true—but incomplete.

Ask someone in a Christian gathering the same question and you'll probably be told that Jesus was God and that his primary mission was dying on the Cross to do something about our sins. Like the first, that response is also true—and incomplete.

Though neither response is complete, Christians these days more likely recognize the defects of the first than of the second.

That's too bad. A lot depends on a full understanding of Jesus' person and mission. The defects of the second "orthodox" answer fuel the kind of religiousness we've been considering: those defects keep us pumping our doubts out of the bilge, keep us pretending to believe things we're naggingly unsure of. They make us religious phonies.

Right images are as important as right doctrines. Our very doctrines originated as code to represent experiences and images. The right image or metaphor will often precipitate a helpful doctrinal phrasing. The reverse isn't always the case, as the destructive careers of doctrinally proper people have demonstrated throughout history.*

How you picture Jesus, how he sounds to you, how you sense him, all that makes a difference in how you receive his ministry to you. We won't qualify for heaven by understanding Jesus doctrinally; we will qualify by yearning for him, by finding him attractive, by responding to his charm.⁺

Two mistakes about Jesus block righteousness and keep us religious. The first mistake, concerning his person, falls into the area of the doctrine of the Incarnation; the second, concerning his work, falls within the area of the doctrine of the Atonement.◆ In the present chapter we examine the Incarnation to make sure that our understanding of it really serves us.

---

* John Calvin's Christology was as correct as any and more so than most. Yet in its service he caused a theological rival—and his wife's former suitor—to be burnt at the stake, ordering that the faggots be green and wet in order to protract the execution. (Servetus' death took three hours.) It is difficult to imagine Jesus urging Calvin on. And of Luther, *de mortuis nil nisi bonum.*

⁺ "On that day many will say to me, 'Lord, Lord, did we not prophesy in your name, and cast out demons in your name, and do many deeds of power in your name?' Then I will declare to them, 'I never knew you....'" Mt.7:22–23a There are, of course, readings of this passage more faithful to its context. But that passage does come to mind.

◆ The doctrine of the Atonement is discussed in the following chapter, examining how some ways of phrasing it actually distance us from righteous fellowship with the First Person.

THE PERSON OF JESUS

THE CLASSICAL DISCUSSION

A brief summary of the doctrine of the Incarnation will help us locate some potential hazards.

"And the Word became flesh and lived among us." (Jn. 1:14) That's the beginning and foundation of the doctrine. Over the next four centuries the church hammered away at that truth, closing off blind alleys and false turns that would lead us away from fellowship with Jesus Christ.

Was Jesus really God or just a human being who was godly? (The Ebionite Heresy.) He was really God, the church answered.

Was his death real, or was a phantasm put in his place on the cross to protect him and fool us? (The Docetic Heresy.) No, his death was real, it was *his* death, not someone else's. One writer had suggested that Judas Iscariot's soul was substituted for Jesus' on the Cross as divine retribution!

Wasn't Jesus perhaps a super creature, similar to God and resembling a human being? (The Arian Heresy.)* No, he was fully God and fully human.

Was his divinity located in one part of him and his humanity in another part; maybe his spirit was divine but his soul and flesh were human? (The Apollinarian Heresy.) No, all of him was God and all of him was human.

When did Jesus become God? Later on, wasn't it? God surely couldn't be an embryo or a fetus—living inside a woman! (The Nestorian Heresy.) At his very conception he was already God and, yes, God lived and grew inside a woman.

Okay, but his divinity must have really swamped his humanity, right? (The Eutychian Heresy.) Wrong. His two natures (divine and human) did not compete within him nor did one obscure or absorb the other.

---

* Arianism gets its name from Arius, a priest in Alexandria who taught that the Son was of "like substance" to the Father, but was not directly divine. Arius' followers were educated aristocrats, most unwilling to believe that the Lord of the Universe in his [sic] human incarnation would be a servant, of all things. The Arians preferred viewing God as the divine model for their patron, the Roman Emperor: sitting in remote elevated majesty, waited on by legions of anxious angels, exercising his power chiefly as violence in the maintenance of his own prestige. (Bennett Sims' phrasing.) That would have shored up the advantage of their own class. The debate was never purely theological.

Jesus Christ is fully God and fully a human being. He is God being a man. So correct belief about him recognizes both natures, divine and human, "...without confusion, without change, without division, without separation," as the Chalcedonian Formula of 451 phrased it.*

Every seminary graduate knows all that and many lay folk know it too. Any person who intends to be doctrinally orthodox, who doesn't intend rebellion against the church's traditional teaching, professes that belief about Jesus. But that belief is a slippery saddle, and it is easy to slide off one side or the other. Devout Christians often pay a lot of attention to one side of that doctrine—the divinity part—at the expense of the other.

THE "FINAL HERESY OF THE ORTHODOX"

Nineteenth-century theologians used to remark, "The final heresy of the orthodox is to deny the humanity of Christ." De-emphasizing his humanity to compliment his divinity is a first and basic misapprehension of Jesus, more dangerous even than denying his divinity. People who don't believe that Jesus is "God" are nevertheless prone to a life-changing fascination with him. But those who de-emphasize his humanity separate themselves from him in ways that blunt his impact. The de-emphasis is rarely, if

---

* Definition of the Union of the Divine and Human Natures in the Person of Christ *Council of Chalcedon, 451 A.D., Act V*

"Therefore, following the holy fathers, we all with one accord teach men to acknowledge one and the same Son, our Lord Jesus Christ, at once complete in Godhead and complete in manhood, truly God and truly man, consisting also of a reasonable soul and body, of one substance (homoousios) with the Father as regards his Godhead, and at the same time of one substance with us as regards his manhood; like us in all respects, apart from sin; as regards his Godhead, begotten of the Father before the ages, but yet as regards his manhood begotten, for us men and for our salvation, of Mary the Virgin, the God-bearer (Theotokos); one and the same Christ, Son, Lord, Only-begotten, recognized in two natures, without confusion, without change, without division, without separation; the distinction of natures being in no way annulled by the union, but rather the characteristics of each nature being preserved and coming together to form one person and subsistence, not as parted or separated into two persons, but one and the same Son and Only-begotten God the Word, Lord Jesus Christ; even as the prophets from earliest times spoke of him and our Lord Jesus Christ himself taught us, and the creed of the Fathers has handed down to us." (Book of Common Prayer 1979, 864).

For a somewhat lengthier summary, found in the third of the church's historic creeds, see the so-called Athanasian Creed (BCP 1979, 864–865).

ever, deliberate. It betrays itself most clearly at the level of imagery, easily viewed in the popular culture.

Let's look, for example, at films. With the exception of *The Gospel According to Saint Matthew*, directed by Piero Paolo Pasolini, there has not yet been a humanly credible, let alone an attractive, cinemagraphic portrayal of Jesus. Max von Sydow played Jesus once—a 120-minute portrayal without one smile. A more recent attempt was Franco Zefirelli's *Jesus of Nazareth*, based on the Gospel of Luke, but not one scene in this film depicts Jesus engaged in recognizable human behavior. For example, Jesus delivers the Sermon on the Mount/Plain drifting dreamily through a rapt and docile crowd in the open air, murmuring his message as though to himself—crowds don't act like that, speakers don't act like that, and the laws of acoustics don't work like that. And then there was Willem Dafoe's portrayal of Jesus in *The Last Temptation of Christ* in which he accurately captured the hollow-eyed neurotic of Nikos Katzanzakis' puzzling novel. The connection between that novel's central character and the central figure of the New Testament seemed accidental. In fact, I heard one Atlanta wag remark, "That picture was so bad, not even a picket line of Fundamentalists could save it!"

All of us know and lament the dearth of helpful images of our Lord. There is a group within the Episcopal Church that concocts advertisements for congregations to run in their local newspapers. An advertisement designed for use at Christmas showed two pictures, one an anxious baleful nineteenth century Christ, the other a Coca-Cola portrait of Santa Claus. The caption read, "Whose birthday party *is* it, anyway?" My secretary glanced at that ad and remarked, "Whose party would you rather go to?" The estranging power of that misbegotten ad demonstrates the danger of getting complacent with contaminated images of our Lord. They do harm.

In conversation with people who have no personal experience of Jesus, I always assume that we're swimming upstream of all that kind of imagery. The Gospels are indispensable resources—if people could just read them afresh. I often offer people a cheap paperback New Testament, one they can mark up without guilt or superstition. I tell them to go through one of the Gospels with colored markers. Yellow, say, is for any places in which they can imagine that Jesus could have been joking or teasing. Red is for any place where he is angry or rude. Green is for places where a normal man would have been sexually alert. Blue is for fear, and so on.

That suggestion always meets with resistance and sometimes it takes several tries to get over what I. A. Richards called "dogmatic adhesions," a reference to the truism that "It's easier to see what you know than to know what you see." Needing to see "righteous indignation" keeps people from being able to spot human anger. Sexual alertness is beyond imagining. And did Jesus ever really joke? Was he ever really what we'd call rude? People need encouragement not to worry about theology or incredulity in the face of miracle. They should simply go after the man's personal style.

When and if they complete that exercise, it's a simple matter to ask if they like the person they've unearthed. If they find they like him, would they maybe be willing to test their surroundings for his personal Presence? Our Lord routinely takes it from there.*

Let's try doing some of that exercise here.

THE HUMANITY OF CHRIST

SEXUALITY

Our problem with Jesus' full humanity shows up in the ways we imagine his sexual sensations and behavior. I just used the words sex and Jesus in the same sentence without any prurience whatever. But the mere linking of these words may feel scary.

To be sure, only a very few are so silly—or so bravely candid—as to deny that "sex is holy, and a gift of God." We can rhapsodize about sexuality with so much false-self enthusiasm that the listener imagines us using church robes for pajamas.† Where this attitude shows its true colors is in the fact that we tend to think of our sexuality and our anger as twin zones of our "badness." We may publicly lament our "heart sins," such as pride or doubt or even gossip, but you catch in those confessions no whiff of the terror of being caught that infects the rarer discussions of sex and rage.

---

* Notice that this exercise involves taking Jesus' humanity utterly seriously. In the church's experience, the discovery that Jesus is God followed the discovery of his human force.

† Sex has indeed become the new piety in our day, which is part of what makes it so difficult to discuss sensibly. Malcolm Muggeridge remarked, "Sex is the mysticism of materialist religion."

The former confessions seem almost to be false-self impostures. It could be that spending time in Jesus' company can soothe us in both fearful areas.

Reflecting on Jesus as a sexually self-aware, human male will bear two valuable fruits. First, it produces healing and soothing in this most inflamed area of our own lives. Dramatic healings in the area of sexuality occur when a person comes to terms with the sexual humanity of Jesus. Second, it forces us to take his humanity dead seriously in ways that link God to our own experience—as a participant as well as a judge.

The reader will discover Jesus as a the sexually self-aware, human male by reading John 4:16–19, 27:

> Jesus said to her, "Go, call your husband, and come back."
> The woman answered him, "I have no husband." Jesus said to her, "You are right in saying, 'I have no husband'; for you have had five husbands, and the one you have now is not your husband. What you have said is true!"
> The woman said to him, "Sir, I see that you are a prophet."
> Just then his disciples came. They were astonished that he was speaking with a woman, but no one said, "What do you want?" or, "Why are you speaking with her?"

Scholars tell us this woman came out at noon, rather than at 6:00 A.M., in order to evade the taunts of sister villagers. She's what used to be called "fallen." Can you feel the playfully flirtatious, somewhat erotically appreciative tingle beneath the surface of that conversation—so strong that it cowed the disciples into embarrassed, perhaps envious, silence? Once you consider it, it leaps off the page, in English or Koiné Greek. Feel the easy way the two move back and forth between playfulness and seriousness, directness and evasiveness. They are thoroughly enjoying each other.

Now consider the outcome of the exchange:

> Then the woman left her water jar and went back to the city. She said to the people, "Come and see a man who told me everything I have ever done! He cannot be the Messiah, can he?" (Jn. 4:28–29)
> Many Samaritans from that city believed in him because of the woman's testimony, "He told me everything I have ever done." So when the Samaritans came to him, they asked him to stay with them; and he stayed there two days. And many more believed because of his word. They said to the woman, "It is no longer because of what you said that we believe, for we have heard for ourselves, and we know that this is truly the Savior of the world." (Jn. 4:39–42)

The woman who had formerly hid from her neighbors on account of her checkered past has been so affirmed that she can use that very past on the neighbors she'd dreaded in order to point them to their own healing. Attention to Jesus' sexuality shows us something we'd never seen before: sexuality as a power to bless.

There is no suggestion whatever that anything untoward took place between the two. Indeed such an occurrence would have made the happy outcome implausible. The sexuality in view is a gracious combination of self-awareness, responsiveness to another person, and self-possession. It transformed that person's community. It can do the same with us.

Or consider Luke 7:37–50:

> And a woman in the city, who was a sinner, having learned that he was eating in the Pharisee's house, brought an alabaster jar of ointment. She stood behind him at his feet, weeping, and began to bathe his feet with her tears and to dry them with her hair. Then she continued kissing his feet and anointing them with the ointment. Now when the Pharisee who had invited him saw it, he said to himself, "If this man were a prophet, he would have known who and what kind of woman this is who is touching him—that she is a sinner." Jesus spoke up and said to him, "Simon, I have something to say to you.""Teacher," he replied, "Speak.""A certain creditor had two debtors; one owed five hundred denarii, and the other fifty. When they could not pay, he canceled the debts for both of them. Now which of them will love him more?" Simon answered, "I suppose the one for whom he canceled the greater debt."And Jesus said to him, "You have judged rightly." Then turning toward the woman, he said to Simon, "Do you see this woman? I entered your house; you gave me no water for my feet, but she has bathed my feet with her tears and dried them with her hair. You gave me no kiss, but from the time I came in she has not stopped kissing my feet. You did not anoint my head with oil, but she has anointed my feet with ointment. Therefore, I tell you, her sins, which were many, have been forgiven; hence she has shown great love. But the one to whom little is forgiven, loves little." Then he said to her, "Your sins are forgiven." But those who were at the table with him began to say among themselves, "Who is this who even forgives sins?" And he said to the woman, "Your faith has saved you; go in peace."

It's possible to read that passage too quickly so as to miss—or avoid—its sensual details. Let those readers who lack a suitable partner with whom to re-enact this scene accept the testimony of others that she performed an act of such pleasantness upon our Lord's feet as to precipitate sexual alertness. It was an inappropriate action, appallingly out of place in this setting, in this company. Yet it was what she did for a living and she was good at it—it was how she related to men.

The utterly startling element in the episode was Jesus' response. He made no move to exploit her evident overtures; he arranged no whispered assignation. Nor, on the other hand, did he shrink back in dainty self-protection, insisting that her ministrations to his right foot were quite sufficient, thank you, no need to bother with the left. He didn't ignore her. He didn't scold, reproach, or lecture her. He didn't deny his enjoyment or gratitude. Meanwhile his gasping host pulsated infra-red, protesting that he cannot possibly imagine where the lady came from, how she found her way to his house, never saw her before in his life, how *could* his guest of honor pay attention to her—and so forth.

With perfect charm Jesus received her offering, dignified her motives, offered her a measure of self-respect, corrected and possibly healed his host, and generally modeled the love of that God who made us physical.

How on earth did he do it? He surely didn't accomplish that feat by thinking of baseball statistics or gulping his wine. That is, he didn't flee into mental or physical sensations to protect himself against the associations stirred by the woman's offering. He was apparently so physically self-aware that her touch meant exactly and only what it meant: a pleasing and moving gift of love wrapped up in skill. The fact that Jesus did not eroticize this act, which in most other contexts would be exclusively erotic, shows us that the act didn't stir up archaic associations in him from childhood deprivation. And the most plausible reason that this episode remained sensually self-contained is that Jesus had on some previous occasion(s) already faced into the infantile pains, terrors, and loneliness that so many medicate themselves against by eroticizing their contacts with others. If we have any record of those occasions, they must be the days and nights Jesus fasted in the Wilderness of Judea, the many pre-dawns that he spent in solitude, plumbing his own depths before his Father.

Consider one other passage.

> Early in the morning he came again to the temple. All the
> people came to him and he sat down and began to teach
> them. The scribes and the Pharisees brought a woman who
> had been caught in adultery; and making her stand before all
> of them, they said to him, "Teacher, this woman was caught in
> the very act of committing adultery. Now in the law Moses
> commanded us to stone such women. Now what do you say?"
> They said this to test him, so that they might have some charge
> to bring against him. Jesus bent down and wrote with his fin-
> ger on the ground. When they kept on questioning him, he
> straightened up and said to them, "Let anyone among you
> who is without sin be the first to throw a stone at her." And
> once again he bent down and wrote on the ground. When
> they heard it, they went away, one by one, beginning with the
> elders; and Jesus was left alone with the woman standing
> before him. Jesus straightened up and said to her, "Woman,
> where are they? Has no one condemned you?" She said, "No
> one, sir." And Jesus said, "Neither do I condemn you. Go your
> way, and from now on do not sin again." (Jn. 8:2–11)

Some scholars think this passage was written for Luke's Gospel
rather than for John's, that it strayed into its present location
through multiple copyings. Wherever it came from, it's a fascinating glimpse at another aspect of Jesus' sexual self-awareness. This
episode shows us how Jesus' self-awareness linked him redemptively to other men.

It's easy to assume that the redemptive linkage in this instance
was with the woman, as in the two previous passages. But the more
interesting linkage was with the crowd of men. We can assume
that the mob comprised men we would consider narcissistic. Nar-
cissists need to look good on the outside. Being religious is an effi-
cient way to do so. Living through their outer carapace, they have
difficulty feeling much of anything, so anything sexually prurient
appeals to them, as does violence.* These men received Jesus' pro-
nouncement, "If any of you is without sin, let him be the first to
throw a stone at her," not as a mob-scattering rebuke but as a com-
munity-forming diagnosis. It's as though he'd said, "Wouldn't it
be simple if we could uproot our own sexual pain by tearing up
women like her!" and the crowd murmured, "Yeah, wouldn't it
though!" Someone had understood them; another man had spoken

---

* The narcissist's emotional palette has room only for rage, lust, and sentimentality.

clearly into their condition. Simply hearing it named clearly empowered them against their own dark impulses. His understanding bonded them together for an instant and siphoned off their violence. They walked away, freed from the projected rage, lust, longing, and fears that had possessed them and sought the woman as a scapegoat.*

Contrary to our usual picture of this and other scenes, we have to remind ourselves that Jesus didn't accomplish this rescue by some otherworldly detachment from his humanness that addressed the crowd across immeasurable metaphysical distances. In such a mode, were it even available to him, he'd have appeared merely prissy. No mob of sexually aroused men with the Law on their side is likely to be readily cowed by a prissy fellow. No, Jesus accomplished that feat by using his alpha-male status within the crowd of violent aroused males, by his human kinship with them—not by distance from them. Jesus pulled it off not by asexuality but by calling on his own sexuality—and his potential for violence, if need be. The picture otherwise just doesn't come together, it doesn't work.

Men who are willing to be good sports about our Lord's sexuality discover that he's our best model of Eros devoid of exploitativeness. His companionship extinguishes fires of urgency and restores us to real power. Perhaps for the first time, non-exploitative friendships with women become possible, game-free, non-ulterior friendships that don't stir mischief.

Women who experience their femininity in response to Jesus' maleness discover new funds of feminine power devoid of seductiveness. They discover the power to affirm each other and men as well without seeking to compete or arouse. Conversations with such women are really about what they seem to be about.

Men and women who submit their sexuality to Jesus—to the human Jesus—discover things about themselves that they'd never imagined. They discover that chaste, godly sexuality becomes the power to bless. Blessing means conferring authoritative permission upon people to be fully themselves, what they're intended to be. Those who join their sexuality with Jesus' call forth God-intended charm and excellence from all and sundry. A blessing, in effect.

---

* It's possible they caught another note in his wry tone: "You fellows must have let the guy get away. Where's he? You fixing to stone *him*?"

But is this how we associate Jesus and sexuality? I suspect not. Rather than imagine him as perfectly self-aware, self-possessed—awakening yet safe—we imagine him inert, harmless, without sensations or feelings. I dare say such a Christ would never have healed anybody of anything at all, let alone of anything sexual. So rejecting one of the most attractive and urgent aspects of God's humanity distances us from his ministry to us—and from his person—rather than drawing us closer.

Few women would want to be courted by the Jesus we usually picture. Few men would want to be like that themselves. More than a few men fear that prolonged contact with such an androgynous cipher might be contagious. We fear time spent in that company will lead us to drop our guard, leaching away the hardihood a man requires if he is to compete successfully to assemble, protect, and feed a family. As long as we maintain the prevalent colorless image of Jesus, it's likely that our alleged love for him comes from the false self. However well meant, it is an imposture.

Our trouble with the sexuality of Jesus did not begin in the twentieth century. In a splendid book entitled *The Sexuality of Christ in Renaissance Art and in Modern Oblivion,* Leo Steinberg demonstrates that the artists of the Renaissance repeatedly and routinely offered Jesus' genitalia as a metaphor for his full humanity. In hundreds of paintings, the Madonna is exposing, touching or pointing to the Bambino's tiny manhood. Loincloths flow like a banner from the Cross, though no breeze stirs the robes of the on-lookers. Yet few critics have ever called attention to these clearly intentional devices. Hundreds of such works have been bowdlerized by subsequent hacks, as X-ray studies and cleaning reveal. Steinberg's discussion is as respectful of Jesus' humanity and free of sniggering prurience as are the paintings themselves. We come away from Steinberg's book with the sense that our civilization lacks the courage to gaze where the Mother points or the loincloth furls. To do so, we would have to allow ourselves to be changed. Surely that is the real stake in this aspect of Jesus' humanity as in so many others. If I take Jesus' sexual humanity seriously, I must take my own seriously. Just as we rightly believe Jesus to have been fully ethical as a sexually self-aware male, so we will have to examine our own ethics, our own repressions; we will have to sign the bill of lading, assuming ownership of the sexuality which it has pleased God to bestow on us.

As a pastor, I am occasionally in conversation with unmarried parishioners who seek help with the matter of being sexually self-aware without spouses. All grown-ups who have wrestled with this situation know it's much deeper than simply being hung-up on legalities. Issues of self-respect, of personal integrity and truthfulness, of suitable companions, and indeed of physical safety are at stake as well. Any number have told me of praying to God, "Oh God, please go ahead and take away my sexuality; I'm so tired of living frustrated!"

"And how has God answered? Has God taken it away?" I ask—knowing the answer in advance.

No, God has not.

We then talk of entering into communion with Jesus, asking about Jesus' own experience of singleness and of sexual human nature. They make the experiment. The next conversation with them is far more joyful—and remarkably deeper—than the first. They now know something that deniers of Jesus' humanity do not. They know God-yielded sexuality as the power to bless, just as their Lord did, a power to bless which is fully congruent with an empowered chastity. In the Bible there is no real knowledge that doesn't change you. This knowledge changes them.

That's frightening, to be sure. Yet until each of us does something like it in our own lives, the Jesus of our theological formulae remains a sub-human cipher, for all the claims our orthodoxy makes concerning him. The Word didn't become a cipher; the Word became *flesh*. Fellowship with the First Person, trusting Jesus as our judge—everything depends on embracing that humanity and its life-changing implications.

ANGER

To explore another scary aspect of Jesus' humanity we might notice that he was never dainty about conflict. Half of his recorded conversations occurred in the context of arguments, a significant number of which he himself provoked. He rounded vehemently on Peter, he rebuked friend and enemy alike, and he single-handedly emptied the forecourt of the Temple by the angry application of a whip. G.K. Chesterton remarks how unaccustomed we are to such a picture:

> In any case there is something appalling, something that makes the blood run cold, in the idea of having a statue of

> Christ in wrath. There is something insupportable even to the imagination in the idea of turning the corner of a street or coming out into the spaces of a market place, to meet the petrifying petrifaction of *that* figure as it turned on a generation of vipers, or that face as it looked at the face of a hypocrite. [*]

Yet we ought to be clear about this aspect of his anger: it gave substance to his affection. If you have your choice of being loved by someone who can fight and by someone who cannot, by all means choose the fighter. Such people are more reliable and trustworthy. Their affections exhibit firm skeletal and muscle structure. Jesus models that for us. Recall him whistling and doodling in the dirt, holding an enraged crowd at bay by the restraint.

A case in point is the following episode:

> He said to them, "Doubtless you will quote to me this proverb, 'Doctor, cure yourself!' And you will say, 'Do here also in your hometown the things that we have heard you did at Capernaum.'" And he said, "Truly I tell you, no prophet is accepted in the prophet's hometown. But the truth is, there were many widows in Israel in the time of Elijah, when the heaven was shut up three years and six months, and there was a severe famine over all the land; yet Elijah was sent to none of them except to a widow at Zarephath in Sidon. There were also many lepers in Israel in the time of the prophet Elisha, and none of them was cleansed except Naaman the Syrian." When they heard this, all in the synagogue were filled with rage. They got up, drove him out of the town, and led him to the brow of the hill on which their town was built, so that they might hurl him off the cliff. But he passed through the midst of them and went on his way. (Lk. 4:23–30)

Have you ever seen a person pass through a mob in real life? Such a person has to be strong, resolute, self-possessed, and ready to take on any number without needing to win—only wanting to dent as many as possible. He looks each person in the crowd in the eye, one by one, with fearless interest, saying, if anything at all, something like, "Who wants to be first?" At that point everybody remembers something urgent they have to do right then—somewhere else. No one deters him as he strides through the gaze-cowed mob.[+] Surely Jesus did something similar on this and any number of other occasions.

---

[*] G.K. Chesterton, *The Everlasting Man* (New York, Dodd, Mead, and Company, 1953), 226.

[+] Women do this as forcibly as men. It has little to do with size.

People have been healed of free-floating rage and temper once they stopped trying to amputate it, once they quit trying to transform it into something they think is called "righteous indignation," once they joined their anger to his and allowed him to transform it. It is wonderful and a little frightening to be with such a person. The proverb, "Beware the wrath of patient people" attaches to such people. No one who's ever stood before a seasoned pacifist—the real thing, not an adolescent imitator—will confuse that posture with passivity. The mature self-possession of such people is never the result of surgically removing their tempers. It can only stem from their admitting the Risen Lord into their internal boilers, making the field of conflict the ground of meeting with their Lord's humanity.

But, we must repeat, is that our common notion of our Lord? Sadly, no. Rather we tend to see his anger as a suspension of his love, not as an operation of it. And it's to our great impoverishment that this aspect of our Lord's humanity finds no acceptance in our normal image of him.

This harms the church as well as individuals. Church leadership would be more healthy and effective if the real Jesus were our model. But the image of Christ we employ in church life and leadership is one whose "love" has devolved into an undifferentiated wad of favorable emotion. This sometimes gets called "unconditional love." We act as though an outpouring of "unconditional" love is enough to dissipate conflict. Rather it works like kerosene on coals, scorching our eyelashes, eyebrows, and mustaches. Since people don't really respect unconditional love, it has no force as an institutional norm to restrain mischievous or toxic behavior. What we offer as "unconditional love" is often seen as feckless weakness. It nets us contempt, not gratitude.

This model of church life shows up among people who really ought to know better. In seminary the typical pastor is taught that her duties rest mainly in making people love her, in ingratiating herself with her congregation, in amassing large quantities of esteem. She then trades in all that esteem like so many Green Stamps, pressing people's reluctance to take on necessary but uncongenial duties. Smiling, cajoling, persuading, placating, being her utterly loving, lovable self, she "runs the church."

And so the church operates—supposedly. The actual harvest of such squishy leadership is confusion, contempt, and rage among the laity and depression among the clergy. If we need to be able to see ourselves favorably reflected in our leaders—and we throw over leaders in whom we can't—we sense that we can't afford to respect soft leaders for fear of self-weakening. Trying to bestow unconditional love, leaders fall into the anxious trap of needing approval from others. Such leadership reinforces, for example, our notion that our dealings with God are commercial, with self-generated esteem as the currency. And yet clergy and laity come by such notions honestly. They arise partially from a mistaken picture of Jesus, one far removed from the Gospels' witness.

Our Lord's anger was what gave cash-value to his love. If he was able to fight with you yet decided not to, maybe you didn't need fighting with right then. His willingness to disagree with you at any point meant that you could trust anything he said to you at any time. That's the kind of leader you can safely follow. Such leadership is clear.

Where in the Gospels do you find Jesus laboring to find just the right phrasing to avoid offending his followers? Where do you see him taking responsibility for how other people feel about his words—or indeed how they feel about his person? Where does he make the slightest effort whatever to cajole? To persuade? To placate? To mollify? Evelyn Underhill somewhere reminds us that when the "Rich Young Ruler"—to conflate three gospels' descriptions—went away sorrowful, because he had much goods (Matthew 19:16–22, inter alia), Jesus did not scurry after him "to quote him a lower price."

Now try imagining a church with such a head. Can you envision such a congregation? Straight-shooting, blackmail-proof, non-manipulative, unsentimental, mutually accountable, candid in the face of active- or passive-aggression, clear about its terms and standards? A church made human by our Lord's humanity would be effective beyond our power to imagine or hope. Our misapprehensions of his humanity keep us institutionally feeble. The Incarnation is no merely ornamental doctrine.

IRONY AND HUMOR

A friend once showed me an instructive book written for the improvement of young women in the nineteenth century in which the gloomy author points out, in an essay against levity, "It is nowhere recorded of our Blessed Savior that He ever smiled."

The sourpuss had a point; it is not recorded. But there are two reasons that might account for that, only one of which our writer considered—that Jesus in fact never did smile. But the more plausible explanation is that Jesus' smiling was the one thing about him nobody had to mention. We tend to be silent to the obvious.

If you read through the Gospels afresh, asking yourself at each point, "Could Jesus possibly have been teasing here? Is there irony here? Could he be joking?" you will discover depths you'd never previously discerned. Indeed it will be difficult subsequently ever to be fully confident that any dominical utterance is entirely unironic.

One way to get at the humor is to recast a story in modern terms. For example, the woman and the lost coin in Luke 15:8–10 gets wry indeed when the woman becomes a suburban Junior Leaguer who left her Visa card at Niemann-Marcus but retrieves it before her husband gets home from his law firm, calling her cronies in for a celebrative Bloody Mary to toast her good fortune. How odd of Jesus to compare the joy of the holy angels to that cocktail klatch....

Or consider the shock his listeners experience to this day when God the Father is compared to a corrupt judge, as in Luke 18:1–7? Or how about your own shock as Jesus teases you as he asks you to imitate the corrupt servant in Luke 16:1–13?

Jesus' abiding sense of irony scares us. Irony and humor are inherently spiritual characteristics, since they require that we process reality at more than one level simultaneously, an act of self-transcendence. To be confronted with one whose understanding of us constantly expressed itself as wry wit is scarier than to be confronted by a humorless square. Furthermore, what if God wanted us to embrace Jesus' irony in our own discourse? Might it not be more difficult to practice self-deception? Or self-admiration?

WHY DENY JESUS' HUMANITY?

Denying Jesus' humanity is evasive. It's a racket. It forestalls frightening growth in our spirituality and our own humanity.

We deny Jesus' humanity in order to avoid becoming spiritually mature. We can survey the miracles of Jesus and then assure ourselves that Jesus performed them by virtue of his divine nature—if indeed we choose to credit them at all. The logic goes like this: "Of course he could heal the sick, he was God after all. If he can make the water, I guess he can walk on it...." The suppressed parenthesis is, "I am excused from healing anybody, because I'm not God." So we deny our Lord's humanity in order to avoid exploring what it was about his humanity that opened up the effective power of God in various settings. If we took Jesus' humanity seriously, we would have to recognize that something about his human manner made the miracle stories sound plausible to those who knew him. We might have to face the question, "Why isn't my *own* expression of humanity that way?"

When we deny our Lord's humanity, spirituality begins to feel like something distinct from fleshly humanity. The fact that God's Word becoming flesh made that notion bad doctrine hardly deters it. By making Jesus' uniqueness something "spiritual," the fruit of his divine nature as opposed to his human nature, many Christians create a special province of existence called "the spiritual," imagining it's a place or condition you can visit from time to time as you feel the inclination. The hidden point though is that when you make "the spiritual" into a special neighborhood you can visit, you also make it a place you can leave, take a break from, or indeed avoid. Ironically, getting straight about the full humanity of Jesus compels you to move into authentically spiritual life. No circumstance can ever again be beneath the notice of God, because God has sought out mundane circumstances as the field for living divine humanity.

By the same token, we can deny our Lord's humanity in order to evade our own. Born-again Christians are not the only people to avoid this point of the Incarnation, though we rarely suspect ourselves of it. Such Christians also like to think of the spiritual realm as separate from the human, the only difference being that we imagine we're more comfortable in it than other people probably are. That illusion probably rests on our discomfort with our physicality—Since my body can die, let me ignore that I'm a body, let me pretend that I'm mostly spirit. Death-fear, once again.

Some Christians assume that physicality impels us towards destructive sexual doings. Consequently, if we are part of the Catholic tradition, we worry a lot about how effectively to "mortify the flesh," or if we are more Protestant, how to transcend the "carnal," so we can avoid getting into a whole lot of trouble. That effort—eventually futile, if headlines inform us correctly—draws energy from a serious misunderstanding of what St. Paul meant by "flesh" or "carnality."

Oddly, the best presentation of Paul's concept of "flesh" comes from a wicked French pagan named Georges Bataille, from his book, *Eroticism*. Here's a hasty summary.

Bataille says *community* is necessary for human life. *Work* is necessary to maintain community. *Violence* disrupts work. Violence stems from community members' *impulses of exuberant self-expansion*, both *aggressive* and *erotic*. If these get acted out on without regulation work stops and the community dies. If, on the other hand, they're utterly repressed, the community gets sullen and explosive. So the community makes *laws*: "No hitting each other," "No hitting *on* each other," etc. The laws *taboo* overt sexuality and aggression for the work period. But to forestall social explosions, there must be periods of *transgression* of those laws, when work is temporarily suspended. You can transgress laws against aggression by athletic games and wars. You can transgress laws against Eros at Mardi Gras, office Christmas parties, New Year's Eve, *Fasching*, weekends at singles' bars, proms, and the like. At the end of transgression periods, the whistle blows, and everyone returns to work.

Taboo periods are non-sacred, feeling normal. Transgression periods, on the other hand, are *sacred*, as they give vent to energies that feel as though they possess us from the outside.

Now this is the important thought Bataille has to offer us about St. Paul, wiping away our caricature notions of his thought. Paul was not some cramped moralist who thought taboo was good—i.e. sacred—and transgression was bad—i.e. profane— "carnal." Paul was a penetrating social analyst. What Paul meant by "the flesh" was not the *transgression* of law by aggressive or erotic acts. "Flesh" means *being caught in the dismal oscillation between taboo and transgression.* Nor did he think either taboo or transgression were sacred or profane in themselves—being caught in that oscillation, on that whole spectrum, was utterly profane, sub-spiritual. What Paul thought of as sacred was allowing our bodies to be indwelt by God's Holy Spirit who helps us transcend the drivenness between transgression and taboo.*

---

* "Enkrateia," the fruit of self-control (Gal.5:22), is not self-suppression. It is "spirit," it is self-transcendence. That is a far cry from fleshly efforts at self-escape, either through asceticism or sensual escapade, that control our modern life.

If you want to work with Paul's moral understanding, you have to be a good sport about the Holy Spirit. Something like what the Pentecostals report—that the Spirit infills us, infuses us with capacities and awareness otherwise inaccessible—is no longer optional. For Paul to make his glorious sense to us, indeed for Paul in our view not to be a toxic older brother of Mrs. Grundy, we would need to be filled with the same Spirit who filled and excited him.

Finally, Bataille notes that subsequent Christian generations defected from Paul's high vision. Frightened of the Spirit's power, Christians quit receiving the Spirit's ministry and began offering God a Spirit-less moralism in religious exchange. Now *taboo became sacred*, as though the suppression of anger and Eros were God's ideal for us—and *transgression was ceded to the Devil*. Ever since that baleful switch, western Christians have snuck out to the Devil's neighborhood whenever being good felt too oppressive, whenever we felt angry or frisky. How ironic: the very self-constricting measures we herniate ourselves with while trying not to be fleshly or carnal lock us into the very essence of carnality, the tedious and corrosive oscillation between being real good and being real bad that makes our lives such misery. The *whole effort* was "flesh."

Bataille's surprisingly astute analysis is yet another pointer to our desperate need for God's humanity. It is said that the Medieval Scholastics debated the following question for many years: "If humanity had not fallen into sin in the Garden of Eden, would the Son of God nevertheless have become incarnate in human history?" Their splendid conclusion was positive. Yes, indeed he would have come among us—just for the joy of participation with us! *That* is the One we need to join us, accompany us, judge us, teach us, lead us, tease us, suffer with us, and transform us. Otherwise our very spiritual seriousness will lead not to correction but distortion.*

Caught in the trap of religiousness we assume that God wants

---

* I have two friends in the ministry who do not like each other. One is a somewhat Fundamentalist Charismatic, the other a somewhat worldly man who scornfully opposes that expression of faith. I asked the latter recently why he dislikes the former. He replied, "Joe does not live in his body." The antagonism is regrettable, to be sure. But the critic's observation is quite serious indeed.

us nonsexual and wimpish in the face of anger.* The clear implication of that assumption is that our humanity is the principal obstacle between God and ourselves. You hear the word human used as a complaint: "Oh, I'm so *human!*" one laments in the wake of a bad mistake. The Incarnation, resulting in a human Jesus Christ, disrupts that notion. The Incarnation establishes our humanity as the field for our meeting with God. Human untidiness can't cancel God's purpose in calling the Son to share human nature with us. No longer may we use "human" as a complaint. Nor may we use it again as a gentle insult, e.g., "Teacher, I used to have you on a pedestal, but now I realize that you're just human like the rest of us"

No, for the last two thousand years the word human has been the universe's second highest compliment. The *Word* became flesh. Let none of us affect shame at our flesh again. God has taken humanity into God's own being where it remains. To be human is a badge of honor. It is the necessary condition for receiving God's fullest self-revelation.

That's an energizing realization. We avoid its strain by refusing to take Jesus' humanity seriously.

Embracing Jesus' humanity—and our own—is righteous but it isn't religious. It opens a wide channel for loving God, for thanking God, for admiring God, for meeting with God, but it's of no help at all in coercing God.+

I'm not a steady mystic; I "receive pictures" from the Lord about as rarely as anybody, I guess. But I saw a hilarious one once. Early one morning at my habitual time for prayer and Bible reading, I was nagged by one or two details in my life that I was reluctant to discuss with God. When you need to hold stuff back from God, any prayer is risky. I experienced the problem as spiritual dryness. I tried to pretend it was God's fault that I was "dry." I also persuaded myself that I was sleepy. Maybe some music would keep me awake. When I switched on the stereo, out poured Irish jig music

---

* That assumption follows from believing that anything fleshly and anything spiritual are distinct if not in fact antipathetic.

+ That should alert us that we are contending with something more than a mistake. Refusing to honor Jesus' humanity is perverse. It is what the Transactional Analysts join Eric Berne in calling a racket. It is a ploy of religion because it keeps Jesus at a distance, on the other side of a spiritual/material dichotomy. It requires him to differ from us so as to parry the challenge of his kinship with us.

by the Chieftains, serving the conscious purpose of keeping me awake and the pre-conscious purpose of keeping God inaudible.

Suddenly I was looking at Jesus from the waist down. His hands gripped his robe, lifting it to mid-calf, and his feet danced a jig. "Your music can't shut me out," he chuckled. I spent the remaining time laughing with the delight of one who has been judged, understood, forgiven, and re-enlisted all in the same instant.

Now the primary point of that episode is our Lord's wit in devising new ways to love us and rescue us. But let me stress a secondary point, what the Book of Common Prayer calls the "devices and desires of our own hearts." Denying Jesus' humanity seeks to keep God at a middle distance across which our religiousness promises to extend some influence. It won't do to have God too close. You have to imagine God needs our report in order to know how it feels to be a creature. Maybe we could arouse God's guilt at not being an involved participant, press it for advantages, play like we're victims? God's humanity breaks up that racket. God is a participant. Jesus knows how it feels, better in most instances than we do. He does not need our information for his own instruction; he listens in order that our telling it might give us comfort. When we have taken his yoke upon ourselves as he commanded, that requires him to be in the same place and situation we are at any moment. That yoke is easy, but it does not bend or stretch. That leaves no room whatever for flight, bargaining, or self-pity. We're in conversation with a fellow participant. It cancels religiousness. Small wonder we reject it.

No less a one than Peter Berger, one of the foremost sociologists of religion in our time, insists that the Incarnation is essential if the Christian is to make any sense at all out of evil and suffering:

> However the metaphysics of this incarnation and its relationship to man's redemption may have been formulated in the course of Christian theology, it is crucial that the incarnate God is also the God who suffers.... Only if *both* the full divinity *and* the full humanity of the incarnate Christ could be simultaneously maintained, could the theodicy [the presentation of God's justice and goodness in spite of the evidence of suffering and evil] provided by the incarnation be fully plausible. *This,* and not some obscure metaphysical speculations, was the driving force of the great Christological controversies in the early Christian church, reaching its culmination in the Nicene condemnation of Arianism.[*]

---

[*] Berger, *Sacred Canopy,* 77.

On weekends Berger is an active Lutheran; but at the office he's primarily a social scientist. From the detached perspective of a sociologist studying religion, it is clear that Christianity does not work unless Jesus really is God and really is human. In Christ, God willingly suffers. Jesus' suffering can be no pretense, not if in him we are to be one with God.

It is of urgent importance that we submit to the humanness of Jesus, permitting the Spirit to make for us images of him recognizable in our terms. As the Spirit does so, we will be charmed out of religion into righteousness. We may even embrace our own creatureliness. In Chapter 9 we will examine a specific episode in Jesus' ministry—the account of his healing a paralytic who'd been lowered through the ceiling—that makes this vivid. Until such an episode occurs for each of us, our relationship with Jesus will not have the effect we longed for at the close of the third chapter: he will not yet have shown us the essential friendliness that lies beyond the terror of God's judgment. If our humanity is the hole we crawl into to escape God, we have to associate it with sin, with disobedience, with our "badness." We can well wonder how much outright craziness results from seeing our humanness as the locus of "badness" in us. Ernest Becker saw this as the underlying element in our horror of our own bodies; we are trapped in bodies—and bodies die. Humanity is mortality.

And if our "spirituality" is the hole we crawl into to escape being mortal creatures, how can we face the very Creator who thought up our physical, mortal being?

THE INCARNATION AND JUDGMENT OF THE FALSE SELF

By now we must sense that much religious striving to be—or appear—"good" springs from a false self. On the flip side, the flight into worldly transgression is not more authentically human either, since it denies the Vision that elevates us to survey, admire, and care for created nature. Licentious behavior springs from a false self no less than fear-driven asceticism.*

God's mercy displays itself in that God does not stand outside and above our caughtness in the human ditch and call to us; God

---

* It is odd how often those seeming opposite patterns get generated by the same insights. The Gnostics of the first few centuries of our era as well as the medieval Cathari each produced both abstemious hermits and prodigal roués.

enters the ditch and ministers to us. God is not fooled or delayed by our false selves. God has assumed the condition of death: God is flesh too. We may approach safely. What was accomplished by Jesus' sufferings will be discussed in the next chapter. But the *fact* of his suffering can be appreciated right here. Indeed we mustn't avoid it. If, as the Fourth Gospel tells us, God gave the Son—*gave*, not merely dispatched—we're already talking about an emotional transaction. That would be impossible if God were imagined as a dispassionate critic. Ignoring the hints we have about God's inner life can only serve to allow us to ignore our own.

So far we have been talking about righteousness as something that people either embody or don't embody towards one another and towards God. But Berger's—and the church's—understanding of the Passion of the incarnate Son of God must be seen and can be appreciated as an expression of *God's righteousness towards us.* The Old Testament had understood God's relationship with humanity in contractual terms: we're in a "covenant" together. Though not many Old Testament passages encourage the notion, we normally assume that if we break our promise to God, God is either permitted or indeed required to break the divine promise to us. God's participation in human experience—especially in our suffering—demonstrates that God has never decided to break that promise, despite our failures of covenant. Divine goodness to us results from God's own nature—love and righteousness. God's mercy is not an involuntary response summoned by our good behavior or right belief. Nor is it the response of heaven's ambulance when sin dials 911. Redemption was always a present element in Creation—and all Redemption is merrily creative.

The divinity of Christ, because it's true, takes care of itself without our anxious protectiveness. We no more have to defend the divinity of Christ than Calvin had to defend the sovereignty of God. Some matters can look after themselves. Jesus' divinity was initially the discovery of people who allowed his humanity to attract them, to catalyze their deepest hopes, their bravest self-confrontation. That—from his charming humanity to his commanding divinity—was the experiential order in which their lives were transformed. We don't achieve that transformation by doing it backward.

Real spirituality, the self-offering of authentic selves to God, is rooted in the humanity of Christ.

CHAPTER SEVEN

THE ATONEMENT

A TROUBLESOME DOCTRINE

In the previous chapter, we looked at two correct—but incomplete—understandings of Jesus. The first comes from Main Street. The second comes from church. I think the standard "church" reply to the question, "What do you think about Jesus?" is as defective as what you'd hear on the street. It goes something like this: "Jesus was God and his primary mission was dying on the Cross to do something about our sins." This statement is directly connected to our understanding of the troublesome doctrine of the Atonement.

To be sure, you could graduate from any Christian seminary on the strength of that answer. A conservative seminary would likely give you an A, while a liberal seminary might give you a lower grade, maybe a C-, unless you said considerably more—but both would pass you. However, orthodoxy notwithstanding, there are several things wrong with it.

First, it is based on a fundamentally wrong assumption that Jesus' (and by extension, God's) only real interest in us is our sin. You probably have no trouble seeing that summation of Jesus' work is…well…stupid; but a heartbreaking number of Christians have believed exactly that through the centuries, clothing and cloaking its stupidity in dogmatic vestments.

Another problem with this belief is that it is by no means clear how the death of an innocent man removes sin from a guilty one. If my state (Georgia) electrocutes an innocent man, a guilty man presumably retains his freedom. That's probably not how Jesus' death works, though I have never heard it expressed in such blunt terms.

But if, for a moment, we assume its validity, how does it work? Psychologists talk about survivor guilt, the guilt, for example, surviving soldiers are said to feel when a buddy dives on a grenade to save them. Talk to the soldiers afterwards and they'll give the expected reply: Yes, they're grateful, of course they are. But after a few drinks the answer will be different. You'll get a sense of the burden of living a life secured by the death of another. People who have actually been died for don't appear all that joyous about it.

Another thing wrong with the statement that Jesus died for our sins is that it reflects a hopelessly superficial understanding of sin. Can sin really be removed from me without changing something in me? Is it really comparable to points on my driving record, something I could get erased if I had a pal working at the Department of Motor Vehicles? Lots of church-talk about being "washed in the Blood" seems to refer to something external like that. If it were that simple, if it was a stain that Jesus can paint over or sponge-out with his detergent blood, wouldn't God put up with me in spite of it? I mean, I put up with all sorts of irritating behavior, mannerisms, and traits from those around me and yet I keep loving them, paying their salaries—and I'm not nearly as nice as God is said to be. So if I can put up with my child, my mate, my associate, why can't God put up with a guy no worse than I am without killing Jesus to make it possible?

So when we say, "Jesus was God and his primary mission was dying on the Cross to do something about our sins," we have mixed up elements of basic belief with a whole bunch of reified metaphors that have hardened around the core belief—the divinity of Jesus Christ. Let's start with sin.

What we normally think of as "sin" is a symptom rather than the disease. If I asked you to tell me your worst sins and gave you little time for reflection, you'd struggle to withhold the predictable reflex answers, because you wouldn't want me to hear them. The reflex answers would likely pertain to sexual thoughts or deeds, substance abuse, dishonesty, betrayals of those who trust you, or maybe to hidden crimes, such as theft. That is, we tend to view sin as a something that has been done rather than as a way of being. Therefore you'd be less likely to say, "I flee God. I refuse to trust God. I scramble to preserve my own life in ways that make me toxic to others. I live caught between my appetitive impulses and the restraining voice of society, so I always feel either deadness or guilty anxiety." In comparison with what sin really is, the "sins" we drag to the Cross are superficial. The actions we identify as our sins are actually symptomatic of our real sin.

Given our shallow understanding of sin, we are likely to misunderstand and distort what the Bible and the Tradition tell us about God's gracious dealings with people caught in our condition. If the atoning work of Jesus is to improve our condition, it's a pretty deeply wounded and wounding condition that needs repair. Again, getting somebody at the Department of Motor Vehicles to erase the penalty points against your license will clear your driving record, but no vaguely comparable process will erase the reality of sin. Certainly not frozen metaphors of sacrifice, ransoms, or substitution, however vivid the metaphors were to those who first used them.

Discussions of the Atonement (i.e., by which I mean, Jesus' work in getting us back into fellowship with God) all too frequently leave us standing by ourselves, cleansed of sexual misdoings, of smoking, of cussing, and the like, but unaccompanied by the Presence. It is as though you could be "justified," made or pronounced no longer liable to punishment, without being "atoned," brought back into a cordial relationship with God. Consequently our understanding of the Cross rarely follows us out the church door.

These questions and objections point to the really damning objection to much church-talk about Jesus' Cross, my sin, and how I get saved: *For many centuries people who have not had the white-hot molten encounter with the Other have taken over the reports of those who have—and fashioned those reports into theological theory.* Those theories are no more credible than any other secondhand gossip. And, if we are looking to achieve a molten state that brings us closer to God, we're not going to get there via metaphors and theories that have ossified through the ages.

METAPHORS INTO THEORIES

If we buy into those theories, we are explaining how Jesus' Cross "saves us from sin" in terms that we do not actually believe. We say Jesus saves us by processes—human sacrifice, hostage swapping, vicarious punishment—that we do not accredit anywhere else in our lives. If any of us were the object of such actions in real life, we would be neither favorably changed nor grateful. So, once we drag it out of church onto the sidewalk, we don't believe our own language. At the heart of our report of what should be the most intimate transaction in any human life there lurks a falsehood. To persist in those explanations creates a constant struggle with cognitive dissonance. It makes us phonies.* Being phonies in turn puts a more painful sin in place of all the sins we decided the Cross removed. Embedded at the center of the "faith" of many a believer is something we secretly suspect is a lie.

In my view, we're here at the very crux of the problem as Christians experience it—the collision between human religion and the righteousness of God. If, as suggested earlier, our enmity with God grows directly out of the death-fearing psyche, that enmity is also reinforced by inauthentic approaches to the work of Christ. Too much of our discussion of the central work of Jesus smacks of contrived sentiment, attempts at enthusiasm for processes that don't spontaneously engage us. That's the activity of a false self.

That's quite different from the experience of those biblical writers and subsequent saints who bequeathed to us our primary language for the Atonement. They were groping for poetic metaphors to convey an ineffable, life-transforming encounter with a Presence. That encounter had left them feeling understood, accepted, forgiven, remade, restored, embraced—"atoned," as we say theologically. The choices of words suggest such experiences as being bought off a slave block or discovering that they are included in a rich man's will. They knew they could no more understand or explain the mystery of God's grace in their lives than your dog can explain your last business trip to his canine colleagues; he can only explain that you came back home with a raw-hide bone. Their figures of speech were attempts to

---

* Recall the schoolboy definition of faith: "Faith is believing something you know ain't so!"

point towards what cannot be satisfactorily spoken, because it's rooted in a reality far above our own.

Had we been contemporary listeners, scowlingly struggling to work out exactly *how* we got "adopted," or "redeemed" (from slavery), or "bought," or "ransomed," the four Evangelists, Paul, and other New Testament writers would have laughed merrily, explaining that we were missing their point. They'd likely tell us to lighten up. We do them no honor by refusing to find fresh language for our own experience of God's atoning work in our lives, by inattention to our actual experience, and recognition of its distinctness from theirs. Contriving enthusiasm for metaphors unrecognized as such (and hence literalized) shores up the God-avoidant false-self.

As Christian teachers discussed the Atonement through the centuries, two critical transitions took place. First, anxious listeners and readers took the metaphors from the first molten souls and constructed a fixed universe in which those figures of speech became perceived as the literal way things actually happen. In that universe "sin" cannot be removed without the shedding of blood, we are being held by the Devil (who actually has the authority to hold us) for an actual ransom, and having another suffer our punishment somehow "counts" to make us innocent. Keeping such a symbolic world from sinking into its own implausibility requires constant sweat at the theological pumps.*

Second, whereas originally the Atonement was happily celebrated as the work of a loving God converting the heart of an estranged humanity, it came to be seen as humanity's vicarious substitute—Jesus—mollifying the wrathful heart of an estranged Father. Past a certain point, it became *God's* heart that needed changing, not ours. Nobody ever said or meant that—but their figures of speech, when literalized, left that distinct impression. The face of that enraged Father so haunts the unconsciousness of

---

* It also keeps us mad at those who don't think it's worth the trouble. My brother once took a crowd out sailing on his boat. One guest kept pressing him to know if he were saved, if he went to church, if he'd accepted Jesus. Cloaking his annoyance behind his deadpan expression, he replied to her, "Ma'am, me and God, we made a deal a while back: he promised me that if I never went to church another day in my life and never said another prayer, that I'd get to spend eternity in hell. And, you know, when you get a deal like that, you just can't turn it down!" She almost jumped over the side.

Christianity (especially in my region, the South) that it is sometimes functionally indistinguishable from that of the very Devil.
Consequently the Christian faith (especially in my region)
becomes indistinguishable from Islam: a critical God placated by
exterior moralism derived from a book that may not be critiqued.
That confusion of images—and of enemies—makes religiousness,
if possible, even more inevitable.

In the following pages, I'll briefly sketch some of the most
influential figures of speech, e.g., the Atonement as "ransom" or
"sacrifice," show their metaphorical value as poetic figures of
speech, and point out the unhappy results when we reify them
into theories. I'll also suggest some alternative approaches the
present-day work of the Spirit extends to us from our biblical heritage, our theological inheritance, and our prayerful reason. I
hope we will end up capable of authentically experiencing and
identifying God's atoning work in our lives—in ways that we ourselves believe.

In this discussion it is important to keep in mind the legacy
attached to the Incarnation and the Atonement. If the discussion
of the Incarnation in Christian thinking has been tangled, however inadvertently, throughout the history, the doctrine of the
Atonement has been even more so. But there is one critical difference: with the Incarnation every Christian who's trying to be
orthodox will assent to the Chalcedonian formula of 451 (BCP
1979, 864); but with the Atonement, there's no comparable standard of orthodoxy and the various theories cannot in every
instance be harmonized. The fact that some theologians think of
them as "theories" is itself a symptom of what's wrong. And just as
automobiles give off clouds of exhaust that pollute the air—yet
who could live without a car?—so the various theories of the
Atonement give off a sort of theological exhaust, inferences not
intended by the theories' various authors. Poetic figures of speech
usually make one point and spread no further. But with theories
of how things are and how things work you don't switch off your
mind as though it were an electric typewriter or computer. When
you've finished thinking about Atonement "theories," parts of
your mind keep hearing echoes of that thought even though your
conscious mind has changed the subject. We preconsciously begin

to construct universes in which those theories will work. Those universes may not correspond to the biblical writers' intentions.

THE CLASSICAL DISCUSSION

The New Testament frequently states the *fact* of the Atonement: "In Christ God was reconciling the world to himself, not counting their trespasses against them...." (2 Cor. 5:19a)

But the New Testament contains no single *theory* of the Atonement. New Testament writers did not experience the Atonement mechanically or theoretically, and remained surprisingly silent on its mechanics. Because they went to no trouble spelling out an Atonement "theory," we must conclude that they felt no need to. Why? The most plausible answer was that they considered the mechanics of their reunion with God too obvious to discuss; writers are always silent to topics they take for granted. And what made the Atonement obvious to them was the *experience* of it. Previously they'd felt lost and frightened; now they knew the company of a God who loved them—and the Cross furnished a way to measure how much. The Atonement was not for them a belief: it was an event, the climax of their autobiographies—in which they ceased to be the central protagonists when Christ became the hero of their life stories.

This points to the primary value you and I must seek in any presentation of it in sermons we hear or in books we read: it has to be capable of becoming an event for us personally. The Atonement remains the great open space at the heart of Christian doctrine, the hole in our bagel. It's there by design, not defect. The Spirit must fill that space for every individual. There's a necessarily experiential, indeed mystical, aspect to each individual's appropriation of the Atonement. Gregory of Nazianzus (329–389) suggested that until each of us has by the Holy Spirit's aid made Christ's personal experience our own, the atoning work of Jesus for each of us is not yet complete. The Atonement must be no longer mechanical but personal, no longer merely a belief but an event. "Salvation" is individual rather than general or universal, so the Bible prescribes no single Atonement "theory." Neither the Bible nor the universal church offers us any single mode of understanding the Atonement. But the Bible does offer hints that we can use to understand the various ways in which the event of the Atonement becomes real in our individual experience.

THE RANSOM METAPHOR FOR THE ATONEMENT

Mark 10:45 offers one such hint: "For the Son of Man came not to be served but to serve, and to give his life a ransom for many."

The "Ransom Theory of the Atonement" emerged in the work of Origen (185–254). He fleshed out Mark's notion, and his presentation was widely accepted among ancient theologians. Origen had to add two elements to the gospel, though, because the original verse specifies neither the recipient of the payment, nor the contract by which he's entitled to receive it. He filled in those blanks thus: the Devil is the recipient; his entitlement to hold us captive originated at the Fall in Eden—in which the Serpent becomes identified with Satan (an identification by no means clear in the text of Genesis 3).

The period that produced the ransom theory offers us comic sermons, which mock the Devil for getting the short end of the bargain:

> He took a body, and face to face met God!
> He took earth, and encountered heaven!
> He took what he saw, but crumbled before what
> he had not seen!
> (St. John Chrysostom, "Easter Homily")

During this recitation, the congregation would stamp its feet triumphantly at each mention of Satan's embitterment. It was and remains great fun.

The metaphor of catching the Devil on a fishhook came in for a lot of use as well: the humanity of Jesus was the bait, his divinity was the hook, and the devil was the fish.* Augustine (354–430)

---

* Rufinus of Aquileia, summarizing the view of Gregory of Nyssa (330-395), phrased it thus: "The purpose of the Incarnation... was that the divine virtue of the Son of God might be as it were a hook hidden beneath the form of human flesh... to lure on the prince of this age to a contest; that the Son might offer him his flesh as a bait and that then the divinity which lay beneath might catch him and hold him fast with its hook....Then, as a fish when it seizes a baited hook not only fails to drag off the bait but is itself dragged out of the water to serve as food for others; so he that had the power of death seized the body of Jesus in death, unaware of the hook of divinity concealed therein. Having swallowed it, he was caught straightway; the bars of hell were burst, and he was, as it were, drawn up from the pit, to become food for others." Quoted in Henry Bettenson, ed., *Documents of the Christian Church* (New York: Oxford University Press, 1961), 49.

used a similar image, suggesting that the Cross was a "mousetrap" baited to catch the Devil. Many early Christian writers had a lot of fun exulting in the fact that the deceiver had been deceived, the ensnarer had been ensnared.

Among the riches of this metaphor is the fact that, by its designation of Satan as the target of Jesus' work on the Cross, it locates the source of evil at a point outside of human experience. There's more wrong with the world than our sinful presence in it. This allows us to grow beyond the sin-based anthropology so central to the Western Christian discussion since Augustine, in which human sin seems almost a necessary signal flare to catch God's attention. If there were no human race, there would still be evil in the cosmos.*

The ransom metaphor suggests with Paul that:

> Our struggle is not against enemies of blood and flesh, but against the rulers, against the authorities, against the cosmic powers of this present darkness, against the spiritual forces of evil in the heavenly places. (Eph. 6:12.)

The ransom metaphor stretches the victory of Jesus onto a canvas the size of the whole cosmos. It unifies the first chapter of Colossians:

> He has rescued us from the power of darkness and transferred us into the kingdom of his beloved Son, in whom we have redemption, the forgiveness of sins. He is the image of the invisible God, the firstborn of all creation; for in him all things in heaven and on earth were created, things visible and invisible, whether thrones or dominions or rulers or powers — all things have been created through him and for him. He himself is before all things, and in him all things hold together. He is the head of the body, the church; he is the beginning, the firstborn from the dead, so that he might come to have first place in everything. For in him all the fullness of God was pleased to dwell, and through him God was pleased to reconcile to himself all things, whether on earth or in heaven, by making peace through the blood of his cross. And you who were once estranged and hostile in mind, doing evil deeds, he has now reconciled in his fleshly body through death, so as to present you holy and blameless and irreproachable before him. (Col. 1:13–22)

---

* The importance of that designation may not be obvious. But think about it a moment. Suppose the only evil the universe contains is *us?* Then the way is paved for the fiercest tyranny: find the people the evil is coming from and do something about them, whether that be a scolding, excommunication, burning at the stake, or—in our century—genocide and ethnic cleansing.

It reaches a crescendo of the eighth chapter of Romans:

> What then are we to say about these things? If God is for us, who is against us? He who did not withhold his own Son, but gave him up for all of us, will he not with him also give us everything else? Who will bring any charge against God's elect? It is God who justifies. Who is to condemn? It is Christ Jesus, who died, yes, who was raised, who is at the right hand of God, who indeed intercedes for us. Who will separate us from the love of Christ? Will hardship, or distress, or persecution, or famine, or nakedness, or peril, or sword? ...No, in all these things we are more than conquerors through him who loved us. For I am convinced that neither death, nor life, nor angels, nor rulers, nor things present, nor things to come, nor powers, nor height, nor depth, nor anything else in all creation, will be able to separate us from the love of God in Christ Jesus our Lord. (Rom. 8:31–35, 37–39)

The ransom metaphor invites us into a deeper understanding of human sin. Sin isn't just a misdeed for which we must be punished; it is a captive condition from which we must be rescued. Sin can be understood as caughtness. Consequently, sin is a problem God has solved. Your sin is no longer the most interesting thing about you.*

To our impoverishment, American Protestantism allows the ransom metaphor little place in preaching or prayer. An understanding of the Atonement that sees the problem of sin and its solution in broader terms than private moral contamination is greatly needed today. Its absence among us more than anything accounts for our scandalous insouciance towards the poor—as direct a disobedience of a clear unambiguous biblical principle as it is possible to imagine.

The New Testament experiences our distress as broader and deeper, stretching beyond private immorality. Talk of sin these days and your listener automatically thinks of something to do with sex or alcohol. Talk of sin in the days of the New Testament and the listener thought of an accusation that the Devil, who presently held humanity's mortgage, made against those God loves.

---

* Frank K. Allan, retired Bishop of Atlanta—himself a splendid theologian—once delighted many and terrified a few of my parishioners by observing, "If you read the Bible attentively, you realize that sin is not all that big a deal. Sin is a problem which God has solved."

Why struggle with the Devil if there's nothing more wrong with us than bad habits? The ransom metaphor takes a wider view of the damage done to creation at the Fall—in effect, the Fall preceded Eden. Nor is the work of a Christian done when she cleanses her life of moral contamination; the contaminated world order remains to be addressed. The ransom theory left room for this understanding. Significantly, it connects the Atonement with the spread of justice.*

As it ceased to be a poetic figure and became "The Ransom Theory," a couple of damning weaknesses became evident. First, it pointed the mind in the direction of a kind of dualism even if its exponents denied that intention. It left people living in a universe in which good and evil are locked in a struggle to break the equipoise between them. That's a Zoroastrian cosmos, not Christian.

See what Gregory of Nazianzus said about it:

> Was [the ransom] paid to the evil one? Monstrous thought! The Devil receives a ransom not only *from* God but *of* God....To the Father? But we were not in bondage to him: and again, how could it be? Could the Father delight in the blood of his Son?[+]

Second, the notion of God tricking the Devil was and remains distasteful. It has been protested by many. When you cheat the Devil, the Devil wins, in that he got you to cheat at all. In Christian theory at least, ends do not justify means, the early Jesuits notwithstanding.

THE SACRIFICIAL METAPHOR OF THE ATONEMENT

Another poetic figure grew up alongside the ransom metaphor—the "sacrificial" metaphor. This is sometimes called the "Classical Theory," since the notion of sacrifice gave rise to subsequent substitutionary theories. It is suggested in the Epistle to the Hebrews 13:10–12:

> We have an altar from which those who officiate in the tent have no right to eat. For the bodies of those animals whose blood is brought into the sanctuary by the high priest as a sacrifice for

---

* Eastern Orthodoxy, merrily ignoring Augustine as a Western barbarian, makes less of the Atonement than we do in the Western Tradition. It follows that they also make less of social justice and the struggle for peace.

[+] J.F. Bethune-Baker, *An Introduction to the Early History of Christian Doctrine* (London: Methuen & Co., Ltd., 1951), 343–344.

sin are burned outside the camp. Therefore Jesus also suffered outside the city gate in order to sanctify the people by
his own blood.

Notice that Hebrews 9:11–12, among any number of similar
passages, emphasizes Jesus' role as priest rather than as victim:

> But when Christ came as a high priest of the good things that
> have come, then through the greater and perfect tent (not
> made with hands, that is, not of this creation), he entered
> once for all into the Holy Place, not with the blood of goats
> and calves, but with his own blood, thus obtaining eternal
> redemption.

This emphasis on Jesus' priesthood over his status as victim
should make us hesitate to assume that the early church saw Jesus
as a *substitute* for sinful humanity. Rather, as a priest, he was our
representative.

This figure depends on a little background: In an Old Testament sacrifice, an animal was substituted for a human sinner to
pay off a moral debt. The one offering the sacrifice would place
his hand on the victim's head, identifying his own life and deserv-
ings with the impending death of the animal. The flawlessness of
the animal, hence expense, kept the transaction from being
entirely painless to the donor. The early church saw the Old Testament sacrifices as a useful metaphor for the work of Jesus.

The value in this metaphor was that it offered the catastrophe
of the death of Jesus as a gift rather than a deprivation, as design
rather than defect. There is much internal evidence in the New Testament that the death of Jesus scandalized his followers, seeming, as
it did, to cancel his claims for serious attention. We see this struggle
and its effective resolution in Luke 24:13–32, the familiar story of
the two disciples on the road to Emmaus, part of which goes:

> Then one of them, whose name was Cleopas, answered him,
> "Are you the only stranger in Jerusalem who does not know
> the things that have taken place there in these days?" He
> asked them, "What things?" They replied, "The things about
> Jesus of Nazareth, who was a prophet mighty in deed and
> word before God and all the people, and how our chief priests
> and leaders handed him over to be condemned to death and
> crucified him. But we had hoped that he was the one to
> redeem Israel. Yes, and besides all this, it is now the third day
> since these things took place. Moreover, some women of our
> group astounded us. They were at the tomb early this morn-
> ing, and when they did not find his body there, they came
> back and told us that they had indeed seen a vision of angels

who said that he was alive. Some of those who were with us went to the tomb and found it just as the women had said; but they did not see him." Then he said to them, "Oh, how foolish you are, and how slow of heart to believe all that the prophets have declared! Was it not necessary that the Messiah should suffer these things and then enter into his glory?" Then beginning with Moses and all the prophets, he interpreted to them the things about himself in all the scriptures.

But suggestions of a sacrificial mechanism in the Greek New Testament aren't as clear as they'd seem in English translation. It's clearly not a direct substitution, as later theologians would claim. In each place where something like "Jesus died *for* us . . ." occurs, the word "for" translates the Greek *hyper*, which means "on behalf of," "with reference to." The word lacks the force of the equally current *anti*, which means "instead of." That linguistic clue suggests that the people closest to the event didn't find a pure substitutionary mechanism for Jesus' atoning work obvious. We must also ask, why did no New Testament writer think to connect Jesus with the scapegoat of Leviticus 16 if a substitutionary understanding was ever intended? Surely the scapegoat image should have thrust itself upon them otherwise, though for all its obviousness it appears nowhere in the New Testament. That it did not occur to them suggests that sacrificial mechanisms were not important to them as more than the bases for occasional metaphors.

SUBSTITUTION THEORIES: ANSELM

At this point, we must begin to refer not to metaphors but theories outright. From Anselm on, theologians may have thought they were describing literally how things actually work.

Augustine's notion of Original Sin formed a sort of watershed in Atonement discussions. Prior to Augustine's invention, there was a widespread understanding in all sectors of the church that Jesus had actually accomplished what God intended for him to accomplish—to restore us to fellowship with the First Person and fill us with the delightful energies of the Third Person. As the Western empire faded and people grew more pessimistic, Augustine explained European humanity to itself in terms derived from the Bible but nowhere close to the Bible's central thrust. In Augustine's theory, the sin in the Garden of Eden was sexualized and made into a sort of sexually transmitted disease. Christian regret about the necessity of sex found its first and loudest voice. The norm for clergy drifted towards celibacy.

One result in Western theology was that the Atonement became more urgent. As people learned to experience themselves as more deeply and thoroughly bad, the reconciling work of Christ got harder. Playful figures of speech and delighted poetic images no longer satisfied: theories with visible moving parts felt necessary.

Despite the lack of clear biblical warrant, theories of the Atonement in later centuries mostly based themselves on some form of sacrifice in which Jesus' substitution of himself for us, taking our punishment, got the work done.*

St. Anselm's (1033–1109) satisfaction theory set a sacrificial substitution theory within the context of the feudalism of his day.

In the Middle Ages, a vassal owed his lord honor, obedience, and a portion of his produce. Because the system depended upon the respect of the vassal for the lord, an insult to his lord was punishable by death. This world view formed a serviceable illustration for the Atonement, one readily grasped by Anselm's contemporaries. Sin was an insult to your divine Lord, a theft of God's honor, which required the "satisfaction" Jesus offered from the Cross. In Anselm's own words from *Cur deus homo?*—Why the God/man?:

> What is due to God? Righteousness, or rectitude of will. He who fails to render this honor to God, robs God of what belongs to God, and dishonors God. This is *sin*. . . . And what is satisfaction? It is not enough simply to restore what had been taken away; but in consideration of this insult offered, more than what was taken away must be rendered back.... (I xi)
>
> Let us consider whether God could properly remit sin by mercy alone without satisfaction. So to remit sin would be simply to abstain from punishing it. And since the only possible way of correcting sin, for which no satisfaction has been made, is to punish it; not to punish it is to remit it uncorrected. But

---

* Hebrew Yahwistic animal sacrifice as reflected in the Old Testament had displaced earlier Canaanite human sacrifice in which families would sacrifice some of their children in order to have representative family members on the far side of death in the spiritual realm working on their behalf. It is heartbreakingly easy to imagine that celibate clergy, dedicated as children by their families to be priests, would readily have agreed with Augustine's dour assessment of humanity—and the need for the sacrifice of a Son to repair it. It is indeed difficult to imagine any other group to which such a notion would make any sense.

God cannot properly leave anything uncorrected in his Kingdom. Moreover, so to remit sin unpunished would be treating
the sinful and the sinless alike, which would be incongruous
to God's nature. And incongruity is injustice. (xii)

It is necessary, therefore, that either the honor taken away
should be repaid, or punishment should be inflicted. Otherwise one of two things follows—either God is not just to himself, or he is powerless to do what he ought to do. A blasphe-
mous supposition. (xiii)

Satisfaction cannot be made unless there be some One able to
pay God for man's sin, something greater than all that is
beside God....Now nothing is greater than all that is not God,
except God himself. None therefore can make this satisfaction
except God. And none ought to make it except man....If,
then, it be necessary that the Kingdom of Heaven be com-
pleted by man's admission, and if man cannot be admitted
unless the aforesaid satisfaction for sin be first made, and if
God only *can*, and man only *ought* to make this satisfaction,
then necessarily one ought to make it who is both God and
man. [Thus Anselm argues the necessity of the Incarnation.]
(Book II vi)

If the Son chose to make over the claim he had on God to
man, could the Father justly forbid him doing so, or refuse to
man what the Son had willed to give him?" [Thus Anselm
attempts to answer the charge that his notion makes God
seem arbitrary and bloodthirsty.] (xix)[*]

Notice that this formulation skillfully matched an eternal
truth to temporary cultural conditions, a task each generation
must undertake. Surely that's a value we would wish to preserve.
As long as we don't literalize it, that's safe.

But notice also how much it left out once we think that's the
way things really are. Where was the whole creation whose groan-
ing was audible to Paul (Rom. 8:19–24) and to his sensitive reader? The satisfaction theory is limited to a small neighborhood of
the whole cosmos—sinful humanity.

If the reader finds Anselm's discussion to be somewhat too
finely argued, too dependent on logical principles and usages we
no longer employ, dipping into Anselm elsewhere will afford no
relief.[+] Even though Anselm reminded us every few pages that he

---

[*] Anselm of Canterbury, "*Cur deus homo?*" In Bettenson, 196–198.

[+] He reads a bit like government statistics and figures: when gargantuan sums
are supplied to the precise dollar and penny, we suspect some bureaucrat is
blowing smoke at us.

was describing an operation of God's love, we may be excused if we lose the sense of it in his details.

We also lose the sense of the original gospel narratives. It was difficult to keep the visual imagery of the actual crucifixion in mind when considering Anselm's understanding of its meaning. We are too intent on human justice being perverted at Calvary to think readily of justice being satisfied. And Jesus' previous career has to be restricted to a fund of moral teachings and of miracles. The latter were understood only to prove his divinity—though the Synoptic Evangelists saw them as models for what the Holy Spirit wishes to produce in each of us.

That's not its most devastating weakness, however. Anselm unintentionally produced a switch in our understanding of what had to happen in order for Atonement between humanity and God to take place. We can grasp that best by asking, "Who had to change in order for the Atonement to happen?"

In all previous presentations of the Atonement it was uniformly understood that we need to change, not God. The joyous proclamations shouted out that God had done exactly that. While we are still in our sins, indeed, "dead in our sins," the First Person purposes our restoration to righteousness, to cordial joy in God's Presence. God's mind does not need to change; that's the very meaning of God's righteousness. *Our* minds badly need to change. Augustine phrased it this way:

> Let not the fact, then, of our having been reconciled to God
> through the death of his Son be so listened to, or understood,
> as if the Son reconciled us unto him in such wise that he now
> began to love those whom he had formerly hated, as enemy is
> reconciled to enemy, so that on that account they became
> friends and mutual love takes the place of mutual hatred; but
> we were reconciled unto him who already loved us, but with
> whom we were at enmity because of our sins.*

By contrast, in Anselm's theory—and in those that derive from it—*God needed to have a change of mind* about humanity. The First Person's wrath must be called off, and such is its momentum that it seemed beyond God's power or will to withdraw it without bloodshed. It was as though the universe contained laws to which even God was subject—a notion any biblical writer would have

---

* *Tract. in Joh.* CX 6, quoted in Bethune-Baker, 351, note 1.

shouted out of the room. All sorts of reasons were trotted out for that requirement, but they amounted to God's freedom being held hostage to our badness. Is that a limitation God would willingly assume?*

One further weakness which has been frequently noted: there was an implicit conflict of wills within the very Trinity in this theory. Exactly *how* willing was the First Person to accept the Son's self-offering? There lingered in the mind an unintended impression that the Son had to press the Father's reluctance to get us saved.

Did our problem of religiousness displacing righteousness begin with Anselm? No. Individual lives accomplish that displacement without benefit of Anselm—or even Calvin. And in cultural history it is possible to detect the root system of truly violent religiousness in the human sacrifice ceremonies that Yahwism suppressed and supplanted.+ Anselm was nevertheless the first major Christian writer within whose writings God began to emerge, however inadvertently, as sinister. The Ogre-God who haunts earnest American Christianity can first be found on Anselm's pages.

SUBSTITUTION THEORIES: CALVIN

The next significant development owes to John Calvin (1509–1564) one of the most influential—and at least in his writings most charming—of all Christian thinkers.◆

---

* It is fascinating to note that at about this period we see the emergence of extraordinary reverence for the Blessed Virgin Mary and a preoccupation with the Devil, who ceases to be mocked and begins to be feared, respected, and—perversely—served. It is as though medieval people felt the need for refuge from the God implicit in contemporary Atonement theories. The Virgin could be entreated and the Devil could be treated with. A standard criticism of Calvin was that his Christ leaves the Devil no function. Perhaps the criticism really belongs at the door of Anselm and the Schoolmen.

+ Scholars speculate that the chilling story of Abraham and Isaac (Genesis 22) is one marker for that suppression. The path Abraham and Isaac had to take up Mt. Moriah led through the Valley of Hinnom where children were routinely sacrificed to pagan divinities.

◆ Even Ernest Becker liked Calvin, despite professional displeasure with the fruit of his thought. In the interview with Sam Keen cited earlier, Becker described his own awakening to faith in its relation to his subsequent illness: "I think of Calvin when he says, 'Lord, Thou bruisest me, but since it is Thou it is all right.'" Quoted in Keen, *Voices and Visions*, 191.

Readers of Calvin's own writings—his towering *Institutes of the Christian Religion* or his many commentaries and countless sermons and letters—will not find the claustrophobic gloom so characteristic of his subsequent followers. To the contrary, few writers have written so well concerning God's glory or God's affection for us. Calvin's steel deserves worthier opponents than it will receive in this brief treatment, so I am at pains to begin with a declaration of genuine respect and gratitude for this greatest and most complicated of the Reformers.

Calvin bequeathed to his descendants the penal or judicial theory of the Atonement. Using his legal training he set the doctrine in the context of law courts. This was a most helpful illustration at the time when, as Calvin wrote, the European bourgeoisie was discovering in the law courts a bulwark against the capriciousness of the titled nobility.

According to the penal theory, a crime had been committed. Justice required a penalty—a death penalty—be paid. By a process lawyers call creating a legal fiction, God pretended that Jesus is guilty in order to pretend that we are innocent.*

Let Calvin speak for himself here:

> If we would assure ourselves that God is pacified and propitious to us, we must fix our eyes and our hearts on Christ alone, since it is by him only that we obtain the *non-imputation of sins*, the imputation of which is connected with the Divine wrath. (II xvi 3.)
>
> This is our absolution, that *the guilt which made us obnoxious to punishment is transferred to the person of the Son of God.* For we ought particularly to remember this satisfaction.... (II xvi 5.)
>
> It follows in the Creed, "that he died and was buried;" in which it may be further seen, how in every respect *he substituted himself in our room to pay the price of our redemption....* [Emphasis added] (II xvi 7.)

Again this doctrine skillfully matched a truth to current conditions. But it contained weaknesses. It added the artificiality of the legal fiction to Anselm's narrowness. "How many legs does a dog have if you call its tail a leg?" asked Abraham Lincoln. "Four," is the answer; calling a tail a leg does not make it a leg. Lincoln

---

* Common legal fictions include the pretense in court that a corporation is an individual with constitutional rights; or that nothing like insurance exists in a damages case. Legal fictions are perfectly proper devices for making the law work smoothly. They simply are not true.

the lawyer had his own doubts about legal fictions. At 2:00 A.M., tossing on the bed and wracked with doubts, many a poor sinner has discovered that the penal theory of the Atonement only works in church.

We must add to it all the criticisms to which Anselm is vulnerable, excepting only the charge of turgid logic—Calvin's logic is clearer than Anselm's. Yet substituting Jesus for humanity is not New Testament teaching, no matter who says it is. Again, in Calvin's theory God seemed trapped in constraining requirements, God's much-vaunted "sovereignty" notwithstanding. Again, it seemed that God's mind must be changed rather than ours. And with the penal theory, we were no closer to the actual events of the Passion than previously—if anything, we were indeed further removed from the *data* of our restoration to enjoying God.

In spite of its vulnerability to common sense, the penal theory of the Atonement has the widest currency of any in American religious practice. It was earlier enshrined in the Westminster Confession of 1643:

XI. Of Justification

> Those whom God effectually calleth he also freely justifieth. . . by imputing the obedience and satisfaction of Christ unto them....They are not justified until the Holy Spirit doth in due time actually apply Christ unto them. [*]

When the Fundamentalists, in their conflict with the Liberals, nailed the "Substitutionary Atonement" to their mast as one of the five fundamental tenets of Christian orthodoxy, it was this theory they had in mind. It is still widely taught, if the broad currency and frequent reprinting of Berkhof's *Systematic Theology* is any indication; the latter's discussion of the Atonement begins thus:

> The doctrine of the Atonement here presented is the penal substitutionary or satisfaction doctrine [*sic*], which is the doctrine clearly taught in the Word of God....In the case under consideration, it means that the Atonement was intended *to propitiate God and to reconcile him to the sinner.* [Emphasis added][+]

---

[*] Bettenson, 348–349.

[+] Louis Berkhof. *Systematic Theology* (Grand Rapids, Wm. B. Eerdmans Publishing Co., 1941), 373.

Virtually all evangelistic procedures in conservative Protestantism apply this theory in the innocent belief that it is "the biblical theory." Charismatics, in our headlong flight from anything "liberal," have adopted this conservative Atonement theory uncritically, never pausing to discern its spirit-deadening defects.

We must be clear about these defects. The primary defect is that it states that God is our enemy, suggesting that God's wrath requires death. Any pastor can tell you how many years it takes the most devout believer thoroughly to expunge that notion, even after the most dramatic of conversions.

Second, when your notion of Atonement—a restored fellowship with God the First Person—goes no further than justification—getting your criminal record erased— you are still liable for trouble. After all, you could slip again. Furthermore, you're confusing righteousness with innocence.* And that's to move from righteousness to religion, willy-nilly. How? Because innocence is a bargaining chip in your negotiation with God, a sign that your dealings with God are commercial, coercive, and meretricious.

As long as you remain concerned about innocence, a concern nourished by any substitutionary Atonement theory, you're caught up in religion. Your gaze remains on yourself, not on Jesus. You still see your contaminated identity as your main problem. That contamination feels dangerous because it reduces your imagined power to control God and others. It reduces your putative entitlement to life. So if you think of the Cross only as removing sins, if you refuse to travel through the Cross to the Throne, the fear of death and the need for personal control have bracketed your personal reliance on God.

In "The Dogma is the Drama," Dorothy L. Sayers satirized such notions with a catechism according to the man-in-the-street:

> Q. What does the Church think of God the Father?
>
> A. He is omnipotent and holy. He created the world and imposed on man conditions impossible of fulfillment; he is very angry if these are not carried out. He sometimes interferes by means of arbitrary judgments and miracles, distributed with a good deal of favoritism. He likes to be truckled to and is always ready to pounce on anybody who trips up over a difficulty in

---

* The Bible does not support our preoccupation with innocence. The word rarely occurs in it and the contexts of its few occurrences (e.g. Phil. 2:15; Heb. 7:26) suggest that the writer meant something like ceremonial cleanliness.

the law or is having a bit of fun. He is rather like a dictator, only larger and more arbitrary.

Q. What does the Church think of God the Son?

A. He is in some way to be identified with Jesus of Nazareth. It was not his fault that the world was made like this, and unlike God the Father, he is friendly to man and did his best to reconcile man to God. He has a good deal of influence with God, and if you want anything done, it is best to apply to him....

Q. What is meant by the Atonement?

A. God wanted to damn everybody, but his vindictive sadism was sated by the crucifixion of his own Son, who was quite innocent, and therefore, a particularly attractive victim. He now only damns people who don't follow Christ, or who never heard of him.[*]

How far this is from the biblical and post-biblical witness, though it's often identified with it. It's the result of centuries of proclamation of substitutionary theories of the Atonement.

As we have seen so far, another spirit-deadening effect of a substitutionary Atonement theory occurs at the level of imagery. If you use such a lens, there is no getting around the view of God as either sinister or silly. A God whose offended dignity requires bloodshed does not readily elicit worship. We all know human beings more admirable, with superior foresight.

Presentations of a substitutionary Atonement display the Father as silly, as though our sins and their consequences were developments unanticipated on high.[+] Such a notion of God elicits no worship, admiration, or trust. A seat on such a lap is no secure perch. You might do business with such a person—religion—but you would not willingly socialize with such a person—righteousness.

Substitution is not a process we accredit in other departments of life. The story is told of a mother who introduced her son to his

---

[*] Dorothy L. Sayers, *The Whimsical Christian* (New York, Macmillan Publishing Co., Inc., 1978) 25–26

[+] We have all heard talks from people who ought to know better saying something like, "God *had the problem* of reconciling his justice with his mercy...." Seems a bit short-sighted, does it not? The church has always viewed Abraham on Mount Moriah suspending the sacrifice of Isaac as a metaphor for God. But this "God-had-the-problem" folly replaces Abraham with Jephthah, whose thoughtless vow and subsequent personal vanity cost the life of his daughter. (Judg. 11:28–40) new teacher, saying, "Eustace is very sensitive; if he misbehaves, just punish the kid next to him!" Our responsive chuckle reflects our understanding that that isn't how things work. And if your plane crashed on the sea, would you live forever affectionately grateful to someone who gave you her lifejacket and then drowned?

As long as Christians use such language, we will never grasp the full work of Jesus in our unconscious minds—from which all meaningful images and symbols emerge and to which they return. Our houses will perch tenuously on sand, they won't rest on rock.

A mere shift in doctrine won't lead us out of this quandary. To develop religious theories is like hitting the Tar Baby; hitting it someplace different won't free us. A helper with turpentine and a wire brush is required. That helper is the Holy Spirit who searches the heart, replacing false images with true. Surely Paul meant something like this when he spoke of "renewing your minds" (Rom. 12:2). We assist the Spirit in this work by washing our minds through the Scriptures, taking their pictures and phrases into ourselves rather than strip-mining them for complete theories. We read the Scriptures to attune our hearts in preparation for our own conscious encounters with God. That's what those figures of speech are for. As we read the Scriptures, we "snuggle up to the data," as a friend put it. That snuggle revivifies the Tradition and nourishes Reason.

THE MORAL THEORY* OF THE ATONEMENT: ABELARD

In the Scriptures we find the basis for yet another theory of the Atonement that is essential for grasping the work of Jesus. This theory has the flavor of original experience left in it. I'll call it the moral theory, though it has also been described as the exemplary, psychological, or subjective theory of the Atonement. It suggests that the real impact of Jesus' self-offering is directed at our hearts, not God's heart, softening us and siphoning off our violence. It's a charming theory, effective indeed by virtue of its very charm. First formulated by Peter Abelard (1079–1142) who may have needed to embrace the Atonement more than most theologians of his

---

* Though I favor it, I don't mind calling it a theory, since it describes things we can actually see happening. Things appear really to work that way.

day,* it has been reworked in detail in the last two centuries. This theory is in bad odor with Evangelicals because "liberals" and Unitarians—or their Socinian ancestors, at any rate—use it. Charismatics have fallen into the Evangelical fashion of abhorring anything "liberal" and are also suspicious of it. But the moral theory of the Atonement is indispensable, notwithstanding the company it keeps, because it comes closest to describing how the Cross affects *us*.

Jesus was the first to point to it: "And I, when I am lifted up from the earth, will draw all people to myself." (Jn. 12:32)

The centurion at the cross was the second: "Now when the centurion, who stood facing him, saw that in this way he breathed his last, he said, 'Truly this man was God's Son!'" (Mk. 15:39)

Described here is Jesus' attractiveness and its impact on those around him. The vision of such a one dying voluntarily at our hands at a moment when we are at our most self-righteous and most cowardly melts our hearts, siphons out our violence, and makes us pliable to the God who gave him. It changes *our* minds—not God's.

Each of us can think of the impact of some Christ-like person. To be in the presence of such a person calls forth our best efforts and courage, strengthening our resolve to be better than we were. Jesus' presence had such an effect on anyone who was not hardened in pride.

Let Abelard present it himself. He began by attacking older notions of the Atonement:

QUESTION

What right to possess mankind could the devil possibly have unless he had received man for purposes of torture through the express permission or even the assignment, of the Lord?

Who indeed doubts that, if a slave of any master seduces his fellow slave by subtle suggestions and makes him depart from obedience to his true master, the seducer is looked upon by the slave's master as much more guilty than the seduced? And how unjust it would be that he who seduced the other should deserve as a result to have special right or authority over him![+]

---

* Abelard was a not altogether honorable lover of his pupil Héloise, his amatory career criminally curtailed by her family who had him castrated. He subsequently haunted the European imagination as a tragic lover.

[+] "Expos. of Epistle to the Romans II," quoted in Eugene R. Fairweather, ed., *A Scholastic Miscellany* (Library of Christian Classics, Vol. X. Philadelphia, Westminster Press, 1956), 281.

Notice the fruit of rejecting dualism in the latter quote; the Devil is recognized as our fellow slave.

> How did the death of his innocent Son so please God the Father that through it he should be reconciled to us—to us who by our sinful acts have done the very things for which our innocent Lord was put to death? Had not this very great sin been committed, could he not have pardoned the former much lighter sin?
>
> In what manner have we been made more righteous through the death of the Son of God than we were before, so that we ought to be delivered from punishment?
>
> Indeed, how cruel and wicked it seems that anyone should demand the blood of an innocent person as the price for anything, or that it should in any way please him that an innocent man should be slain—still less that God should consider the death of his Son so agreeable that by it he should be reconciled to the whole world![*]

Now Abelard puts forward his own theory:

SOLUTION

> Now it seems to us that we have been justified by the blood of Christ and reconciled to God in this way: through this unique act of grace manifested to us—in that his Son has taken upon himself our nature and preserved [sic] therein in teaching us by word and example even unto death—he has more fully bound us to himself by love; with the result that our hearts should be enkindled by such a gift of divine grace, and true charity should not now shrink from enduring anything for him."[+]
>
> Yet everyone becomes more righteous—by which we mean a greater lover of the Lord—after the Passion of Christ than before, since a realized gift inspires greater love than one that is only hoped for. Wherefore our redemption through Christ's suffering is that deeper affection in us which not only frees us from slavery to sin, but also wins for us the true liberty of sons of God, so that we do all things out of love rather than fear—love to him who has shown us such grace that no greater can be found, as he himself asserts, saying, "Greater love than this no man hath, that a man lay down his life for his friends."[◆]

---

[*] Ibid., 283.

[+] Ibid.

[◆] Ibid., 284

Anyone can see at a glance that this is not a complete presentation of Jesus' work. It does in fact ignore the sacrificial passages in the New Testament. And it places perhaps too much emphasis on humanity's faith response, almost to the point of suppressing God's initiative.* Yet the moral theory makes so much else intelligible. Our normal lives occasionally offer examples of heroic people whom we love staying honest at tremendous cost during difficult and stressful periods that press us to compromise our own honor; their subsequent delight in us sweeps us up past self-justification into a realm of self-acceptance, generosity and understanding towards others, and the passionate wish to be our best selves in response. We know that happens and that it really changes us. So Abelard's theory describes something we can experience: it makes God's judgment friendly. Our terror of God's judgment blocks us from our rightful place on God's lap; the charm of Jesus, to which the moral theory points, melts that terror.

Let us examine Jesus as judge. An initial example of the principle friendly judgment in my own life may help before we look at specific passages.

One day my mother walked into my room in college unannounced. She remained her cordial self as she gazed around at *Playboy* centerfolds on the walls, long-unchanged sheets on an unmade bed, and heaps of dirty laundry. Without her saying a word I received judgment at the hands of a merciful person. No "problem of justice and mercy" was there; the two qualities were united. That episode energized a campaign on my part to live more hygienically, if not altogether more neatly. In real judgment a truthful person precipitates truth as much by presence as by word or action.

Such an understanding helps us through the apparent contradictions about judgment in the Gospel of John. In some places Jesus says that he has come to judge (Jn. 5:30; 9:39), in others he says that he did not (Jn. 3:17; 8:15). In fact, he has come to precipitate judgment by his very presence. We can form an image of our Lord in his charming humanity producing change by the responses people offer, in which, "...to all who received him, who

---

* Anselm's understanding, it must be noted, did just the opposite—it left little room at all for humanity's faith response. In hot debate, exaggeration begets counter-exaggeration.

believed in his name, he gave power to become children of God."
(Jn. 1:12)

He has no need to rant, rave or "lecture," as we used to call it
when we were children. "When they kept on questioning him, he
straightened up and said to them, 'Let anyone among you who is
without sin be the first to throw a stone at her.'" (Jn. 8:7)

That is judgment.

"Therefore, I tell you, her sins, which were many, have been
forgiven; hence she has shown great love. But the one to whom little is forgiven, loves little." (Lk. 7:47)

That is also judgment.

"Martha, Martha, you are worried and distracted by many
things." (Lk. 10:41)

More judgment.

"When he had said this, he cried with a loud voice, 'Lazarus,
come out!' The dead man came out, his hands and feet bound
with strips of cloth, and his face wrapped in a cloth. Jesus said to
them, 'Unbind him, and let him go.'" (Jn. 11:43–44)

Death itself is judged. And the final judgment on this world is
the Cross. By submitting to his death Jesus demonstrated that the
world order as constituted by death-fearful humanity and as polluted by the Devil will not tolerate righteous life. The Cross compels us to recognize that.

THE PROBLEM OF INNOCENCE

A remaining obstacle barring us from the understanding of
Jesus as judge arises from the moral theory of the Atonement.
That obstacle is our preoccupation with innocence, which distorts
our view of ourselves and of Jesus as well. To want to be innocent
is not to want the truth. For in truth you are not innocent. This
condition has deep roots. Becker put it this way:

> If you took a blind and dumb organism and gave it self-con-
> sciousness and a name, if you made it stand out of nature and
> know consciously that it was unique, then you would have nar-
> cissism. In man, physico-chemical identity and the sense of
> power and activity have become conscious. . . . When you com-
> bine natural narcissism with the basic need for self-esteem, you
> create a creature who has to feel himself an object of primary
> value: first in the universe, representing in himself all of life.
> (DD, 2–3)

G.K. Chesterton once marveled that the modern world had rejected the doctrine of Original Sin: "I should have thought," he remarked, "that it would be the only Christian doctrine clearly demonstrable by empirical observation!"

You cannot attain innocence in the sense of an unblemished record without incurring innocence in a second, more destructive sense. This latter innocence is the refusal of knowledge, the suppression of what you really know. As a religious impulse, innocence is dangerous, because you'll harm others to preserve it. If your record has to remain unblemished, you'll cast blame elsewhere, regardless of truth or justice. I have vivid memories of assisting seriously devout families with the discovery that their children routinely lied about various misbehaviors, some quite reprehensible. In these households innocence had replaced righteousness, so truth could not be told. Personal darkness couldn't be discussed in such a setting, so it grew like mildew in a damp unventilated cellar. This becomes such a habit that you're not aware of the distortion. Innocence in this sense is a competitive blood sport, the preoccupation of people like Pontius Pilate washing his hands and Judas Iscariot flinging back the money.

We can't attribute innocence to Jesus; sinlessness, yes, refusal to be separated from God, yes; but not innocence. Here we tread near a delicate mystery. On the one hand it is nowhere recorded, nor is it easy to imagine, that Jesus ever behaved in a base or dishonest way. Yet he shows no trace of the cloying daintiness of the innocent. Somehow he *knows* that, "...it is from within, from the human heart, that evil intentions come: fornication, theft, murder, adultery, avarice, wickedness, deceit, licentiousness, envy, slander, pride, folly." (Mk. 7:21–22)

His tone is not that of an observer. As we saw, when he said, "Let anyone among you who is without sin be the first to throw a stone at her," (Jn. 8:7), he formed a personal bond with the accusing crowd. "Every one of us has had trouble with this stuff, haven't we?" he is saying. "If you think you can kill your problem by killing her, have a shot." You can't fake that kind of knowledge. They know he knows, and he knows they know it. An innocent Jesus doesn't fit that tableau. How could he fit ours?

To sit in God's lap we must know God's truth is friendly to us. We must let our fictitiousness melt away; we must shed our false selves; we must allow our creatureliness to re-emerge. We will only have that courage if beckoned by one who is recognizable and true in our terms. Surely something like that is what he meant when he said, "I am the way, and the truth, and the life. No one comes to the Father except through me." (Jn. 14:6)

He did not offer us those words to support our bigotry or to justify the horrors that have been committed under this banner. Jesus was stating a fact: no human being, dead in sin, will dare approach God unless God, with gracious tact, assumes a human nature to beckon to us, unless God shows kinship with us.

The notion of innocence distorts Jesus' humanity past recognition. The polar paradox remains; both terms—innocence and humanity—generate the mystery. Jesus was without sin—and yet he *knows* human badness in a way that makes his presence judgment. To verify the second pole of that paradox, Jesus' worldly wisdom, is not to falsify the first.

In addition to my own encounters with God's judgment over the years, I have been privileged to hear the accounts of any number of parishioners and friends. Such encounters reflect a pattern. Each is preluded with terror, each recreates the person, each restores the person to a sense of being God's creature rather than his own, each leaves her wiser and more accepting of others. And, strangely, in each encounter our Lord feels to us like an *insider*, like someone who knows all about it. "All will be well, and all will be well, and all manner of thing will be well," Jesus told Lady Julian. In each encounter his charm draws us into righteousness while his authority rules out bargaining. You emerge with a joyful sense, "He knows all about it. He knows me. He still came. It's all right."

In whatever expression we claim our restored place on God's lap, that expression must disclose God as friendly, as beckoning. The problem of human sin is bitterly real and, in ways that surely Augustine himself must have sensed, it *is* hereditary, "original." As "sociobiologists," often called "evolutionary psychologists," and psychoanalysts have been insisting to us, the conditions of our physical lives and our urgent drive to ensure individual and species survival make us competitive with and exploitative of one another and our environment. Yet, if others are to tolerate, assist, and not destroy us, we must internalize the behavioral limits of the surrounding culture. This tension is not naturally resoluble— it is always there. We may cope with it by becoming Goody Two-Shoes on one end or Charles Manson on the other—but there is no natural means to achieve comfort with it. Both of those postures try to reduce the tension for the other end of the spectrum, but each has obvious disadvantages. I have been suggesting that its spiritual expression is religion, the effort to exploit and placate God.

The first few generations of the church left us records which report encounters with Jesus of Nazareth which rapidly and gradually resolved that tension. Those encounters made it possible to say with "John the Elder,"

> And by this we will know that we are from the truth and will reassure our hearts before him whenever our hearts condemn us; for God is greater than our hearts, and he knows everything. Beloved, if our hearts do not condemn us, we have boldness before God; and we receive from him whatever we ask, because we obey his commandments and do what pleases him. (1 Jn. 3:19–22)

Jesus' faithfulness in the face of death itself, his enduring love for his faithless friends even as he was being annihilated, and his delight in reconfronting them that first Easter night made the niggling voices of their vanity-driven consciences sound foolish. They were impelled to "accept their acceptance" and in the process discovered that they were, for the first time, moral and spiritual grown-ups. In every account of the Resurrection of Jesus, they became aware at some point that his Spirit had settled into occupancy within them.* That Spirit empowered them to live in a gleefully paradoxical relationship with their own "badness" (the irresoluble tension between biological drive and social constraint). Once they were Spirit-filled, their badness was no longer a necessary life resource nor was it any longer a threat to their own or others' lives. In Jesus' resurrected presence, they could both acknowledge its truth yet live largely independent of it. God's authority in their lives if anything actually grew; but their dread of God was gone.

Now *that's* Atonement.

The acceptance of our humanity within God's embrace invites

---

* Sources vary as to when. Matthew 27:50 says Jesus poured out his Spirit from the Cross itself—that's why Matthew tells us about the veil of the Temple tearing and graves opening. Mark may agree, but phrases it more vaguely (Mk.15:37). Luke places it at Pentecost (Acts 2:1ff). John places it in the Upper Room Easter night (Jn.20:19ff.). Paul says it happened to him three days after the encounter on the road to Damascus (Acts 9:17). It happens to us when we slow down, get quiet, pay attention, and let our lives catch up with us.

us to a Christian doctrine of humanity—a theological anthropol-ogy—that takes in the full scope of the Scriptures' description of the human condition, which is no longer purely sin-based.

> When I look at your heavens, the work of your fingers, the moon and the stars that you have established; what are human beings that you are mindful of them, mortals that you care for them? Yet you have made them a little lower than God, and crowned them with glory and honor. You have given them dominion over the works of your hands; you have put all things under their feet, all sheep and oxen, and also the beasts of the field, the birds of the air, and the fish of the sea, whatever passes along the paths of the seas. (Ps. 8:3–8)

> If the Spirit of him who raised Jesus from the dead dwells in you, he who raised Christ from the dead will give life to your mortal bodies also through his Spirit that dwells in you. (Rom. 8:11)

> He destined us for adoption as his children through Jesus Christ, according to the good pleasure of his will, to the praise of his glorious grace that he freely bestowed on us in the Beloved. In him we have redemption through his blood, the forgiveness of our trespasses, according to the riches of his grace that he lavished on us. With all wisdom and insight he has made known to us the mystery of his will, according to his good pleasure that he set forth in Christ, as a plan for the full-ness of time, to gather up all things in him, things in heaven and things on earth. In Christ we have also obtained an inher-itance, having been destined according to the purpose of him who accomplishes all things according to his counsel and will, so that we, who were the first to set our hope on Christ, might live for the praise of his glory. (Eph. 1:5–12)

It's easily possible to miss those elements in present day dis-cussions of God's ways with us.* Our expression of God's image, our co-creator privileges, the privilege of contributing to God's joy with our worship, the honor of "making up in [our] own suf-ferings that which is lacking in the sufferings of Christ" (Col. 1:24), the requirement to express God's love to others through service and sacrifice—all these elements discovered in the Bible

---

* The Reformation—especially Luther—was properly thrilled with a recovered sense of "justification by grace through faith," matching the requirements of a new widespread individual self-consciousness in Europe. But when you've found a ham-mer, everything looks like a nail. To this day many Protestants assume that "justifi-cation by faith" is what Paul thought he was talking about. The baleful outcome has been to confine the operation of God's affectionate power exclusively to sin-removal. Surely in our day it is time to embrace a broader anthropology than the Augustinian Original Sin that Luther recaptured in order to solve.

require a relationship with God which consists of an unselfconscious trust and delight in God.

Whatever Atonement description you embrace, make certain that it allows the restoration of that broader anthropology. Make sure it operates by processes you believe possible. Make sure it's one you believe on the basis of experience rather than pretense. Make sure that it knows Jesus as your fellow human being—more than a Lamb or an impersonal hematological function. Use your courage to obey God—don't use it up trying to manage cognitive dissonance. To settle for less shuns Jesus. I can't put it plainer than that.

For Jesus to reconcile us to God, his humanity must be authentic, not a theological formula. It must have the same ontological weight as his divinity. Nor can he be innocent as we normally use the term, because that sort of innocence is a subhuman falsehood. He must see past our behavior; he must decide that our sin is not our most interesting feature. He must see us into a fresh relationship with the First Person, one based on self-acceptance in judgment and truth. And so he does. But the unexpected, gratuitous element in his judgment is his *merriness*, the merriness of one giving a party.

Julian of Norwich describes that party:

> My mind was lifted up to heaven and I saw our Lord as lord in his own house where he had called his much-loved friends and servants to a banquet. I saw that the Lord did not sit in one place but ranged throughout the house, filling it with joy and gladness. Completely relaxed and courteous, he was himself the happiness and peace of his dear friends, his beautiful face radiating measureless love like a marvelous symphony; and it was that wonderful face shining with the beauty of God that filled that heavenly place with joy and light.[*]

No matter how skillful we are at avoiding stepping on the cracks in the moral sidewalk, throwing moral salt over religious shoulders, you and I will never be *righteous* until we hear that celebration—and join it.

---

[*] Julian of Norwich, *Revelations of Divine Love*, Revelation (or "Showing") Six, chapter xiv.

CHAPTER EIGHT

A RELIGIOUS BREAKDOWN

A friend caught W.C. Fields reading a Bible on his deathbed and demanded what he was doing. "Looking for loopholes, looking for loopholes!" was Fields' reply.

I doubt that many of us has consciously scanned the Scriptures for loopholes, exactly, though possibly some of us have scanned the Bible for new rules to follow, hoping perhaps to change our luck or find some shortcuts. However, the Bible demands more of us. Such scrutiny will not yield the sort of understanding we are developing in this discussion. The scrutiny required here must include a resolute confrontation with our deepest fears and our shadow characteristics alongside biblical texts. It must include permission to see what we really see, to suspend temporarily the operation of our conventional understandings. As Jesus told his opponents, "You search the scriptures because you think that in them you have eternal life; and it is they that testify on my behalf." (Jn. 5:39)

The thoughts we have been considering, about the fear of death, about the preference of religion to righteousness, about the cultivation of a false self, and the urgent necessity of God's judgment—all these do in fact correspond to the Bible according to the reading strategy I and many others employ.* It is easy to read the Bible so as to miss them, however. So it may be helpful to look at a prominent part of the Bible where all the themes I have been discussing come together.

Let turn now to a few important places in the Old and New Testaments, seeking God's company. Specifically we want to see if the distinction between religion and righteousness can be discovered and sustained because if God could rescue us from religiousness and offer us righteousness, we would have "come to God for that life" indeed.

The Old Testament furnishes many detailed pictures of much that we have considered so far. But one book protrudes in alpine splendor, illustrating the sharp contrast between religiousness and righteousness. It is the story of a heroically religious man whose religion fails him; he is brought to righteousness through a judging, repression-stripping encounter with God; his crisis leaves him able to converse with and love God as a friend. The work in question is the Book of Job. A detailed look at that book will illustrate many of the points we have been considering.+

POETRY AS A BIBLICAL GENRE

Before we begin, a few words about biblical interpretation are in order. Every English edition of the Bible since the Revised Standard Version of 1946 has been typeset with more care than was taken with the Authorized Version. Consequently, modern readers can distinguish poetry from prose at a glance. Casually leafing through Job shows that most of it is poetry. Scholars have reached consensus that the poet took an older folk tale—the prose sections on either end of the work—and used it as the setting for his poem. In so doing, he made the original tale his own and transformed it.

We do not interpret poetry the way we interpret prose, particularly a prose history. Prose focuses the imagination; poetry frees

---

* That is, on approaching a passage, one goes first for whatever one can surmise about the human author's likely intention.

+ The following thoughts owe a debt to Aloys von Orelli, M.D., a Basel psychoanalyst and thoughtful Christian. He generously shared these thoughts with me in an unpublished essay entitled "Job: Attempt at a Psychological Explanation," written for and presented to the *Médicine de la Personne Entière* XXVI International Meeting in Bristol, United Kingdom, July 21–27, 1974.

it. The Books of Samuel and Kings ask to be read as history, indeed as journalism, allowing little interpretive license. But in Job, the Spirit has inspired poetry with all the imaginative liberty that entails. So when we exercise interpretive license with a poetic book, we are not playing fast-and-loose with the meaning or authority of the text. Rather we are taking seriously the Spirit's selection of poetry as the proper medium for this revelation. To treat Job as history or journalism is not being faithful to the Word; it is being pridefully unfaithful to the discipline imposed by the actual form the Word takes.

THE BOOK OF JOB

JOB'S RELIGION

"There was once a man in the land of Uz whose name was Job." (Job 1:1a) No one knows where Uz is. The book begins in effect by saying, "Once upon a time, in a land far away."

"That man was blameless and upright, one who feared God and turned away from evil." (Job 1:1b) That is, in that land there lived a man who was in our terms "religious." By his behavior he was trying to control how much God loved him. Fascinatingly, biblical Hebrew contains no single words corresponding to our words "religion" or "religious," so the tale has to describe how a religious person acts. Job thinks that God's favor to him is a response to the attractiveness he generates by his morality and his correct cultic practices. In Aloys von Orelli's words,

> Job knows exactly what is good and what is evil. He is a blameless man. According to the story, he has even attracted God's attention as being an extraordinary specimen of this otherwise dubious race. He keeps strictly to that which he considers correct and feels that he is in the right.

His prosperity should have assured him that he was doing fine but he is not serene in that confidence. His relationship with God is not righteous, as we have used the term. There is no comfort in it, no relaxation.

> There were born to him seven sons and three daughters. He had seven thousand sheep, three thousand camels, five hundred yoke of oxen, five hundred donkeys, and very many servants; so that this man was the greatest of all the people of the east. (Job 1:2–3)

He is worried about staying innocent.

> His sons used to go and hold feasts in one another's houses in turn; and they would send and invite their three sisters to eat and drink with them. And when the feast days had run their course, Job would send and sanctify them, and he would rise early in the morning and offer burnt offerings according to the number of them all; for Job said, "It may be that my children have sinned, and cursed God in their hearts." This is what Job always did. (Job 1:4–5)

See him shake his head at the beer-cans in his children's yards after a long weekend; he sacrifices on their behalf so their hell raising will not stain his own record. Their gratitude for this unsolicited ministry is not recorded.

JOB'S UNCONSCIOUS

Beginning in verse 6, "God" and "the Satan" make a bet about this anxious man as though he were a laboratory rat:

> Then Satan answered the LORD, "Does Job fear God for nothing? Have you not put a fence around him and his house and all that he has, on every side? You have blessed the work of his hands, and his possessions have increased in the land. But stretch out your hand now, and touch all that he has, and he will curse you to your face." The LORD said to Satan, "Very well, all that he has is in your power; only do not stretch out your hand against him!"(Job 1:9–12a)

As von Orelli puts it:

> This wager of God with Satan at Job's expense is probably one of the morally most offensive texts in the Bible. How can the all-bountiful and omniscient God, merely to satisfy a malicious doubt of Satan's, drive his most loyal servant to despair, almost to suicide?

Under what circumstances might we imagine the God and Father of Jesus Christ taking part in such a deal? Some such question has occurred to every morally alert reader of Job since its very composition. Here von Orelli's interpretation comes to our rescue, drawing as he does on his understanding of God and of the unconscious mind:

> We must try to understand the various persons in the drama from Job's subjective point of view, i.e., as a projection of the psychological functions of Job....

> With his idealistic way of life his image of God is bound to be
> a projection of his ideals at a cosmic all-powerful level. "God
> cannot be less good than I am. But I am a virtuous, upright
> man avoiding evil; therefore all the more God must be
> upright, virtuous and just and avoid all evil." God cannot be
> less good than an upright man. He must put into practice at
> an absolute level the qualities, which Job is aiming at, in his
> human restrictedness. However, fundamentally an ideal never
> includes more than half the reality; the other half is in the
> shade. An ideal God can never be total. Thus an ideal-projec-
> tion cannot be the God who created the world, whose pre-
> rogative is Totality, Oneness and Entirety. This God of Job is a
> very special god, one might say "God" in inverted commas,
> therefore Job's image of God.

This is in fact *not* God as God self-reveals elsewhere; such dealings cannot be attributed to God. It is Job's religious image of
"God" projected onto the clouds, dwelling not in heaven or eternity but in Job's imagination. It is the notion of "God" that Job
claims to love but actually resents. It is "God" in Job's image, the
image of a fallen human being's notion of goodness. It is the projection of that part of Job's cookie-dough that fits inside the dia-
mond-shaped cutter as discussed in Chapter 3.

Likewise "the Satan" is the projection of Job's own badness—
as he religiously conceives his badness. If "God" here is the projection of Job's conscious, if idealized, ego, "the Satan" is the projection of Job's unconscious Shadow. He is the dough that falls
outside the cutter. He is the image writ large of everything that
Job represses in himself to stay afloat. And it is rising up to haunt
him. Von Orelli makes this clear:

> The identification of the ego [Job] with the ideal ["God"]
> leads to a misinterpretation of one's own nature and this stim-
> ulates the unconscious shadow. If the shadow is not con-
> sciously accepted, its effects will be subconscious, foreign to
> the ego. It will then be experienced as a blow of fate, as an
> individual or collective tragedy.

It is important that we understand the internal conflict Job
projects onto the clouds. To understand this "God" and this
"Satan" more firmly, let us analyze Job's condition in the very
beginning of the book.

Genesis 2–3
(Excursus)

Job is a true child of Adam and Eve (Gen. 2–3).* The fruit of the Tree of the Knowledge of Good and Evil (Gen. 2:17; 3:1–7) is tucked in his cheek where he can suck on its poison. Do you know what that fruit does to us? It *restricts* our knowledge to the categories of good and evil. "You will be like God, knowing good and evil," the serpent told them (3:5). What he did not tell them was the appalling limitations that knowledge would impose. Eating that fruit, we can no longer know a thing simply in itself; we can only judge its qualities in positive or negative terms. For Job, the consequence is that his perception of everything around him consists of judging them either good or evil. Sacrificing is good, wild parties are bad. That is what that fruit does to people. Job is stuck where the human race has been stuck since Eden. He cannot experience something for itself: "And the two were naked and were not ashamed." (Gen. 2:25) He must judge: "And they saw that they were naked; and they knitted for themselves aprons out of fig leaves." (Gen. 3:7)

Judging everything, Job understands nothing. The reader will discover the same mental law. You can either judge or understand; you cannot do both simultaneously. When you judge, your understanding has hit its ceiling. When you understand something, your inclination to judge it recedes. "*Tout comprendre, c'est tout pardonner,*" said Voltaire. It is as though our minds contain a switch that can be engaged in only one of two positions: JUDGE or UNDERSTAND. God alone can do both at once. We must choose between them.

Placing your finger at Job 1 and flip back to Genesis 2–3 for a dramatization of this dilemma.

In Genesis 2:19, the "Adam"—"human being," not yet specifically masculine—receives power to name the beasts.

---

* Genesis 2–3 seems to have been written not to describe sin, a word which does not occur in the account, but simply to account for human mortality. Until Paul, Jewish scholars paid little attention to the story, and would scarcely have extrapolated a notion like Original Sin from it. The terms "fall" and "sin" do not occur in the story itself and were likely not what the writer had in mind. However, Christian interpretation of the account has transformed it into a metaphor of almost allegorical specificity for the origin of sin in human experience. Since that later, superimposed understanding lies so ready at hand, it is too temptingly apt not to use.

Since the time of Lactantius in the fourth century C.E., down to Carl Jung a few decades ago, various people have interpreted the Eden story as a fall "upward," as though eating the fruit had produced an intellectual awakening. This interpretation founders against Genesis 2:19. Our normal interpretation of the Adam naming the beasts states that s/he has authority over them, because possessing the name confers the power to control. But the power and authority to name the beasts also implies a cognitive penetration into the very essence of the animals. To name it correctly, the Adam has to understand it utterly. Here we have a clue to what biblical writers often mean by understanding: to experience something in the presence of God, allowing God to interpret it. In fellowship with God, the Adam gazes at a beast, understands it, speaks a name. But the Adam does not judge the animal. Prior to the Fall from fellowship with God, the Adam has no need to judge anything, no need to call a rose good or poison-ivy bad. God's Presence serves that function, warning against harm and pointing out delights. The distinction between good and evil is there to be made. But it is not the Adam's job to distinguish it, it is God's. Human understanding results from receiving God's judgment.

When Adam and Eve, the now sexually differentiated human beings,* eat the fruit in 3:6, when they ingest that poison into hitherto uncontaminated tissues and "become what they eat," a *decline* in intellect results. From now on, one sole consideration overrides every perception and thought: Is this good or is it bad? As we saw in the example of nakedness, they quickly judge that the other person's physicality is dangerous—"bad." They judge God unfriendly—"bad"—and hide at the sound of God's approach. They judge the truth harmful—"bad"—so they tell something else. Their bodies have not changed; their judgment of their bodies has. God has not changed; their relationship with God has. The truth has not changed; their trust in it has.

Their experience substantiates Becker's insights into the effect of the awareness of death over us: "[T]hey have to be preoccupied with evil, even in the absence of any immediate danger; their lives become a meditation on evil and a planned venture for controlling it and forestalling it." (*EE*, 148)

---

* The differentiation of a previously hermaphroditic "Adam" takes place in 2:21–22.

God predicts that they will experience death as an enemy. They will resent the fact of being made out of dust. They will judge that death is evil and fear it.

They whirl in a vicious gyre. They have disobeyed God and refused to repent and receive God's judgment, which for them would result in understanding. Separate from God, they must replace God's functions; they must do for themselves what God once did for them. Judging the goodness or badness of things was formerly God's job, freeing them to appreciate, hence understand, other qualities of things. The more distant they get from God, the more it is up to them to make judgments. This is the ongoing "meditation on evil" that Becker says they need to keep themselves safe. Judgment in turn cancels their power to appreciate. The more they judge, the further away from God they drift, the less they understand, the more sterile their perceived world becomes.

Some relationship with God remains necessary. But because it is frightening, it becomes religious. Adam and Eve hope that they can negotiate with God for the wherewithal to live. They are caught in pride as theology understands it: they must rely on themselves, bargaining with God from that posture as best they can. Pride is not mere conceit, and vanity is only one of its minor expressions. The Bible understands pride as self-reliance in contrast to reliance on God. The opposite of pride is not modesty; it is righteous faith.

The Collapse of Job's Religion

Now let's turn back to Job.

A religious man whose way of knowing consists of making judgments, Job thinks that God is just the same as he is, only bigger. God must be a connoisseur of good behavior, one who prefers morality to milk. If Job can remain a little copy of that image, he will experience well-being. But that cookie cutter leaves out a lot of dough; what is to become of all that unused material, all that unlived life? The "Satan" holds it for him. Not that it is all evil, mind you; but Job can find no place for it in his conscious ego ideal. So he projects it outside himself and experiences it coming back at him as though from outside. That is the way of projections.

When we project our internal lives outside ourselves, the cosmos becomes a cramped little cinema in which our own movies are played back at us—over and over.

When such powerful forces contend within a person, things are bound to pop. Seemingly random, capricious events will fly at you from external sources, generated or attracted by your inner condition. Each of us knows people who are accident-prone, people who seem to attract misfortune. In Yiddish they are called "shlimmazels" and wise Jews counsel us not to invite them home. Occasionally we sense that the events that befall them obey some unconscious summons. So it is with Job.

For example, what might be the meaning of the Sabeans turning on their religious neighbor (1:14–15)? Von Orelli's understanding is both simple and profound:

> Why are the neighbors evil, envious enemies? Experience teaches that precisely virtuous people such as Job who achieve success through real, excellent accomplishments are not accordingly esteemed but easily become the victims of other people's envy and hate. They overestimate the model of their behavior, which has proved good for them, and lose the capacity to understand others. They provoke them with tactlessness and unintentional insults: thus neighbors become enemies.

But readers may enjoy deciding for themselves what internal circumstances the external forces correspond to. What about the fire from the sky (1:16)? Or the wind that kills his children in their house (1:18–19)? Von Orelli finds each of these symbolic of the unconscious forces that contend *within Job*. By these disasters, Job is stripped of family, wealth, health, and marriage. Still he clings to his religiousness for dear life like a ruined financier clutching his last sinking stock.

At the end of the second chapter, three friends come to offer Job comfort. Their seven-day silence is an ancient custom for mourning the dead. The message is clear: Job's life is effectively over. Only the autopsy remains. Von Orelli describes it thus:

> Now follows a long, exhausting, emotional discussion with the friends. This also is to be understood on the subjective level i.e., as a representation of Job's inner argument and his own antiquated ideas.
>
> It is touching and at the same time annoying to see with what Philistine perseverance they all praise the "justice of God" and radically condemn Job for purely theoretical, moral reasons on no realistic grounds. That is the classic idealistic religion. It is based on the exact knowledge of good and evil, a religion that also exists in us.

The process as it unfolds with gathering intensity in the next few chapters, can be seen today in any prayer group. Job's lament that his religion has not worked is not unfamiliar: "Why is light given to one who cannot see the way, whom God has fenced in?" (Job 3:23)

His friends reply by criticizing his doctrine and behavior, insisting that his ill fortune is the result of personal wrongdoing:

> "But now it has come to you, and you are impatient;
> it touches you, and you are dismayed.
> Is not your fear of God your confidence,
> and the integrity of your ways your hope?
>
> "Think now, who that was innocent ever perished?
> Or where were the upright cut off?
> As I have seen, those who plow iniquity
> and sow trouble reap the same.
> By the breath of God they perish,
> and by the blast of his anger they are consumed." (Job 4:5–9)

Job insists bitterly to his friends that he is innocent:

> "Teach me, and I will be silent;
> make me understand how I have gone wrong.
> How forceful are honest words!
>
> But your reproof, what does it reprove?
> Do you think that you can reprove words,
> as if the speech of the desperate were wind?
> You would even cast lots over the orphan,
> and bargain over your friend.
>
> "But now, be pleased to look at me;
> for I will not lie to your face.
> Turn, I pray, let no wrong be done.
> Turn now, my vindication is at stake.
> Is there any wrong on my tongue?
> Cannot my taste discern calamity?" (6:24–30)

Things simply are not as tidy, pat, and neat as he had previously believed. Though they are friends—witness the distance they traveled to reach him, the time they devote to him, and that they willingly contaminate themselves ritually by sitting with him—they prefer their own religious doctrine to their friend's comfort. Why?

They are in the same religious position Job was in as recently as last month. No wonder they clutch their doctrines for dear life. Religion works. Period. If it does not work for Job, it is because he is either mistaken or lying about practicing it correctly. Done correctly, religion always works; life and control over life alike depend upon the stability of religion, the human technology for influencing the powers of the universe. Over these chapters, the following argument is played and replayed:

"Religion didn't work."

"Of course it works; you're just not doing it right."

"No, I've been doing it right; it doesn't work."

"Then there's *sin* in your life, Job."

"There is no sin in my life, friends; it's religion that doesn't work."

So it goes for many pages, each side expressed as poignantly as anywhere in human literature.

WHERE DID JOB'S FRIENDS GET THEIR OPINIONS?

One aspect of this debate will trouble many. Job's friends are speaking familiar words. The familiarity derives from two sources in the Bible.* The first source of Job's friends' speeches is other parts of the Old Testament. Compare Eliphaz's statement:

> "For consider, what innocent man has ever perished?
> Where have you seen the upright destroyed?" (4:7)

with Psalm 37:25:

> "I have been young, and am now grown old
> and never have I seen a righteous man forsaken."

Much of Job's friends' material comes almost verbatim from the Psalms or Proverbs. There is no getting around it: part of the Bible is correcting—nay, *satirizing*—another part.+ When Job's friends get through offering him all the platitudes in Psalms and Proverbs, God himself will say to Eliphaz, "My wrath is kindled against you and against your two friends; for you have not spoken of me what is right, as my servant Job has." (42:7)

That is unsettling in view of the fact that the three friends had simply repeated the Bible verses they learned in Sunday school, whereas Job has been as skeptical as Tom Sawyer about it all.◆ To take Job seriously is to recognize the dialectic tensions that

---

* You will readily see this in a Bible with connected references in a center column.

+ That may make some of us uncomfortable, especially if we have never wrestled through this sort of interpretive issue. But efforts to avoid recognizing the critique of Psalms and Proverbs in Job do more damage to all three books than they prevent.

◆ In Fowler's terms, the friends are in Stage 3; Job's crisis has propelled him into Stage 4. He is not yet in Stage 5.

express the mind of God in the Scriptures. That ought to make us cautious about sweeping statements beginning with "The Bible says...."

The second source of the familiarity is our own backgrounds. Were not most of us reared on the doctrines Job's friends are defending? How many of our hopes rest on such a foundation? When we read of airline crashes, do we not wonder what Jonah was on the flight, what the victims had been up to? When misfortune strikes a "good" person, do we not speculate about hidden vices? We are reading stern stuff here. It is ourselves, our own deep beliefs, that Job critiques.

Job's Conversion

The Collapse of the Old

The argument rocks back and forth in the pages of Job, but after a few chapters, no new ground is broken. Much of the poem offers "variations on a theme." Yet there is one development within Job himself. He more and more throws over his old notion of "God" as a projected ego ideal. He grows bold enough to challenge God to fight:

> "There is no umpire between us,
> who might lay his hand on us both.
> If he would take his rod away from me,
> and not let dread of him terrify me,
> then I would speak without fear of him,
> for I know I am not what I am thought to be." (9:33–35)

Though nothing initially comes of this challenge, Von Orelli observes: "He [begins to] express his deep conviction in a divine reality beyond his experiences which he cannot understand."

While his old ego ideal is fading, a new hope, a mature longing grows in the vacuum created by "God's" death. In Chapter 19, Job reaches out in hope towards another whose presence and reality he is beginning to suspect.

> "For I know that my Redeemer lives,
> and that at the last he will stand upon the earth;
> and after my skin has been thus destroyed,
> then in my flesh I shall see God,
> whom I shall see on my side,
> and my eyes shall behold, and not another." (25–27)

Previously God had said, "Do not carve images of me for yourself. Do not seek my nature among angels, human beings, animals, especially not among sea-monsters and demons. You cannot focus me that way." (paraphrase of Deut. 5:8–9) God commanded us to leave his image blank in order that God might fill it: "I will be who I will be." Job is discovering the purpose of the second commandment. Bereft of his graven, moralizing image, he begins to detect another. Paul Tillich ended his best book with the line, "The courage to be is rooted in the God who appears when God has disappeared in the anxiety of doubt."* Job's "God" disappeared exactly so and another is about to appear.

A further development occurs: Job recognizes his religiousness and its underlying pride, the illusory control over life that he hoped it would afford him.

> "When I went out to the gate of the city,
> when I took my seat in the square,
> the young men saw me and withdrew,
> and the aged rose up and stood;
> the nobles refrained from talking,
> and laid their hands on their mouths;
> the voices of princes were hushed,
> and their tongues stuck to the roof of their mouths.
> When the ear heard, it commended me,
> and when the eye saw, it approved;
> because I delivered the poor who cried,
> and the orphan who had no helper.
> The blessing of the wretched came upon me,
> and I caused the widow's heart to sing for joy.
> I put on righteousness, and it clothed me;
> my justice was like a robe and a turban.
> I was eyes to the blind, and feet to the lame.
> I was a father to the needy,
> and I championed the cause of the stranger.
> I broke the fangs of the unrighteous,
> and made them drop their prey from their teeth.
> Then I thought, 'I shall die in my nest,
> and I shall multiply my days like the phoenix;
> my roots spread out to the waters,
> with the dew all night on my branches;
> my glory was fresh with me,
> and my bow ever new in my hand.'" (29:7–20)

Here we see Job's goodness as moral embalming fluid, a way of outwitting death, of perpetuating life indefinitely. Had Job

---

* Paul Tillich. *The Courage to Be* (New Haven: Yale University Press, 2000), 190.

"sinned"? He had certainly avoided stepping on cracks in the moral sidewalk. Yet this very posture is the essence of sin: it is reliance upon self to the exclusion of God. How ironic that the currency of this sin should so often be called virtue.

Religion, though, is not dead in Job:

> "I have made a covenant with my eyes;
> how then could I look upon a virgin?
> What would be my portion from God above,
> and my heritage from the Almighty on high?
> Does not calamity befall the unrighteous,
> and disaster the workers of iniquity?
> Does he not see my ways,
> and number all my steps?" (31:1–4)

You do not reason your way out of religion, anymore than Br'er Rabbit walks away from the Tar Baby. Job has seen the problem, but he remains stuck to it. Enlightenment is not enough. He needs rescue.

You might ignore the Elihu speeches, from Chapters 32 to 37. He wrecks the architecture of the poem, uninterrupted up to this point, and he disrupts the meaning. The composer of his speech—likely a later editor, anxious at so radical an attack on the conventional wisdom represented by the three friends—peeked ahead in order to make him appear a prophet. But he is only a recrudescence of the Psalms/Proverbs perspective gasping for continued life in the face of reality's evidence.

MYSTICISM

In Chapter 38, God—the real one—appears and answers Job. Before reading his speech, be clear how it should sound. Resist hearing that voice as an anxious baritone hollering into an oil barrel; that is the God of children's Bible story recordings. Human parents may sound that way when pushed to the wall, but the heavenly Father never does. None of God's speeches in the Old Testament will make their intended sense until you hear the severest of them delivered in a voice of serene compassion and affection. In the sermon quoted in chapter 3,* George MacDonald tells us why Moses was not allowed to see the face of God (Ex. 33:20ff.) when he asked to:

> But . . . how could Moses have understood, if he had seen the
> face instead of the back of that form that passed the cleft of

---

* See page 58.

the rock amidst the thunderous vapours of Sinai? Had that form turned and that face looked upon him, the face of him who was more than any man; the face through which the divine emotion would, in the ages to come, manifest itself to the eyes of men, bowed, it might well be, at such a moment, in anticipation of the crown with which the children of the people for whom Moses pleaded with his life, would one day crown him; the face of him who was bearing and was yet to bear their griefs and carry their sorrows, who is now bearing our griefs and carrying our sorrows; the face of the Son of God, who, instead of accepting the sacrifice of one of his creatures to satisfy his justice or support his dignity, gave himself utterly unto them, and therein to the Father by doing his lovely will; who suffered unto the death, not that men might not suffer, but that their suffering might be like his, and lead them up to his perfection; if that face, I say, had turned and looked upon Moses, would Moses have lived?

Though it emerges from storm and wind, hear this voice as gentle and somewhat playful.

God's speech has puzzled interpreters for centuries. Why does God ignore Job's questions? Not once does he speak of Job's morality, either to confirm or criticize it. God sweeps aside Job's religious frame of reference without acknowledging it. Instead he draws Job up to considerations higher, wider, and deeper than Job's cramped judgments had ever allowed him to explore. If we listen for more than reproach, we will hear God's glee at the creation which he teases Job into sharing; there is an invitation in the apparent mockery:

> "Have you commanded the morning since your days began,
> and caused the dawn to know its place,
> have you entered into the springs of the sea,
> or walked in the recesses of the deep?" (38:12,16)

The actual matter of judgment is vaster and deeper than Job's morality-focused lenses allow him to perceive:

> "Have the gates of death been revealed to you,
> or have you seen the gates of deep darkness?
> Have you comprehended the expanse of the earth?
> Declare, if you know all this.
>
> "Where is the way to the dwelling of light,
> and where is the place of darkness,
> that you may take it to its territory
> and that you may discern the paths to its home?" (38:17–20)

In such passages we can imagine Job learning to spit out the fruit of the Tree of the Knowledge of Good and Evil. He is undergoing experiences that can be embraced, appreciated, and submitted to—but which defy evaluation.

God says, in effect, "Is Mount Sinai of such interest to you, Job? All right. But we will not talk of tablets of stone. Let me show you how I *made* the mountain, the up-thrust of the plates that formed it. Let me show you the lizards that bake on its boulders, the jack rabbits that frolic and spawn on it."

What is God doing? God is going outside the cookie-cutter Job had crammed over himself, compelling Job to reclaim the unused portions of God's creation. God is gathering up the leftover dough, calling it back to life, revivifying all the parts that Job could not fit into his self-perception. While Job is apart from God, all that unformed material is frightening because it is not controllable. That is why Job had repressed it. But in God's presence it becomes safe to explore. Job need not be afraid of his unconscious material; he need not judge it good or bad.

Perhaps Job, like so many religious people, had repressed his sexuality. That would explain the delight God takes in confronting him with the reproductive cycles of the mountain goats and deer:

> "Do you know when the mountain goats give birth?
> Do you observe the calving of the deer?
> Can you number the months that they fulfill,
> and do you know the time when they give birth,
> when they crouch to give birth to their offspring,
> and are delivered of their young?" (Job 39:1–3)

Had Job ever thought of that being of much interest to God, let alone delight, something God would display to God's child with joy?

In Chapter 40 God euphemistically but unmistakably points to the male genitalia of Behemoth, the legendary land monster, the prototype of all kine:

> "Look at Behemoth, which I made just as I made you;
> it eats grass like an ox.
> Its strength is in its loins,
> and its power in the muscles of its belly.
> It makes its tail stiff like a cedar;
> the sinews of its thighs are knit together." (Job 40:15–17)

In Chapter 41, God sports with Leviathan, the great monster of the deep that haunted the nightmares of the ancient Near East:

"Its back is made of shields in rows,
shut up closely as with a seal.
One is so near to another
that no air can come between them.
They are joined one to another;
they clasp each other and cannot be separated.
Its sneezes flash forth light,
and its eyes are like the eyelids of the dawn.
From its mouth go flaming torches;
sparks of fire leap out." (15–19)

"But in my presence you are safe to look at them. You do not know their purpose. But do not judge them, for they are mine." As Von Orelli says:

The description of these two primeval creatures is the most intense manifestation of the vital aspect of God. Here is the opposite pole to the moral-legal aspect, which up to now for Job is the only valid one. Here a completely different aspect appears which must cause an enormous shock; the manifestation of God in the creation.

The footnotes in your Bible should disentangle the first 6 verses of Chapter 42. Verses 3a and 4 have broken loose from an earlier speech of God's and have lodged here by repeated copyists' errors. It should read like this:

"I know that you can do all things,
and that no purpose of yours can be thwarted.
Therefore I have uttered what I did not understand,
things too wonderful for me, which I did not know.
I had heard of you by the hearing of the ear,
but now my eye sees you;
therefore I despise myself,
and repent in dust and ashes."

The point of Job's speech is that he repents. We may ask, "Repents? Repents of what?" He has done nothing immoral, nor has God accused him of such. He repents his *religious* apprehension of God. "I formerly thought of you in terms of things I had heard or imagined, but you are nothing like that. I need to change my whole life. You are not what I thought you were; I am also not what I thought I was." As Rilke might have said, "*Ich muß mein Leben ändern.*" Job has encountered what theologians and psychologists call "ontological guilt"—the sensibility that made my friend, who experienced the Presence of God, fall to the ground and try to bury his head, crying, "I'm sorry. I'm so sorry!" Job discovers he is not the same sort of thing that God is; he experiences the difference as guilt. Guilt nearly always accompanies any breakthrough into a realization of our creatureliness, our finitude, of the futility of our pretenses to specialness. He has slammed into divinity and his self-generated "goodness" is not much help. Von Orelli describes this breakthrough:

> At this moment Job is able to declare himself guilty. Now he discovers wherein his guilt lies....It is true, Job has done nothing evil. The friends were mistaken. All the reproaches they made were pure imagination and hypothetical postulates. And yet Job was guilty because "he knew what was good," he knew "how things should go" and therefore he was not open to the sense of contrast wherein lies the only possibility of meeting God.

This discovery brings light into his life again and he develops a deeper insight. He has grown out of the youthful, idealistic attitude to a mature dialogue [with God]. He has become a wise man who has beheld God.

God rebukes the three friends for their continued religiousness.

> After the LORD had spoken these words to Job, the LORD said to Eliphaz the Temanite: "My wrath is kindled against you and against your two friends; for you have not spoken of me what is right, as my servant Job has. Now therefore take seven bulls and seven rams, and go to my servant Job, and offer up for yourselves a burnt offering; and my servant Job shall pray for you, for I will accept his prayer not to deal with you according to your folly; for you have not spoken of me what is right, as my servant Job has done." So Eliphaz the Temanite and Bildad the Shuhite and Zophar the Naamathite went and did what the LORD had told them; and the LORD accepted Job's prayer. And the LORD restored the fortunes of Job when he had prayed for his friends; and the LORD gave Job twice as much as he had before. (Job 42:7–10)

Less honest or courageous than Job, they are not converted to righteousness with God. They can only do what they know how to do, which is to offer sacrifice. They do this in Job's presence, but Job himself does not take part. He no longer requires such procedures, he who once offered them superstitiously. Job prays for his friends, speaking directly to God without an intermediary. And as Job exercises righteous intimacy with God for the first time, God spares and restores his friends. Do we detect a deeply respectful wink and a grin passing between Job and the Ancient of Days?

Where is "the Satan"? Vanished along with "God." They were both projections of conscious and unconscious energies that God has made safe and helped Job reclaim as his own. As projections they have vanished like the image of a slide on a screen when you turn off the projector. Von Orelli describes it this way:

> If he [Job] keeps up this attitude, Satan has not only lost the second round but is not even mentioned anymore. It is very astonishing that in the end Satan is not summoned and given a rebuke. For Satan is either the projection of the repressed shadow—and Job has accepted his shadow—or the projection of man's desire to live by his own law [rather than God's]. Job has renounced autonomism and has surrendered to God. He trusts in the meeting with God and therefore Satan is ignored.

Job is sitting with God *and* his ice-cream cone. He will put down his ice cream when God tells him to, not when the Book of Proverbs or its swarming legion of interpreters tell him to. The restoration of his fortunes seems anticlimactic after Job has entered righteousness.

Interestingly, Job's new daughters, unlike his first children, are described and named. Clearly they are individuals, not his chattels. This detail suggests that after his conversion Job is able to appreciate the personal uniqueness of others at a new level.

Von Orelli ends his discussion of Job thus:

> From now on Job in his actions and decisions will no longer rely on his limited [goodness] but on the perfection and boundlessness of God. This experience of Job is the faith which he only finds through the devaluation of all values: the experience that God listens and answers, that God wants him to become his image and that in the dialogue with God he will find his own personality. This transition limited by objects and social structures to a new existence in the direct meeting with God is the anticipation of what Paul later says:
>
>> If anyone else has reason to be confident in the flesh, I have more: circumcised on the eighth day, a member of the people of Israel, of the tribe of Benjamin, a Hebrew born of Hebrews; as to the law, a Pharisee; as to zeal, a persecutor of the church; as to right-eousness under the law, blameless. Yet whatever gains I had, these I have come to regard as loss because of Christ. More than that, I regard every-thing as loss because of the surpassing value of know-ing Christ Jesus my Lord. For his sake I have suffered the loss of all things, and I regard them as rubbish, in order that I may gain Christ. (Phil. 3:4–8)

To understand the Book of Job as von Orelli helps us do is to have our own lives change. It is to have a model of what we ourselves must go through to get from religiousness to righteousness. Not that we must lose our fortunes or our families—though some of us may—but we *must* discover religion's futility and be energetically rescued from it. The little book you hold will be put aside, misplaced, lent out, or forgotten. But your Bible will not be, and if you lose it, you will get another. There Job will be, kinsman and model, pointing out the path God will take to reach us. There Genesis is, showing us the condition in which God finds us.

RELATED SECTIONS OF THE OLD TESTAMENT

What fun it would be to go on and on, to see all through both Testaments the contest between religiousness and righteousness. In Exodus we would conclude that God wrote on tablets of stone so people would not wave the Law around. We might conclude that when we are beset by adulterous impulses, God does not want us fleeing to the Seventh Commandment; God wants us to flee to God.

We would notice a fascinating pattern in Exodus 25:10–22:

> They shall make an ark of acacia wood; it shall be two and a half cubits long, a cubit and a half wide, and a cubit and a half high. You shall overlay it with pure gold, inside and outside you shall overlay it, and you shall make a molding of gold upon it all around. You shall put into the ark the covenant [the two stone tablets containing the Ten Commandments] that I shall give you. Then you shall make a mercy seat of pure gold. You shall put the mercy seat on the top of the ark: and in the ark you shall put the covenant that I shall give you. There I will meet with you ... above the mercy seat.

Can you see the picture? (I did not see it until a Fundamentalist Primitive Baptist preacher showed it to me—and I have been grateful ever since.) Moses reads the Law to the people, calling their attention to their need for the Spirit's work. Then he puts the Law in a box and has eight or nine fellows place a slab of gold on it—imagine the weight!—so the Law cannot jump out onto the people, nor can they play with the tablets at will. Then God sits above the slab, called the Mercy Seat, between the people and the Law, and deals with them *personally*. Is that not Gospel? No detail is accidental.

In that passage the Spirit is saying to us, "When you feel an impulse to sin, do not flee for help to the Law; flee to God. Do not cover yourself in the 'Blood'; enter the Presence of Jesus personally."

We were not given the Law as a tool to make ourselves good, to make ourselves attractive to God. The Law is a description of what we look like when the Spirit works in us without obstruction. The Law is given to show us where and when we need God's judgment and mercy. We can no more make ourselves good by keeping the Law than we can cure our illnesses by eating a stethoscope. The Law does not heal; it is an instrument of diagnosis. Jesus heals, drawing us by the Spirit to the Father whose judgment alone can heal and release us.

◆ ◆ ◆ ◆ ◆

The ultimate failure of the Charismatic Movement, like that of so many other spiritualities, lies in our refusal to put our weight on such truth. We prefer Law to Life. We prefer method to fellowship with God. In this we copy both Catholics and Evangelicals who failed before us and have for generations retailed God's grace to sinners at the cost of a lifetime of legal observances. The failure rests in our persistent return to religiousness, preferring our doctrines to God's reality, preferring debate to prayer, making Christian life something else to get good at, proving how saved we are by demonstrating how sanctified we are—and jostling each other out of line to do so. The failure rests in going off by ourselves to fashion lives that we judge as good, intending to trade them to God like so many books of stamps.

God has not asked that of us. God offers us hearts of flesh, circumcised hearts. That is hardly an order to do heart surgery on ourselves; it is an offer, not a command.

Job shows us where all that must lead and what, by God's mercy, it leads us to. God must judge us to free us. As we receive God's judgment, knowing ourselves as God knows us, we are ready to be in God's personal company, to dare to claim our place on God's lap.

On the assumption that God's judgment still may not feel entirely friendly, let us have one more look at it in the next chapter, this time in the New Testament.

CHAPTER NINE

THE COMMUNITY OF THE SON OF MAN

In the previous chapter we watched God's judgment remaking Job, an individual human being. We undertook this examination to watch some of the themes of this discussion in operation: religion vs. righteousness, the dread of God, stages in faith development, the confrontation of cognitive dissonance and the false-self. We saw that Job had to have his crisis essentially all by himself, abandoned by his wife and upbraided by his friends. But he made it. He became a molten individual.

The Book of Job gives us a poetic depiction of an individual whose religion collapses, who abandons his struggle against cognitive dissonance at the risk of atheism, and accepts righteousness with God in an expression that pushes him into Fowler's Stage 5 towards if indeed not into Stage 6. His transformation takes place despite his conventional Stage 3 faith community. He may or may not take leave of that community, but clearly, by the end of his journey, he contributes more to it now than he draws from it.

Job's solitary breakthrough leaves him spiritually and emotionally isolated. Ideally there should be a community there for him, one that understands and receives his reports of what he has suffered and learned. How will he find it? The poem does not take him—or us—that far.

In the many centuries since the last New Testament documents were finished, humanity in the West has evolved an individualized self-consciousness. We tend to be somewhat more aware of self than of tribe—much more than were our ancestors.* Perhaps for that reason, we like Job better than previous generations did, if their sparse and shallow references reflect their grasp of Job accurately. (I am thinking here of previous generations that viewed Job as a model of "patience." Can they have ever *read* it?) We likely understand him better. We know that individualized self-consciousness is a mixed blessing, and as our addiction to television, its canned laughter, and false community reveal, we flee it regularly. Being an individual is as strenuous as it is bracing. We read Job with a poignant recognition characteristic of modernity, recognizing a brother.

THE PROBLEM OF COMMUNITY

Like Job, we cannot indefinitely cultivate spiritual isolation however individually we get spiritually awakened. As much as Henley's *Invictus*—"I am the master of my fate: / I am the captain of my soul"—stirs something adolescent in me, it sobers me to recall that the poet died an alcoholic suicide, the direction in which such a pure posture ultimately must lead. Spiritual individuals require spiritual companions. We need a faith community.

The principle and purpose of any community is the enhancement of life. What a single individual cannot accomplish working around the clock in her own interest a community can accomplish on her behalf with time to spare. This is not a matter of mere convenience; the issue is survival. Reflect for a moment on the likely quality—or duration—of your own life without the complex coordination of medical, educational, commercial/industrial, transportation, communication, government, entertainment, hospitality, and public safety communities on your behalf.

We choose our communities with some care. Accurate selection of a community is a matter of such urgency, real or apparent, that it cancels objectivity. Listen, for example, to college freshmen discussing fraternities or sororities just before Rush Week;⁺ compare

---

* It is interesting that virtually all words for "I" in western languages derive from "ego." One would expect a pronoun so central to our awareness to be less fluid.

⁺ *Extra ecclesiam nulla salust* is not limited to the Roman Church.

what you hear with the revised version a couple of weeks afterwards.

A critical component of these choices seems to be our requirement that the communities we inhabit display obvious—to ourselves, at least—advantages over others. At issue is the ability of a given group to preserve and enhance life—either literally—e.g., the Marine Corps, where presumably you get the best combat training available—or symbolically—Harvard, whose alumni typically make more money than graduates of lesser institutions.

Feelings run high on such issues. Within living memory, two sovereign nations in the Western hemisphere have waged war against each other over a matter concerning their respective soccer teams, and relations between England, Belgium, and Italy—hardly "banana republics"—more recently were strained severely by an incident of lethal soccer chauvinism.

The depth and urgency with which we justify our community choices offer us a measure of the idolatry involved in this issue. Communities collect literal taxes and bestow symbolic life in return; more flows into them than returns to us. "Leaders"—whether presidents or movie stars—wear wealth on behalf of all of us, allowing even the poor among us to enjoy that wealth vicariously. Communities maintain loyalty to themselves by gathering internally generated tensions, antagonisms, and hostilities and diverting them outward towards rival communities. In fact, some social psychologists think that outward hostility diversion is the primary function of leadership.

Communities get away with all this by persuading us that such a system is necessary if we are to harvest life. That is how idolatry operates. It is henotheism exploiting polytheism, rivaling radical monotheism, which may explain why we feel such rage when an attractive person leaves the congregation we love and joins another. The departure of a fool makes us stronger; that is all right with us; it adorns us. Indeed a fool's departure suggests that our superiority is refined beyond the appreciative capabilities of grosser sensibilities. We affect sadness but secretly rejoice. But how about the departure of a person whose attractiveness seems to embody a vitality we have not yet fully synthesized for our own uses? That is another matter entirely.

Suppose a young surgeon, new to town, visits our church with his charming wife and lovely children. Let them visit us a couple of weeks, during which time they are also choosing country clubs and getting located professionally. After a few weeks let them cease attending; we learn later that they have become members of another congregation. Now let's try to avoid the realization that something about our church itself or our reputation locally or the *class niveau* we project seems less capable of sustaining life than does another group. Such events dispute our group's claim to have "found it." Perhaps our congregation will not be able to keep us attractive to God and safe from ill fortune. *They* certainly seem to think not; they never came back. Such people challenge our social idolatry even while pursuing their own.

Examine the dilemma. We must be social for survival. *Homo sapiens* is among the most individually vulnerable of mammals, making us the most gregarious of the higher mammals. Isolation cancels viability. Yet virtually every community we inhabit functions as a rival deity both to God and to all other communities. Simply to have resolved the matter of religiousness versus righteousness at the individual level is to have achieved a short-lived victory. Radical monotheists still inhabit henotheistic collectives. Our communities reopen the issue for us, willy-nilly, requiring our assent to their life-giving powers as an unexpressed condition for membership.

WHERE CAN JOB GO TO CHURCH?

So return to Job for a moment. Job will have to live carefully among his fellows. He will not lightly join another sacrifice-based cult. He took the cure. And yet, what else is there for him? His new inner peace and joy, his new self-possession, must shortly collide with society. Will he be admired and copied? He will eventually find being imitated wearisome in the absence of peers. Job survived his personal testing by God's grace and judgment. At that point, he was able to resist the voices of his community—his wife and three friends—because their offerings threatened his integrity. It will only be by the same grace and judgment that his righteousness will survive the seductiveness of his community when its combined voices seem to testify to his integrity.

Will he be resented? That is equally wearisome, eventually pressing him either to withdraw from the community or submit to its standards.

Ironically the foregoing has little application to spiritually inert congregations. A Christmas-and-Easter Presbyterian need not fear corporate idolatry—at least not in church. Those of us in spiritually lively congregations are in the most jeopardy. How quickly our "boasting in the Lord" becomes boasting in our buildings, in our leaders and their teaching, boasting in our programs, our new family life center/gymnasium, boasting in the manifestations of spiritual power evident among us. The fact that ours is a "Christian" community in no way protects us against idolatry. Henotheism is alive and well in the American Church.* The only protection against community idolatry is the judgment of God.

As we have seen with Job, God's judgment is an operation of divine mercy. It does not destroy but restores. It strips from a person what is self-made and draws one closer into God's image. And if God's judgment operates redemptively with individuals, should we not hope for the same operation in communities, particularly those that, however corruptly, have gathered in God's name?

Defining our "goodness" as something opposed to another's "badness" plays out at every level of society. In the last couple of decades the United States lost its monolithic geopolitical enemy, the dreaded Soviet Union, and is suffering a dangerous bereavement. Since there is presently no single external enemy worthy of our steel to project our internal hostilities upon, those hostilities have no place to go. The "enemy" is now some fellow citizen.⁺ As of this writing, "mainline" denominations mirror the internal stresses of American society. Except for groups that have formed around a single political pole, denominations and congregations that attempt Christian charity beyond their own "life-style enclaves" are finding that posture difficult to sustain. Polarities yawn wider as mutual forbearance wanes. Schisms within such groups seem likely.

In the face of such conditions, parties of opinion within denominations offer lists of congregations they can accredit as

---

* An Episcopal bishop recently remarked, "The Gospel was proclaimed in Judea and became a faith community; it sailed to Athens and became a philosophy; it crossed the Alps to Rome and became an institution; it crossed Europe to England and became a culture; it crossed the Atlantic and became a commercial enterprise."

⁺ Of this, the art critic Robert Hughes wrote, "The 'Enemy At The Gate' has become 'The Fairy At The Bottom Of The Garden.'" He was referring to the autoimmune convulsions of the American people since the fall of the Iron Curtain.

sharing their own positions reliably. Charismatic groups issue cat-
alogues of Charismatic congregations. Christian Gay and Lesbian
advocates issue lists of welcoming congregations. Conservative
partisans compile rolls of "biblical" congregations.

Where could we look for a list of congregations that readily
accept, support, and deploy Job? Such groups would need to live
comfortably with ambiguity and paradox. They would need non-
repressive and non-capitulative norms for conflict management.
They would need a purchase on the Bible, the Creeds, essential
doctrines, and the imperative for justice, which is respectful,
exploratory, grown-up, and non-idolatrous. Such groups would
foster group norms within which members could seek and discuss
mystical encounters with God—without experiencing embarrassment or incurring scorn. They would need to be committed to justice and charity—while remaining merry. Their worship would
need to reach eternity and the depths of contemporary souls
simultaneously. They would need to be conversationally candid, as
interested in actual personal reality as in ideal personal profiles.

No list of such congregations exists. And those characteristics
describe no existing denomination *in toto*, past or present. If we
were eventually to inhabit such a group, it could not be by discovery. It must be the result of building.

However frustrating and incomplete such community building must always be, it is worth the constant effort it requires. The
community-building project will proceed more satisfactorily if we
have some notion of what is important and what is less so, what
helps and what deters.*

The Book of Job shows that issues we consider important may
be readily discerned in a spiritual/philosophical text more than
ten times older than our civilization. A more recent set of biblical
texts will allow us to focus on a few principles that must undergird
any Christian congregation that seeks to be hospitable to Job—or,
we may hope, ourselves.

---

* "Ideals" may not serve us, since ideals depend upon mental images our efforts
will never entirely resemble. We need principles—because we can apply principles in pitch-black darkness, where no images or ideals are visible.

THE COMMUNITY OF THE SON OF MAN

The New Testament supplies us with examples of Jesus of Nazareth building a principled community; these examples help us cooperate with his work in our congregations. Let's start with a portion of the Gospel of Mark, beginning with the Marcan account of the healing of the paralytic:

> When [Jesus] returned to Capernaum after some days, it was reported that he was at home. So many gathered around that there was no longer room for them, not even in front of the door; and he was speaking the word to them. Then some people came, bringing to him a paralyzed man, carried by four of them. And when they could not bring him to Jesus because of the crowd, they removed the roof above him; and after having dug through it, they let down the mat on which the paralytic lay. When Jesus saw their faith, he said to the paralytic, "Son, your sins are forgiven." Now some of the scribes were sitting there, questioning in their hearts, "Why does this fellow speak in this way? It is blasphemy! Who can forgive sins but God alone?" At once Jesus perceived in his spirit that they were discussing these questions among themselves; and he said to them, "Why do you raise such questions in your hearts? Which is easier, to say to the paralytic, 'Your sins are forgiven,' or to say, 'Stand up and take your mat and walk'? But so that you may know that the Son of Man has authority on earth to forgive sins"—he said to the paralytic—"I say to you, stand up, take your mat and go to your home." And he stood up, and immediately took the mat and went out before all of them; so that they were all amazed and glorified God, saying, "We have never seen anything like this!" (Mk. 2:1–12)

I think that passage was used in "Mark's" community in order to front-load apprentice Christians with an understanding of how the Savior regarded human community.

The scene opens in a house in Capernaum,* crowded with people who are there for the purpose of hearing and discussing "the

---

* The house seems to belong to Jesus. That opens fascinating possibilities. Joseph was, after all, a combination architect and building contractor; there is no reason to assume that he was poor. Stables were the normal accommodations of the poor; only the rich would have asked about a room in an inn. So the detail in Luke about full inns and open stables, while unlikely to be journalistically accurate, may preserve details about Jesus' economic status. Jesus subsequently demonstrates the table manners of an aristocrat on several occasions. His parables display a knowledge of the conditions of wealth and culture. Thus his poverty ["The Son of Man has no place to lay his head."] is not an accident of birth but an adult choice.

word." What word? So far Jesus has been saying, and is presumably saying here: "The time is fulfilled, and the kingdom of God has come near; repent, and believe in the good news." (Mk. 1:15)

That is, "The climax of human history is occurring right now. God is fully present in all your circumstances. So change all your assumptions about how things are. Begin to rely on God and assume that God is *for* you."

A crowd of people wants to hear more about it, especially in view of the reports of exorcisms, healings, and the cleansing of leprosy that precede Jesus wherever he goes. Who would not cram himself into a cramped room to hear a sermon with such illustrations?

Now comes a group of men, four of whom carry a paralyzed friend on a stretcher.*

These men hold specific beliefs about the paralytic. Along with the rest of the community, they believe that his paralysis results from moral guilt. They believe that as firmly as we believe the law of gravity. That reality is morally symmetrical was scientif-ic truth in those days. Life is *quid pro quo.* Do good and good befalls you. Do bad... We have already met this belief among Job's friends, who were so sure that his misfortune stemmed from moral defect.[+]

We should not smirk prematurely. When something bad happens to someone we know, do we not say, "And she is such a *fine* person..." the suppressed parenthesis being "...but I wonder what she could have *done* to get in such a fix?" Some Christian groups today hold people responsible for their own illnesses on the grounds that sufficient faith should either heal them or have prevented the misfortune in the first place. The conclusion of such belief is inevitable: misfortune is the result of personal defec-tiveness. These four men and their community do not differ so very much from us.

In those days, guilt was a permanent social condition. Once you had done something bad, there was no living it down. Forgiveness

---

* Here the story is so familiar to us that we shall likely miss its meanings unless we slow down. For the first meaning, use your visual imagination. The four lower an inert figure down into a hole, where he meets Jesus and receives the power of movement. What is the picture? You are watching a funeral—with a happy ending. At the bottom of the grave, the corpse meets Life. Such gospels-in-miniature are frequent in the Bible.

+ The belief is common in Fowler's first four stages.

and restoration were not realistic hopes or expectations. It still seems so. Chappaquidick, Watergate, and Whitewater are national projections of local conditions.*

Enter any new community with a lengthy history and someone will describe the various members to you in terms of their past mistakes. If the lifeboat grows too crowded, if the hostility in this community reaches critical mass, we will need that information to decide who gets tossed overboard. Guilt makes a handy weapon.⁺

So the friends believe the paralytic is guilty of something. Otherwise he would be walking around like the rest of them. Obviously he cannot be forgiven, because forgiveness does not figure in their catalogue of human experience. They have never seen it, have never felt it, have never extended it. Perhaps like Job, they have contrived to live so as never to need it.

Still a previous contact with Jesus must have impregnated them with another attitude, hope: inchoate as a fetus, but growing. The paralytic's guilt and consequent paralysis may not be the most important thing about him—in the presence of Jesus, that is. Rather than confirming their previous religious beliefs, Jesus has disrupted their clarity with a radiant ambiguity. Were we to ask them what they expect to happen as they drop the man into Jesus' lap, they will not be able to answer; they have no image for such a thing. Probably the most they could say is that something about Jesus makes this absurd action seem like a good idea.

Picture Jesus for a moment. As he is engaging the crowd, some dust falls on his head. Nothing unusual about that; a rat could have done it, or a pigeon, maybe one of those white lizards one sees indoors in the East. Then down comes a stick or two, some straw, and some plaster. Picture him looking up with interest. He sees thirty-two grubby fingers and an occasional thumb clawing

---

* In an introductory essay on Gandhi, Thomas Merton observed that all tyranny is based on a heresy: the heresy of the immutability of evil. That is, once wrong or sin has been committed, it cannot be changed, repaired, or erased. That delivers us into the hands of blackmailers, doing worse and worse things to protect our standing, unaware that repenting and asking forgiveness could break the purchase of evil. Merton somewhere says that is the only way to understand Washington, D.C.

⁺ Evolutionary psychologists suggest that our fascination with gossip is hardwired into our DNA. In the "ancestral environment" possession of such information could help you in astute mate-selection.

their way into his house, into his presence. He stops his talk and gazes up in amused fascination. Four self-conscious faces—house breakers, after all—peer down at him, expecting rebuke. Reading the mixture of embarrassment, *chutzpah,* doubt, and imageless hope playing across their expressions, Jesus laughs and signals them to lower away.

In what follows, Jesus responds as much to the friends as to the paralytic. In their daring hope he sees soil for the seed. I like to imagine that he looks up and sees what the church can be, sees a church in embryo. A lovely image of the church, is it not? —the trustful bringing the helpless to Jesus in raw reliant expectation. The man's paralysis and alleged moral failings have not excluded him from their friendship. That's something Jesus can build on.

He then supplies an astonishing example of how God's judgment works. In one action he is going to accomplish four results. He will heal a sufferer, reward four risk-takers, offer an analysis of human community for all time, showing it for what it is, while calling a new manner of human association into existence. He does all that by simply saying something like, "Hi, Bro'—your sins are forgiven."

Does Jesus think the man is guilty? We don't know. In John 9:1–3 he clearly rejected the automatic connection of sin with physical affliction:

> As he walked along, he saw a man blind from birth. His disciples asked him, "Rabbi, who sinned, this man or his parents, that he was born blind?" Jesus answered, "Neither this man nor his parents sinned; he was born blind so that God's works might be revealed in him."

So in an unrelated account Jesus obviously did not find the sin theory airtight. In pronouncing forgiveness he is not necessarily imputing guilt. He is simply meeting the man and the spectators where they are. The spectators and friends assume the man is guilty of something. The man imagines himself guilty, even if he can't think of anything that he did wrong.

Why should the man think himself guilty? For two reasons, one conscious, one unconscious. The conscious reason is that every one of us has something on our consciences.*

---

* In a famous practical joke a financier sent anonymous telegrams to six colleagues, saying, "FLEE AT ONCE STOP ALL IS DISCOVERED STOP"—Four slipped out of the country that night.

The unconscious reason the paralytic assumes his own guilt is that the assumption he'd done something to cause his affliction gives him an illusion of control over his circumstances. "I don't have to be this way. It was once in my power to be otherwise. We inhabit the same moral universe. I may not embody the standards of this community—but at least I embrace them; please don't shun me." That is the unconscious message of his guilt—and of ours.

One thinks of the guilt parents heap upon themselves for their children's actions, as though guilt could lead them back through time to some unrecognized turning point, which, if lived differently, would have formed different characters or produced better grades.

Guilt serves religiousness. It keeps us stuck, postponing our realization of helplessness and prolonging our sense of being in control. In our commercial dealings with God and each other, we use our guilt the way exiled politicians are said to traffic on their lost titles: e.g., "I may look like a mendicant to you right now, but I was the Minister Plenipotentiary of Agriculture, Termite Control, and Space Exploration in the former Republic of Limostho!"

Jesus knows the crowd also thinks the paralytic guilty. Their reasons too are partly unconscious. The unconscious root of their belief is the relief of having limited responsibility for the man, no need for pity, no requirement for charity beyond that minimum needed for public order.* Their blame also relieves them of the suspicion that the same condition might visit any of them. "Bad things happen to bad people," they assume. "If we stay good, we stay well." Jesus must puncture those attitudes if a new community is to be born, one in which one's defects and sins are not one's primary attributes.

So Jesus addresses the paralytic in an exquisitely affectionate way—"*teknon*" comparable to something like "little Buddy"—"You are forgiven. You are restored to your dignity and your right to it. You are as good as any citizen here." After two thousand years of being taught this story, we assume that Jesus' forgiveness means that sin is something bad that God puts right—a truth indeed, but hardly the point of this action. Here what Jesus attacks is not sin *per se* but the stratifying function of guilt in human community, its

---

* A cursory study of the history of social welfare in the United States, especially recently, suggests parallels.

application allowing us to divide people into groups of good and bad, up and down, in and out.

It is fascinating to notice that he says this "seeing *their* faith," referring to the paralytic's friends. A community that affirms this man is already in place to receive him; there already exists a group, which "keeps no reckoning of wrongs," that "does not rejoice in iniquity." If forgiveness is to take hold and flourish, it requires social expression. Jesus recognizes and gives definition here to a society that makes such a thing possible. The Marcan catechetical teachings insist that new members agree to such standards.

The Scandal of Forgiveness

Some in the crowd are furious. Why? They are scared of something—anger rests on fear. Their complaint suggests what it is they fear: "Who can forgive sins but God alone?" Then as now, the phrase "God alone" is synonymous with "nobody." "What time will this plane take off?" someone asks us. "God knows," we reply, which means, "Nobody can say." They do not think real sin, the kind that makes you sick, poor, or crippled, is forgivable.* Jesus is playing at something they regard as impossible and, of course, they resent it.

Now does it make sense for a group to resent forgiveness? Yes it does. Recall the image of a lifeboat. Stripped of its pretenses and coverings, human life is a competitive scramble with every fellow creature. The chief elements of the competition are prestige and reputation. Forgiveness erases the scoreboard, making scorekeeping impossible. Thus forgiveness is more than an ironic nuisance. In a world-view that sees us in a struggle with one another, real or symbolic, for our very lives, forgiveness of others is a death threat to ourselves because it unloads our guns and shatters our defenses.

By forgiving this man Jesus has disarmed the crowd's prestige system. Life must now be negotiated on some basis other than competition. His action imposes a novel condition: you can no longer tell how safe you are by comparing yourself to other people. That you are materially better off is no longer an ultimate advantage; that you are worse off is no longer an ultimate disqualification. We

---

* The penitential rites of the day dealt mainly with ritual impurities; they offered little provision for sins against one another or society. To get rid of those you were at the mercy of your erstwhile victim, and that mercy was as conditional as our own.

can be tempted, when mastering this point, to play with facile ironies: e.g., "There goes the neighborhood!" Such joking masks fear. When a person first encounters a community in which real forgiveness reigns, if indeed one ever does, one's first reaction is disorientation, perhaps even panic.

Now Jesus asks, "Which is easier, to say, 'Your sins are forgiven,' or to say, 'Get off your stretcher, stand up, and walk'?" This is an indictment as well as a question. He means, "Among you people, forgiveness is as difficult and as rare as a cripple playing hop-scotch." He knows they regard both as impossible—possibly undesirable. So he connects them, so that in what follows one will imply the other.

WHO IS THE SON OF MAN?

Jesus' next remark requires some background to be understood. But it is worth effort, because our grasp of God's judgment on human community depends on it.

Jesus says, "The *Son of Man* has both power and authority on earth to forgive sins,"—and heals the paralytic to prove it. What is the importance of the title "Son of Man" in this context? What does Jesus mean by it?

Scholars studying the Second Gospel coined the phrase "the Messianic Secret." This refers to Jesus' constant refusal to let people or demons speak of him as the "Messiah" or "Christ." Study of the titles used in this gospel—a fruitful project in any of the four—exposes a tension between the titles "Messiah/Christ" and "Son of Man." When someone uses the former title on Jesus, he normally parries it with the latter.* At stake between the two titles

---

* That tension is evident in the following passages of Mark's Gospel: in 8:29–31 notice the shift in titles and Jesus' displeasure with Peter that follows directly upon it. The tension is implicit in 9:9–12, if we assume that the disciples had been using Messianic terms; see their lack of understanding in 9:31–32. In 9:41, Jesus' description of them as "followers of Christ" seems ironic, since it occurs in a hyperbolic example. His talk of the Son of Man in 10:33–34 provokes the two "Sons of Thunder" to a misunderstanding clearly based on a triumphalistic Messianism. Jesus attacks the Messianism of the Jerusalem leadership in 12:35–37. In 13:21–22, Jesus warns that the notion of messiahship lends itself easily to counterfeiting, and speaks of the emergence of the Son of Man in 13:26. Three self-references as Son of Man occur within the Passion Narrative: 14:21, 41, 62, without any self-reference as Christ. From these it seems more plausible than fanciful to subscribe to a tension between the titles in the self-understanding of the Marcan Jesus.

is Jesus' analysis of what is wrong with humanity, of what we really need.

By attachment to Jesus, God the Son of God, the words "messiah" and "Christ" have radically shifted their original meanings. They meant something different and shallower back then, and we ought to understand the different theological and historical analyses upon which their meaning rested.

"Messiah" comes from the Hebrew *mesheach* just as "Christ" comes from the Greek *christos*; both mean "one who has been anointed with oil." No implication of divinity attaches to either term, though the anointing may result from divine selection. The Jewish model for such a person was, of course, David, but there were other examples. In Isaiah 45:1, God calls Cyrus the Persian "my messiah," referring to his selection as the means by whom the Jews will be released from exile. Another pagan example of a messianic figure was Alexander the Great, a charismatic military, religious, and political figure who briefly united the known world under his own rule. More recent would have been Julius Caesar who had scraped up the fragments of Alexander's empire, adding to them Gaul and Britain. The "messianic expectation" of those days, which Jesus fulfilled for some—reluctantly in the Marcan account—was the hope that God would supply another Caesar-like figure, only Jewish this time. A military and political figure as well as a religious exemplar, he would overthrow the Romans and everyone else and inaugurate Israeli rule over the world.

That hope rested on a shallow analysis of the human condition. It saw the human problem as susceptible to political solutions. It says there is nothing wrong with the world that a change from Italian to Israeli administration will not cure. Simple reupholstery will heal history.

In contrast to the messianic title, the Marcan Jesus used another of himself, the "Son of Man." As we might expect, this title contrasts dramatically with the first. It rests upon a more penetrating analysis of the human condition. Let us briefly examine its development.

Originally—in Ezekiel 2:1, for example—the term "Son of Man" simply meant "man" or "mother's son." But in later centuries it took on a specialized meaning, one we discover in Daniel 7:13–14:

> As I watched in the night visions, I saw one like a human being coming with the clouds of heaven. And he came to the Ancient One and was presented before him. To him was given dominion and glory and kingship that all peoples, nations, and languages should serve him. His dominion is an everlasting dominion that shall not pass away, and his kingship is one that shall never be destroyed.

Those who delve into the Pseudepigrapha* will find the same figure in the Fourth Book of Enoch:

> And there I saw one who had a head of days, and his head was white like wool, and with him was another being whose countenance had the appearance of a man, and his face was full of graciousness, like one of the holy angels. And I asked the angel who went with me and showed me all the hidden things, concerning that Son of Man, who he was and whence he was, and why he went with the Head of Days? And he answered and said unto me: This is the Son of Man who hath righteousness, with whom dwelleth righteousness, and who revealeth all the treasures of that which is hidden, because the Lord of the Spirits hath chosen him. (46:1–3)

A particular expectation grew up around this figure that had little connection with the messianic expectation. It was an *apocalyptic* expectation. This was the belief that the present age is irretrievably evil, so far gone that it is no longer susceptible to reform. Reupholstery, a change of administrative personnel, would be as futile as bandaging a gangrenous wound, washing dishes aboard the sinking *Titanic*. The present age must be diagnosed, condemned, closed, and replaced with a new age and order.

Furthermore, this transformation cannot be initiated within the framework of the present age itself since this age is incapable of self-renewal. An epoch cannot change itself; it can only rearrange itself. As we have seen, genuine second-order change only comes as an insertion from outside the frame. The agent of this cataclysm, the judge of the old, the inaugurator and ruler of the new, is the Son of Man. His humanity, emphasized by his title, assures fairness in his judgment. No non-participants, such as angels, would be licensed to do any judging, though they might execute the judge's orders. The judge must be a divinely appointed human being if the outcome is to count as just. Hence the title.

---

* Jewish and Christian writings of the centuries straddling the turn of the millennium, excluded from the Bible by the Paraclete's express mercy.

Whenever Mark has Jesus using this title of himself, pay close attention. Something about that episode will display God's judgment of the present age so we can see it for what it is and turn to the new age, which the same action will in some way introduce.

FORGIVENESS AS JUDGMENT

Now let us apply that understanding to the scene we are inspecting. "In order that you may see that the *Son of Man* has power and authority on earth to forgive sins,"—he said to the paralytic, "Stand up, get your stretcher, and walk home." We should understand Jesus' instruction to mean, "I hereby remove every physical, moral, psychological, and social impediment to your health and dignity. You may and can return to your rightful place in the community." Jesus does this overtly as the Son of Man. That means that two things are happening. First, he is bringing the present age under judgment. Second, he is calling a new age into being, one that he governs.

The distinguishing mark of the new age is forgiveness.

Weigh that.

Not, mind you, forgiveness exclusively in the sense that God forgives us, though that's surely radical enough. No, something more: that we forgive one another.

Will we dare grasp how amazing this is? God's *judgment* of human community takes the form of introducing *forgiveness* among us. It is difficult to imagine another act that could express the First Person's nature with such wit, charm, or economy. "If you have seen me, you have seen the Father," he said. Indeed we have, and our image of the Father is changed forever. We may approach God from now on not only with awe, but also with a heightened awareness of everything in us that requires God's mercy, with the anxiety that we might feel just prior to badly needed surgery—but never again with dread.

Furthermore, the operation of God's forgiveness can be blocked by one human action alone—the refusal to forgive another.

> And forgive us our debts, as we also have forgiven our debtors.
> For if you forgive others their trespasses, your heavenly Father
> will also forgive you; but if you do not forgive others, neither
> will your Father forgive your trespasses. (Mt. 6:12,14–15)

> Then Peter came and said to him, "Lord, if another member
> of the church sins against me, how often should I forgive? As

many as seven times?" Jesus said to him, "Not seven times, but, I tell you, seventy-seven times." (Mt. 18:21–22)

> "Then his lord summoned him and said to him, 'You wicked slave! I forgave you all that debt because you pleaded with me. Should you not have had mercy on your fellow slave, as I had mercy on you?' And in anger his lord handed him over to be tortured until he would pay his entire debt. So my heavenly Father will also do to every one of you, if you do not forgive your brother or sister from your heart." (Mt. 18:32–35)

That requirement is unambiguous.*

And if we receive this judgment as community members, it means our communities will change and express the new age. The Second Gospel thinks the church is the community in which the terms of the new age are to be lived out.

The Matthean account of the paralytic's healing has a thoughtful punch line: "When the crowds saw it, they were filled with awe, and they glorified God, who had given such authority to human beings." (Mt. 9:8)

Indeed such power had been given to human beings, if the human community was willing to receive it.

ANOTHER ACCOUNT OF CHRISTIAN COMMUNITY

The Marcan anecdote is quickly told, over nearly before it starts. Nor are the Lucan or Matthean versions any lengthier. Yet it outlines a major aspect of God's redemptive program in Christ. The central frustration recorded in the Old Testament is the failure of a heroic community to evolve, for all of the admirable individuals so candidly depicted there. Seen against that background, the New Testament emerges as the victory of God with human collectives. If we yearn for authentic righteousness, if our caughtness

---

* It may also be the one social ethical teaching peculiar to Jesus. Over two decades, I have asked recent converts to Christianity from other religions whether the religion they formerly occupied contained equivalents to our prohibitions of theft, adultery, murder, and the like and whether they contained positive injunctions to charity and truthfulness. The uniform reply is always "Yes." When I ask for the equivalent to Jesus' command to forgive our personal enemies, the reply is usually a chuckle followed by "No." I have had such replies from former Buddhists, Hindus, Moslems, and Jews. The official teachings of those religions may state otherwise, but this small sampling remained unaware of that obligation. I think the command to forgive enemies is the unique Christian contribution to humanity's social ethics.

in religion saddens and sickens us, we can afford to neglect no hint about God's work in community. For all of its risks and absurdities, the church is indispensable to those who seek to grow in righteousness. And Godly community results from the practice of mutual forgiveness. To move a congregation towards God's intention, the Gospels agree, you must practice, teach, and insist on forgiveness. There is more to it, to be sure—but there is never less.

The human community has to be both willing and able to receive the power to forgive, if individuals are to live righteously with one another and with God. As each of us knew a long time ago, the community normally exercises determinative influence on the individual. Few of us are strong enough to withstand concerted social, economic, or political pressure. And communities exist by funneling aggressive energies off onto despised "others," whether those be outsiders or deviant members. Jesus' norm of forgiveness confronts that need for aggression at its very core. So it follows inevitably that an authentically "Christian" community would feel weird to most of us—liberals because people pray openly and talk about Jesus personally, conservatives because it contains people they're confident God dislikes.

What would it look like if a community could follow Jesus' lead and make forgiveness the hallmark of its life?

We can infer an answer to that from the story of the rescue of Thomas in John's Gospel:

> When it was evening on that day, the first day of the week, and the doors of the house where the disciples had met were locked for fear of the Jews, Jesus came and stood among them and said, "Peace be with you." After he said this, he showed them his hands and his side. Then the disciples rejoiced when they saw the Lord. Jesus said to them again, "Peace be with you. As the Father has sent me, so I send you." When he had said this, he breathed on them and said to them, "Receive the Holy Spirit. If you forgive the sins of any, they are forgiven them; if you retain the sins of any, they are retained."
> (Jn. 20:19–23)

When the Spirit of God is the life of a community, that community is always aware of Jesus' presence. Jesus' presence makes mutual forgiveness urgent. He also clarifies that disturbing bit about pronouncing sins unforgiven. He sharpens the community's intuitions to discern bogus repentance, helping the group recognize that some soul's problem is not fully uprooted, to know when forgiveness would be harmfully premature.*

Thomas had been absent when Jesus breathed the Spirit onto his ten colleagues, so he did not receive the Spirit-mediated authority to forgive or retain sins.

> But Thomas (who was called the Twin), one of the twelve, was not with them when Jesus came. So the other disciples told him, "We have seen the Lord." But he said to them, "Unless I see the mark of the nails in his hands, and put my finger in the mark of the nails and my hand in his side, I will not believe."
>
> A week later his disciples were again in the house, and Thomas was with them. Although the doors were shut, Jesus came and stood among them and said, "Peace be with you." Then he said to Thomas, "Put your finger here and see my hands. Reach out your hand and put it in my side. Do not doubt but believe." Thomas answered him, "My Lord and my God!" (Jn. 20:24–18)

Thomas' friends report to him their visit with the resurrected Jesus. Perhaps they expect him to be happy with them. But Thomas scorns his friends' report. Tradition says he doubted, and "Doubting Thomas" has been a reproachful nickname ever since. But Thomas does not doubt—he pouts. He refuses to credit phenomena that fell outside the compass of his own experience. He might even be willing to allow this refusal to disrupt old friendships.

Yet eight days later he's still with his friends when Jesus visits again. That "eight days later" indicates a social miracle. Something in the other ten has changed since the days they were competing with each other for status. They're straight with each other now, they've dropped their old caginess. In Paul's phrase, they "speak the truth in love." Now they're able to hold on to their truth against Thomas' scorn and yet hold him in their midst lest he abscond like Judas. And just as the men lowering the paralytic to Jesus catalyzed the miracle by their faith, the ten hold on to Thomas long enough for Jesus to reach him. Jesus does reach him and breaks him out of his sulking. Jesus judged him, in effect. And he could do so because the community moved in concert with him like a basketball team around a trusted center.

This is the community of the new age in action. It is the nec-

---

* Once after I had lectured on the Gifts of the Holy Spirit in another parish, a man approached me and with wry irony said, "I seem to have had a charismatic gift for pronouncing sins unforgiven!" Thank God he was joking.

.essary condition for individual righteousness. Human history has not seen anything like this before.

Marks of Christian Community Today

Do we see such communities today? Periodically, in places, yes we do. But no denomination (even my own) holds the patent or copyright on the gospel and the Son of Man's new age. Some repressive policies of various groups clearly impede it. Partisan theologies do not induce or guarantee it, though they can retard it.

We see such community when and where God-broken men and women gather, consciously seeking to pursue righteousness rather than religion.

We see it where people have lived with their eyes open long enough that they no longer repose much confidence in all our huff-and-puff doctrinal urgencies. Such communities have outgrown both the submissive credulity of children and the dismissive incredulity of adolescents; they can engage the Scriptures and the Tradition with appreciative prayerful Reason.

We see it where cognitive dissonance is embraced as friendly, as a step toward rescuing truth from an over-tight confinement.

We see it in groups that trust the operation of the Spirit enough to encourage another to pursue her current train of thought, however anxiety-producing that course might be.

We see it where people's love of God momentarily feels more energetic than social embarrassment, allowing them to speak of and to God in the presence of others. Such groups grow in comfort with acknowledging God's Presence in the room in conversation, prayer, and worship.*

We see it where the sins, the roles, and the prestige of others do not interest the members so much as the interior of the person, as how they have grown, as what they can teach.

Such groups view conflict as preliminary to growth, not to social collapse.

Such groups have received enough divine mercy to want to

---

* Years ago a parishioner got angry, prophetically, as it turned out, during an adult Sunday school discussion. She hollered, "What is it with you people? A month ago I walked in and told somebody I felt anxious; they offered me Valium and the name of their therapist. Last week I told somebody I had a headache—they offered me aspirin. Doesn't anybody here know how to *pray*?" "But, Jenny," someone responded in horror—"that was *at the Coffee Hour!*"

extend it more widely as generosity and justice.

All of that takes place against a distinct background: a periodic vision of ineffable magnificence, goodness, and delight.* Such groups' inability to cram that vision fully into any theoretical expression—like it or not, they know they're stuck with metaphors—opens them to paradox without too much discomfort.

Do not look for that church in the Yellow Pages.

Pray, work, encourage other people, give, testify, yearn, serve, teach, confront, and forgive within the congregation you have already chosen.

Build it there.

---

* A seminary classmate once asked a famous elderly preacher, Dr. Walter Russell Bowie, how he had managed to keep coming up with something fresh to say from the pulpit week after week for so many decades. The old man, addressing the personal anxiety beneath the question, replied, "Keep ever before your eyes an image of magnificence!"

CHAPTER TEN

STAYING MOLTEN

THE MOLTEN INDIVIDUAL

In conclusion, let's consider what each of us as individuals can do to stay susceptible to mystical encounters with God, to remain subsequently molten enough not to harden within dysfunctional molds, and to promote congregational life that works for, rather than against, spiritual suppleness.

Whatever success I have enjoyed in those endeavors has resulted from blending Evangelical procedures for spiritual initiation, classical (largely Catholic) procedures for spiritual endurance, Charismatic procedures for spiritual growth, and "liberal" approaches to the Bible and to group dynamics for spiritual sanity. Biologists speculate that life may have begun in some pond or puddle where lightning—or something—forced separate amino acids to bond, forming the protocol for eventual DNA. The religious scene in the United States currently needs a lightning bolt to jump-start an authentically mystical national religious life that is responsive to God.

If that process is already underway, it has so far escaped public notice. Evangelicalism and its Pentecostal offshoots are, at present, rushing to become family-maintenance systems based on restrictive notions of what families really are. We could think of that religious expression as "conservative Republicanism at prayer"—if its prayer were only more evident. Most expressions of Catholicism in America are curatorships of past values. Anglicans who think of ourselves as "catholic" function as curators of old customs. Roman Catholics function as curators of old authority structures with their vanishing prestige. By choice, Eastern Orthodox expressions remain isolated beyond the discussion.* Liberalism combines knitted brows, pursed lips, and intellectual/cultural self-congratulation. Our dwindling numbers persuade us that high standards are not for everyone.

The fire of God has its work cut out for it, but there are ways we can prepare the altars.

MEETING JESUS

The earliest records—the Pauline letters in the New Testament—display what is unique to Christian spirituality: a sense of Jesus' Presence in the room with us decades after his physical departure. That Presence was not available to everyone. People off the street presumably could not discern it. But those who had known Jesus when he walked the earth found it unmistakable.

We can to some extent replicate their acquaintance with Jesus by studying the four Gospels to begin to know him. The Gospels give us a sense of Jesus' personal style. As I suggested in Chapter 6, it helps to mark up a copy of the Gospels with colored highlighter pens, different colors for different traits. Important traits include: humor, anger, sexual self-awareness, fear, delight, sorrow, glee, and rudeness. Any of these elements can be startling, but they will help us to recall that the whole point of the Incarnation is that God became a human being. A person who manifests none of those traits does not pass our tests for being human.

Once you have a sense of Jesus' style, ask yourself whether or not he appeals to you. Do you find him attractive? Do you have

---

* A liturgical scholar was teaching an ecumenical summer course in the history of liturgical worship a couple of decades ago. He reported that on an essay exam two Eastern Orthodox priests wrote single identical sentences—something like, "The Divine Liturgy of the Orthodox Church reached a pinnacle of perfection in the thirteenth century and is in no wise susceptible of improvement." He thought it remarkable that they had attended at all.

some sense of why seasoned fishermen would take his advice about where to drop nets? About why he scared clergy and politicians? About why women felt comfortable, safe—and smart—around him? About why people behaved a little better towards each other in his presence? Does he awaken hope, a sense of your own possibilities?

If the answer to any of that is "yes," it is time to enact your hope. Assume the Presence you seek to discern, addressing the Unseen with your wish to know him personally. Assume that God occupies the air around you and the spaces between your constituent atoms—and talk to God. (Do not, however, try it aloud on an occupied elevator.) The experience of many generations of Evangelicals and several generations of Pentecostals offers us specific conversation topics it helps to begin with.

The first conversation topic is *confession*. This consists of a frank assessment of your life in Jesus' unseen Presence. You acknowledge the actions, words, and attitudes you would have felt shabby about had you known his Presence at the time. You offer to quit rationalizing them, to abandon excuses, to stop calling them by pretty names. Instead you *grieve* in his Presence for the regrets about your own person you detect. You open the tension you feel between the impulses of your nature and the strictures of those around you. You ask him how his own struggle with all that felt.

Pay attention to what happens. In Chapter 7, I outlined several understandings of how Jesus' death has been understood as reconciling us to God. I suggest here that you collect the experience itself before seeking a theory to explain it. Don't cram it onto a theoretical matrix or compare it with anyone else's report until you have communed with the experience itself for a while. It may help to delay talking to others about it for a couple of weeks. Sit with your grief and feel it being addressed by Jesus'—and, by extension, God's—understanding, acceptance, cleansing, correction, insight, encouragement, empowerment, and delight in you. You are experiencing some of what various Christians call being "saved." If you tell Jesus at that point that you welcome and need that gift, you are in effect "accepting Jesus as your Savior"—a good thing to do even if it sounds tacky. That is, you are recognizing Jesus as your most treasured and valuable resource in all circumstances of your life. It will not surprise you to carry a sense of Jesus' presence around with you routinely from then on, regardless of what you are doing.

The second topic is *forgiving others.** Much of the wrongdoing you acknowledged previously was in reaction to things others had done to you. At the moment that you are aware of God's profound acceptance of you, it will be possible to extend that acceptance beyond yourself to people who have wounded you. That is a deeply godly act, one that very intimately expresses God's image. In response you will be aware of God's deep pleasure at what you have chosen to do with your own acceptance. You will discover in the Gospels that it is an obedience: Jesus commands us to forgive others. You will sense the Presence is deeply pleased by your obedience in forgiving others, resulting in a further sense of empowerment, a deeper understanding of things. This would then be a good time to promise that you will attempt to obey every instruction Jesus gives you. That is quite similar to what others call embracing Jesus as "Lord," one whom you serve obediently.

I think it is good to use these early conversations with Jesus as occasions to identify and *close rival bank accounts.* You can identify Jesus' rivals in your life by completing the sentence, "If Jesus disappoints me, I can always…" Rival resources include reliance on understandings contrary to what God reveals to you, various possessions, alternative life-giving relationships, or social status. Any alternative source of personal power and support, accessed apart from God, is a rival bank account—and will deplete you spiritually. Some of us must in fact be told to "Sell all you possess, give it to the poor, and come follow me!" Others will be given other instructions. Some people may be urged to switch careers. Others will be told to mend a broken relationship by asking forgiveness. Whatever you are told, you will find that obedience leads to a deeper sense of peace and righteousness. Delay results in your life feeling jammed and disorderly. Eventual obedience is the remedy.

Subsequent conversations with Jesus can delight you both as you offer up area after area of pain, confusion, interest, fear, curiosity, gratitude, and wonder into his Presence and get a sense of how Jesus wants you to relate to each right now. Expect the answer to change as you develop. Ask Jesus how he himself experienced whatever issue you bring to him. His answers will change you. Real Christian mysticism is the fruit of taking God's humanity utterly seriously. That is what you are doing in all these conversations.

---

* See Appendix B for a fuller discussion of this essential matter.

The Gifts of the Holy Spirit

All through this book I have stressed that we get into trouble when our spiritual fluidity, our moltenness, hardens into some group's mold, a mold that, in all probability, requires rigidity and an element of phoniness. The problem of staying supple in God's hands, of staying molten once you get that way, needs attention.

Many conservative Evangelicals have hit on revivalism as a conspicuous solution to that problem. In a revival both the individual and the community attempt to repeat their initial entry into a sense of God's grace. A speaker with a voice less familiar than the regular pastor's comes in to deliver several rousing presentations. These include—if, indeed, they do not confine themselves to—a fresh approach to sin. The sin message allows the previously "saved"* listeners to re-experience themselves as spiritually imperiled in order to repent and re-experience grace in the form of pardon. Pardon, after all, may be the only work of grace the community is practically aware of. The community feels reconstituted as its old members revive their enthusiasm and new converts join them.

I am not a revivalist and do not belong to such a community. The one revival I attended years ago found me an unreceptive candidate—callow and cynical, in fact. Clearly there are advantages to such procedures; otherwise revivalism would not be so widespread. However, I'll report my hunch—substantiated by any number of reports from revival veterans—that it eventually gets to be pretty much the same thing, over and over and over.

Here we can borrow helpfully from Pentecostalism. Pentecostals and their Charismatic understudies stress spiritual growth in ways that go (occasionally dangerously) beyond repentance and getting justified. It is called sanctification—growing holy, set apart for God. Along with catholic⁺ spiritual disciplines, Pentecostalism

---

* I put "saved" in quotes not as satire but as a mark of my discomfort with an assumption that the term, as conventionally employed, begs. That is, people who use that term these days usually refer to a spiritual breakthrough that occurred on a datable occasion during their lifetimes. My theological daintiness makes me want to use the term to point to what Jesus did about two thousand years ago for all humanity ["He descended to the Dead...."] rather than (in my case) 1957. I don't put quotes around *breakthrough, conversion,* or *encounter,* terms for what others mean by "saved."

⁺ This use of "catholic" includes Anglicans, Eastern Orthodox, High Church Lutherans, and classical Pietists along with Roman Catholics.

makes a place for periods of spiritual aridity that does not reproach but empowers the sufferer. Unlike standard catholic spiritual exercises, it places heavy stress on the "charismata," the gifts of the Holy Spirit to the community exercised by individual believers.

Thousands of books and pamphlets explain the charismata in charming detail; to read the descriptions is to flirt with Pentecostal conversion willy-nilly.* I shall not replicate their discussions except to stress a few points for readers who may find the whole matter either bizarre or distasteful or both.

People who pray for and receive the gift of "tongues" or *glossalalia* possess an advantage over the rest of us that the controversy it invariably stirs should not be allowed to obscure. That is, one who can turn loose her tongue and address God without intellectual filtration is able to accomplish within thirty to ninety seconds something that those of us who study "centering prayer" may fail to achieve in an hour. Furthermore, she will find that she can do so during a period of aridity. Spiritual dryness will deprive her only of the desire, not the ability. +

Those who offer Charismatic ministries to others—such as healing, prophecy, wisdom, and knowledge—feel drawn to God more firmly in their offering. There are few more breathtaking spiritual delights than watching God honor your prayer for another—right before your eyes.◆

---

* My favorite book both to read and recommend is John Sherrill's *They Speak With Other Tongues*. Dennis Bennett's *Nine O'clock in the Morning* is another winsome classic. The best book so far written about Charismatic spirituality and theology is Jean-Jacques Suurmond's *Word and Spirit at Play*.

+ I think the inner struggle launched by the topic of tongues is almost always fruitful. Questions like, "Would God give me something to embarrass me?" or "Would God ignore my request?" are healthy to confront. Any mention of this topic is likely to stir up what Pentecostals call a "spirit of rejection," an urgent, teary inner sense that God does not love me enough to grant this request. The fruit of such struggles makes the hassle of mentioning the gift of tongues as a desideratum worth it.

◆ Once at a conference where I spoke, I was steadily beset by a man who gained no sense of God's love for him from my presentations. As the event concluded he was reporting his disappointment one last time when another man broke in, reported suffering a splitting headache, and asked to be prayed for. On a not-altogether-unmischievous impulse, I turned to the complainer, instructing him to place hands on the sufferer's head and pray for his healing. With great reluctance and hesitation he did so. The recipient gave a gladsome whoop of celebration and reported that his head suddenly felt fine. His erstwhile reluctant minister stood dumbfounded, grinning with a new awareness of how God feels.

Charismatics, of course, harden and rigidify at the same rate as the rest of us. Some of our forms and molds combine all the recessive traits of other spiritualities, especially those of Fundamentalism. All that notwithstanding, the engagement with God enabled by exercising the charismata is unmistakably authentic. One who is faithful and regular in practicing the gifts will experience enough vicissitudes, enough roller-coaster ups and downs, to stay at least semi-molten.*

PRAYER

If there are hundreds of books on the Charismatic gifts, square and cube that number for books on prayer. However, no amount of reading will keep you as molten as will daily prayer. There are as many varieties of prayer as there are of any mode of discourse. The spectrum covers everything from devoted attendance at a Solemn High Mass, through corporate prayer services (the Daily Office, in some traditions), through private structured devotions, all the way to wordless, imageless attentiveness. It is as futile to ask, "Which is best?" or "Which is right for me?" as it would be to ask similar questions about the offerings of a mile-long cafeteria. The only reasonable reply is, "Try as many as you can and see."

The single point I urge from this discussion is that the difference between religion and righteousness guide one's selection and practice. We do not pray in order to cajole or constrain God, nor to press God's reluctance. We pray in an attitude of trust, knowing that God loves us. That allows us to be open to listen as well as speak. The most memorable times of prayer are invariably those in which God has spoken more than we have.

THE BIBLE

The inspiration of the Bible is a fruit of inductive experience with it; it is not the deductive, authoritative starting point of Bible reading.

> The fact of the inspiration of Holy Scripture has impressed itself as an unshakable conviction on generations of sincere Christians.

---

* Should you choose to exercise this form of spirituality, read some of the New Testament passages in Appendix A and then include the request in your conversation with Jesus. You may wish to get someone who already lives with God in this manner to accompany you as you make the request.

> Belief in the inspiration of Scripture moreover grows on men as they live with the Bible and work with it in the service of Christ Himself. James Denny once wrote, "Belief in the inspiration of Scripture is neither the beginning of the Christian life, nor the foundation of Christian theology; it is the last conclusion—a conclusion which becomes every day more sure—to which experience of the truth of Scripture leads."*

The discussion in Chapter 5 was presented to clear away misconceptions about the Bible's authority in order that its real power be accessible to us without distortion. The Bible is a splendid launching pad for prayer. Calling the Bible the "Word of God" is something of a misnomer. But one who reads the Bible prayerfully will shortly be caught up in the real Word of God. Passages suddenly light up, become incandescent. Something you have read a hundred times suddenly strikes you as strange—and something tells you and Toto that you are not in Kansas anymore. If you are faithfully following a lectionary schedule of daily readings—and if the editors were not too busy with their scissors—you will find perfect gems in the middle of trackless wastes. Previously I called your attention to the passages in Exodus 25 and 40, which describe the ark, the tablets, and the Mercy Seat. Another of my favorite oases occurs in the middle of a tedious list of "begats":

> Jabez was honored more than his brothers; and his mother named him Jabez, saying, "Because I bore him in pain." Jabez called on the God of Israel, saying, "Oh that you would bless me and enlarge my border, and that your hand might be with me, and that you would keep me from hurt and harm!" And God granted what he asked. (1 Chr. 4:9–10)

What a treasure. Jabez asked God to cancel a familial script injunction and that is exactly what happened. A reader who launches a prayer from that discovery might find all sorts of family nicknames and scripts he wants God to exorcise.

The Bible is mostly freeze-dried.+ It only becomes food when we add water, stir it, and heat it. To inflate the briefest story, to address it as though we were casting directors for a movie, dwelling

---

* Ronald S. Wallace. "Principles of Biblical Interpretation," in New American Standard Bible: Study Edition (New York, A.J. Holman Company, 1975), 1320.

+ Hebrew writing is quite compressed—it did not even bother with vowels. Copiers of Greek manuscripts of the New Testament did not bother with punctuation and spaces between words and sentences.

on its details and its possible meanings, expands our interior spaces. Meditative imaginative Bible reading makes room for God.

WORSHIP

The word "worship" comes from the earlier English word, "worthship." It means to attribute worth to another—in effect, to admire them. Worship is admiring God. Its value rests in the fact that we come to resemble whatever or whomever we admire.* Worship is the main engine by which God restores us to the divine Image. Real worship cracks us open, melts us, and leaves us ready to set up in a more godly pattern.

Attendance at worship is helpful in staying molten. Even in a lackadaisical worship service, contacting the heart of God on behalf of the rest of the congregation is a fruitful exercise; we can admire God for them. In an energetic service whose norms repel you, it is fruitful to offer your discomfort to God as a sacrifice on behalf of others, congratulating God's vast taste. In a service that suits you, it is wonderful to allow yourself to get swept up and carried in adoring admiration, paddling with the stream as you lift your own voice.

To those not accustomed to it, sacramental worship appears superstitious. Its object, however, is to sensitize worshipers to the fact that all of life is sacramentally porous to the Presence of God. All food is God's self-offering (the Lord's Supper), every shower, bath, or swim a cleansing caress (Baptism).

The effort of rubbing your heart against God's in the middle of a congregation builds a quality of spiritual muscle not otherwise cultivable. If corporate worship does not displace private prayer, neither can the private be allowed to supplant the corporate. They occur as a set.

FELLOWSHIP

Relationships with a few others who are striving to stay molten before God are an indispensable resource. People who employ

---

* Clearly that reality underlies all the Old Testament strictures against idolatrous worship. The God speaking in the OT does not want people coming to resemble animals, monsters, or imaginary spiritual beings. In the OT, God does not use images for self-disclosure, instead requiring us to wait for the Presence before we can admire. A friend recently pointed out that God's self-introduction to Moses—"I will be who I will be"—is meant eventually to describe creatures in God's image: us.

catholic procedures often use clergy or mature lay Christians as confessors. Some may seek out mature Christians to serve as spiritual directors or companions. In my experience, as essential as those two offices are, I still need, in addition, a small group of peers to whom I give permission to ask tacky questions and make personal observations. When I am trying to cultivate any other skill—such as white-water kayaking—I seek rather than object to critical feedback so as to improve. That applies to life before God as well. Others help.

MINISTRY

By ministry, I refer to your own, not the preacher's. Wherever Christianity flourishes vital ministry is widely distributed, and it is not confined to the ordained—it is the proper activity of all believers.

In this context, it helps to distinguish between ministry and "church-work." The latter is something you are already good at which you offer the church. A good thing to offer, to be sure, but church-work can usually be done without prayer, since you so rarely get in over your head. Church-work by itself does not foster spiritual growth. On the other hand, ministry is something that God directly calls you to do. Ministry requires prayer, because it often seems beyond your normal ability. Consequently, you will be aware of God's power operating in and through you as you offer ministry. There is nothing like ministry to accustom you to living in tandem with God.

STEWARDSHIP

Stewardship is the recognition that everything we possess is gift. Specifically it involves claiming freedom to give some back. Its outward expression is a conspicuous change in getting and spending. Gifts are much more fun than personal purchases, we discover. Real wealth is not the power to amass, but the power to make a gift. The much-misunderstood "grace of poverty" is the resolution not to possess more than you can actively use or care for. In this sense, holy poverty—while invisible to the world—offers relief from care. Though you would not suspect it, a keen awareness of your stewardship for all you've been given is much of what makes converted Christian life so delightfully merry. Making the tithe the first check you write produces constant fresh conversion—because it is always a struggle. Your checkbook becomes a holy setting, a battleground in the struggle between fear and trust. Your stomach gets more relaxed each month you approach it. When in need, make a gift.

JUSTICE

Experiencing God normally entails a vision of what the New Testament calls the Kingdom of God—human society arranged so as to fulfill God's love for humanity. Spiritual enlightenment cannot remain a private position without spoiling. If you want to maintain a steady molten condition before God, you can do no better than to engage in some personally costly activity on behalf of God's poor. There are glimpses of God's glory that are only available to us in the context of passionate joint efforts for justice.* Christians who engage in lobbying, demonstrating, and hands-on service to poor people rapidly discover the applicability of the "spiritual warfare" section of Ephesisians:

> Finally, be strong in the Lord and in the strength of his power. Put on the whole armor of God, so that you may be able to stand against the wiles of the devil. For our struggle is not against enemies of blood and flesh, but against the rulers, against the authorities, against the cosmic powers of this present darkness, against the spiritual forces of evil in the heavenly places. Therefore take up the whole armor of God, so that you may be able to withstand on that evil day, and having done everything, to stand firm. (6:10–13)

It is not enough simply to do charity work case by case, we eventually realize. It was not for his case-by-case charity work that the authorities lynched Jesus; it was for his ringing denunciations of the power relations by which they exploited others. An auto repairman who gets asked to repair a whole lot of punctured tires on southbound cars will eventually want to know what is in the road north of the station that's puncturing all those tires. Likewise, when Christians actually engage with poor people, discovering how hard they must work and how little use they make of public services, the bland assurances that the poor are at fault for their own condition no longer pass as truth—or pass unchallenged. Call that

---

* The fraudulence of much American public Christianity is nowhere more clearly evident than in its blame-the-victim insouciance for minorities and poor people. One misses God.

politics if you must. Politics is just the Greek term for citizenship. It is also stewardship of your citizenship as a Christian American. Such ministry will keep you scared and upset enough to cultivate prayerfulness. In such struggles, the Devil inadvertently tells you a lot of what he knows about God.

All those elements make up the ingredients for what the catholic tradition calls a "rule of life." At their best, rules of life keep us in a steady state of spiritual adventure.

The previous list of elements out of which we could construct a spirituality includes what I regard as the best features of Evangelical, Catholic, Pentecostal, and activist spiritualities. Intense experience in each has led me to believe not a single one is complete in itself. If it were, the contemporary religious scene would not be so fragmented. The string section alone is not a complete orchestra—neither is the brass. We yearn for a blend, for harmony, for complementary rhythms. That harmony must begin within the self before it spreads to theological movements and religious denominations. Surely the antagonism between Fundamentalists and "secular humanists," between "progressive Christians" and "conservatives," between "pietists" and "activists," displays the internal discord of the individuals who make up those movements. That antagonism is at least partially the reflection of our own unclaimed individual proclivities, abilities, temptations, and dreads, leading us to join groups whose fears look like ours. If we were each more courageous in facing our private internal contradictions, would we not be wiser and more charitable conversation partners? However much or little human effort contributes to the establishment of the Kingdom of God, it's clear that souls which are no longer molten, which are frozen into the mold of some religious group or other, can scarcely contribute much to that Kingdom's emergence. Kingdom building starts on the far side of Stage 4. What's on the near side is "empire-building"—something else entirely.

It is enormous fun to imagine what would be turned loose on our national scene if members of "country club churches" would explore the high adventure of stewardship; if "liberal/activist/progressive" Christians would assay the high risks of repentance and "accepting Jesus as Savior"; if "conservatives" would dare roll up their sleeves and get to know people in the ghettos, then go "have a word of prayer" with the mayor and council. Imagine the combinations yourself. What if the votaries of each perspective could simply appreciate what it offers, remain aware that there is yet more, and refuse to define their commitments in adversarial terms? Paul tells us:

> For the creation waits with eager longing for the revealing of the children of God; for the creation was subjected to futility, not of its own will but by the will of the one who subjected it, in hope that the creation itself will be set free from its bondage to decay and will obtain the freedom of the glory of the children of God. We know that the whole creation has been groaning in labor pains until now. (Rom. 8:19–22)

Those groans, if not indeed our own well-being, might prompt us to authentic growth, might empower us to melt again.

THE MOLTEN COMMUNITY

Needless to say, it would be difficult to spot a molten faith community in the Yellow Pages of your local phone directory. If you seek directions to such a community, not everyone you ask will understand what you are looking for.* It is usually necessary to build such a group—and an existing group is in many ways a better place to start than a fresh one. Following are four qualities that, if embraced, will allow a congregation to develop into a lively, growth-fostering community of faith.

WORSHIP/FELLOWSHIP/MINISTRY

Earlier in this chapter I discussed worship, fellowship, and ministry as components of a molten individual's rule of life. Taken together—and in that order—they are essential for spiritually molten communities as well. When communities bend every effort to offer worth and admiration to God, their hearts rub against God's. Individual worshipers crack and melt a little bit. There is a momentary window of opportunity for personal change. At this juncture, fellowship is indispensable. The fellowship of other recent worshipers encourages us to trust the changes

---

* One of the best compliments ever paid St. Patrick's was delivered by a new family from across the country. I asked them how they had found us. They replied, "We called the diocesan office. We knew better than to ask for a spiritually alive congregation—the receptionist would have been duty-bound to report that all were. So we asked, 'What congregation has the highest per capita giving?' 'Oh, that's simple—it's St. Patrick's!' the receptionist replied. So we knew that's where we would find life."

the Spirit forges in us during worship. We cultivate friendships in which candid discussion of our actual relationship with God is acceptable and expected. Those friendships become the support system necessary for our taking up ministries that force us to grow in trust. The results of those ministries in turn recycle into worship, as we thank God for what has resulted (or grieve about the results, as the case may be), and report to each other.

Keeping those three elements in proper order is as important as it is counterintuitive. Worship, unfueled by previous ministry, which does not issue into fellowship, devolves into a duty-driven curatorship of moribund customs, as lifeless as it is fussy. Fellowship, unfueled by worship, which does not lead to ministry, swiftly devolves into boozy, gossipy cliquishness. Ministry, unfueled by spiritual fellowship, which does not lead into worship, becomes prideful and turf-preoccupied.

The single reason judicatory-level and denomination-level programs accomplish so little is that they do not arise from an active fellowship of worshipers. Consequently they are nobody's active priority except for their paid staff's. The most fruitful expressions of ministry occur among friends who worship God together. The most fruitful friendships treasure common worship and joint efforts in the service of causes beyond oneself as their substance. The most nourishing worship arises from bands of active committed friends.

A congregation that consciously embraces those three elements as its priority will swiftly become a group within which a spiritually adventurous soul can flourish.

KEEPING SHORT ACCOUNTS

Conflict, an element of any group, can produce hostility, but it need not. Nor does conflict necessarily arise from hostility. Anytime two people's fields of intention collide upon the same plane, there is conflict. We generally manage that reality with courtesy and etiquette. Traffic intersections are a case in point. At an intersection, my field of intention falls afoul of the fields of three other groups, those coming from the left and from the right and those wishing to turn in front of me. That is why God made traffic lights and stop signs. It is possible to drive in traffic decently yet remain merry.

There are norms built into Christian community that make

conflicts more fruitful—and more fun.* Think of those norms as keeping short accounts with other people. It requires us to cultivate three habits.

The first habit is to forgive other people when I feel bruised by their behavior.⁺ "Then Peter came and said to him, 'Lord, if another member of the church sins against me, how often should I forgive? As many as seven times?' Jesus said to him, 'Not seven times, but, I tell you, seventy-seven times.'" (Mt. 18:21–22)

This exchange indicates that the community that produced Matthew's Gospel, possibly the church in Antioch, thought Jesus wanted mutual forgiveness to be a reflex among his friends. For a moment, imagine living in a community in which you could always count on being forgiven.

The Matthean community prized a corollary norm, the second habit: "So when you are offering your gift at the altar, if you remember that your brother or sister has something against you, leave your gift there before the altar and go; first be reconciled to your brother or sister, and then come and offer your gift." (Mt. 5:23–24)

That is, if I have reason to believe that I have caused offense to another, I need to approach them and ask forgiveness prior to approaching worship.◆ Imagine a community in which seeking

---

* I recall a conversation with a wise older friend when I—a pacifist—was struggling with whether or not to encourage my small sons to learn self-defense. She pointed out succinctly, "If they cannot fight, they cannot talk." She went on to explain that every conversation is a potential fight—if one is frightened or inept at fighting, one cannot converse freely. If they learn to fight, they may not have to. Pacifism is an adult commitment, embraced after one knows alternatives.

⁺ A procedure for forgiving others can be found in Appendix B.

◆ *Disciplinary Rubrics*

> If the priest knows that a person who is living a notoriously evil life intends to come to Communion, the priest shall speak to that person privately, and tell *him* that *he* may not come to the Holy Table until *he* has given clear proof of repentance and amendment of life.
>
> The priest shall follow the same procedure with those who have done wrong to their neighbors and are a scandal to the other members of the congregation, not allowing such persons to receive Communion until they have made restitution for the wrong they have done, or have at least promised to do so.
>
> When the priest sees that there is hatred between members of the congregation, *he* shall speak privately to each of them, telling them that they may not receive Communion until they have forgiven each other. And if the person or persons on one side truly forgive the others and desire and promise to make up for their faults, but those on the other side refuse to forgive, the priest shall allow those who are penitent to come to Communion, but not those who are stubborn.
>
> In all such cases, the priest is required to notify the bishop, within fourteen days at the most, giving the reasons for refusing Communion. (Book of Common Prayer 1979, 409)

forgiveness was the norm. Conflicts would be no big deal. Imagine how freely discussion could range.

The third habit is to stop judging each other. Judging people and circumstances comes easily and naturally to us—but it forestalls understanding. Dorothy Parker was once asked what she noticed first when meeting a person. "Whether they're a man or a woman," was her reply. But, of course, additional discernment follows closely: is this person an enemy to be opposed or a resource to be exploited? Since Eden, we have rushed to file people in predictable classes: right/wrong, in/out, up/down, good/bad, top/bottom, master/servant, etc. Dreary. Researchers speculate that such tendencies lodge in our "old brains," the so-called "reptilian complex" comprising the brain stem and the medulla oblongata that we share anatomically with the crocodiles. It takes deliberate effort to transcend that tendency with a willed decision to respond to people from our mammalian mid-brains and our human cortices.* But that effort produces immediate happy results. When a spiritual community embraces that value, life improves markedly for all. We cannot know the quality of a person, an event, or a circumstance until we have experienced them in God's presence.

Surprisingly enough, the matter of not judging includes favorable judgments. I recall leaving a party I had dreaded attending, talking to Jean about how happily surprised I had been that this person was not as obnoxious as I had recalled, how that person had grown, how entertaining a third person was, and so on. Within ten minutes I was glum, having forfeited the pleasure of the evening. Even favorable judgments are toxic—because *all* judgment is toxic.

There are objections that pop up the minute someone proposes non-judgment as a community norm. For example, some dread that non-judgment leaves a group vulnerable to obstreperous

---

* Many readers will recognize the "triune brain" studies of Paul MacLean, helpfully summarized by Arthur Koestler in *Janus* and by Harville Hendrix in *Getting the Love You Want*. It would be great fun to see this understanding finally make it to church. You could furnish far worse summaries of the Gospels than the struggles of the mammalian Jesus against the reptilian Pharisees; likewise you could describe the best work of the Holy Spirit as unifying our relatively poorly connected brain sectors. Alongside that project, we ought to investigate the theological implications of the fascinating differences in structure and function between male and female brains.

individuals. A moment's thought will demonstrate the possibility of setting limits and assigning consequences to clear misbehavior. For another example, people assume that such a norm implies that there is no distinction to be made between good and bad, that everything is a relativistic mish-mash. Nonsense. The distinction persists. It simply is not our task to forge it. Distinguishing good and evil is God's job; our job is to be attentive to God's report. We do that best in a molten spiritual condition. For still another example, people speculate that without judgment there would be nothing to talk about. Those of us who are taciturn introverts would no doubt welcome the resulting silence. In fact, that leaves ample scope for reporting our reactions to things *as our reactions* —which is usually closer to the truth. Finally some object, "But God gave me the gift of discernment; am I not supposed to exercise it?" I usually reply, "Bless your heart—give it *back.*" The serious point is that it is fruitful to assume that one no longer has any "discernment." Facing the day with such a sobering realization would require constant prayer to know what is what; God's faithful reply to each prayer constitutes what we should have meant by discernment in the first place.

Nobody is perfect, nor is any community. People routinely defect from those habits. But public embrace and discussion of those principles is a great resource for any community that wants to maintain its zest. Communities that practice and proclaim those habits take on a quality of realism and delight. Speech is freer and clearer. Laughter and humor are celebrative, non-corrosive. Such a community is molten, porous to God's presence in every detail of corporate life. It is the best setting for staying personally molten.

A MOLTEN BIBLE

In Chapter 5 we discussed the Bible's place in the church. As appreciative as we should be of biblical scholarship for all that it discloses, we should also recognize that its disclosures are preliminary to the Bible's use in the church. In church we seek what some have called a "post-critical naïveté." That is, knowing what we know about the Bible and the myriad ways of misusing it, we now proceed to open it with one another in the Presence of God and watch what happens. Virtually every word in the Bible was written in order to be read and discussed publicly. When the sort of community we have been considering turns itself loose on the Bible, wellsprings of fresh insight, encouragement, direction, and creativity burst open.

Biblical paradigms have often offered indispensable service in Christian history. It is difficult to imagine the emergence of African-American culture over the last three hundred years without a Bible within which to see their own position, their survival, and their eventual victory reflected. Something like that may have recently occurred behind the Iron Curtain, where a disproportionate amount of resistance to Communist regimes was grounded in churches. Imagine how our current political/social conversation would proceed if Christians were seriously reading and discussing Deuteronomy or Amos or Isaiah or Jeremiah or Micah? What would church life feel like if multiple groups were always gathering around the Sermon on the Mount in Matthew or the Sermon on the Plain in Luke?

What is important is not that the Bible be taught from a lectern or preached from a pulpit. What is essential is that the Bible be thrown into a circle of people, that it be read and discussed. In such settings, the Bible will always be catalytic. Any community that wishes to become and remain spiritually melted before God will distribute Bibles to its members and say, "Go to it!"

LOVING THE WORLD

The Epistle of James tells us: "Adulterers! Do you not know that friendship with the world is enmity with God? Therefore whoever wishes to be a friend of the world becomes an enemy of God." (Jas. 4:4)

It is possible to read that and be able to avoid a profounder teaching in the Fourth Gospel: "For God so loved the world that he gave his only Son, so that everyone who believes in him may not perish but may have eternal life. Indeed, God did not send the Son into the world to condemn the world, but in order that the world might be saved through him." (Jn. 3:16–17)

Connect that with this: "Jesus said to them again, 'Peace be with you. As the Father has sent me, so I send you.' When he had said this, he breathed on them and said to them, 'Receive the Holy Spirit.'" (Jn. 20:21–22)

This combination of readings does not allow our communities to ignore the surrounding world, nor to offer themselves to

frightened members as pure alternatives to that naughty world.*
If indeed Jesus was serious when he said to us through Peter,
"'And I tell you, you are Peter, and on this rock I will build my
church, and the gates of Hades will not prevail against it.'" (Mt.
16:18), then we need to discuss why it feels so important that we
shelter ourselves against a supposedly invasive world. Jesus did not
envision a church on the defensive. If congregations are not
scared of their own members, the world will not scare them either.

A spiritually molten church, therefore, is in the world. It takes
its place at the table. Its artists produce real art. Its thinkers produce real thought. Its members do productive work in the world.
And so when it gathers for prayer, it offers its own voice to God
discerningly on behalf of those who do not know to—or who do
not know how to—pray for themselves.

THE TASKS BEFORE US

Anyone who pays attention to the news remains aware that the
human race not only faces many serious problems today—the
human race *is* a serious problem. We harness technological inge-
nuity to our appetites to medicate our dreads—and make the
world thereby more dreadful. Wherever human culture permits
exploration, technology takes off at an exponential rate. The
result is a common standard of living, at least for Westerners,
superior to that of the very gods of our ancestors. It also pollutes
and adulterates the natural environment. It produces enough
conspicuous inequity to fuel constant revolutions. It arms ancient
tribal rivalries with vastly more power than wisdom. It supplies us
all with enough leisure to contemplate our emptiness—driving us
back to consumption. And on and on it cycles.

What we call evolution has brought humanity to a point no
other species on earth has yet reached: that is, the driving force of
human development is now culture rather than passive engagement with the natural environment. Nature no longer determines
which individual will make it. To a large extent—God help us—
groups of us decide what aspects of nature will make it. Several features had to come together at once to produce culture. Language

---

* It is truly said that when you build a wall to keep out the tiger, you wall yourself in with him.

and memory, a sense of time, and self-awareness emerged as the human brain added layers to the brain structures we inherited from earlier common species. The opposable thumb allowed us to manipulate matter. Erect locomotion allowed us to carry stuff—the beginning of our preoccupation with it. Agile physiology and metabolism allowed us to flourish in a bewildering variety of natural settings—not just the marshes from which we are said to have arisen. Put all that together and you get vulnerable individuals capable of collaboration with others over distance and time. Culture is the result, both enabling and imperiling individual survival.

Two Challenges to Human Evolution

The future of human evolution lies with culture. That makes for enormous hope. To be sure, the very cultures we inhabit may erase or cripple each other before we can take the next necessary steps. Yet culture works at such blinding speed to solve problems, it may be that we will find ways to address two vast challenges to the human species' future.*

Those two problems occur at the different levels this book has addressed—the individual and the corporate. At the individual level, culture must complete the job of brain development that biological evolution has bequeathed to us. As Paul MacLean has pointed out, the human brain is really three largely separate organs stacked over each other.[+] The "Old Brain" resembles that of large reptiles and governs such behavior as feeding, fighting, fear, reproduction, and the like. The "Mid-Brain" adds the mammalian capacities for play and nurture. The outer "New Brain" is the thick neo-cortical layer possessed only by humans and dolphins; it allows us memory, imagination, and the manipulation of symbols. The difficulty we face—and that we pose to others—is that these layers are not well connected and can function without reference to each other. Can we remain aware of the extent to which our thoughts serve our appetites? To what extent does our reason have to mop up after our lusts and dreads? Until we learn to pay attention to how awkwardly our brain components work together, how can we know ourselves?

---

* Arthur Koestler's last book, *Janus*, addresses these twin problems in helpful detail.

[+] Paul D. MacLean, *The Triune Brain in Human Evolution* (New York: Plenum Publishing Corp., 1990).

Indeed, the lack of coordination among our brain sectors partially informs what Western Christians since Augustine have called Original Sin. Two internal struggles make us bipedal civil wars. First, the tension between our mid-brain—which loves and enjoys—and our old brain—which dreads and growls—puts us constantly in circumstances where we emerge as "bad." Second, what we as individuals want and need regularly collides with what the culture requires. To survive within culture, we internalize its demands. These demands war inside us with our private urgencies.

Paul wrote about this struggle:

> I do not understand my own actions. For I do not do what I want, but I do the very thing I hate. Now if I do what I do not want, I agree that the law [the "culture"] is good. But in fact it is no longer I that do it, but sin [the drives of the old brain] that dwells within me. For I know that nothing good dwells within me, that is, in my flesh. I can will what is right, but I cannot do it. For I do not do the good I want, but the evil I do not want is what I do. Now if I do what I do not want, it is no longer I that do it, but sin that dwells within me. So I find it to be a law that when I want to do what is good, evil lies close at hand. For I delight in the law of God in my inmost self [Paul knows culture is in some sense God's gift], but I see in my members another law at war with the law of my mind, making me captive to the law of sin that dwells in my members. Wretched man that I am! Who will rescue me from this body of death? (Rom. 7:15–24)

At the cultural level another problem awaits solution. Human communities compete with each other like species rivals. The competition has always been destructive of nature as well as human populations. Within recorded history human strife has altered the previously fertile environments of North Africa and the Middle East. Gazing at the appalling results, we are tempted to think it was all done by bad people. But in reality it was done by good people in the service of ultimately destructive causes.

Private human virtues make corporate vice possible. As Koestler reminds us in his book, *Darkness at Noon,* the self-sacrifice of dedicated Marxists produced the horrors of Stalinism. Nazism arose within the wounded patriotism and personal heroism of individual Germans and Austrians whose parents had taught them to be proud of their culture's arms. The horrors of life in the Balkans will never subside as long as parents greet newborn sons saying, "Hail, Avenger!"—and as long as those sons are "good"—

were those sons "bad" (lazy or cowardly) the Balkans would be as peaceful as Iowa. Love of kin and neighbor, courage, loyalty, heroism—all these produce mischief at the public level.

Ironically, when individuals are selfish and acquisitive, the resulting economy (capitalism) is the only system we know capable of generating wealth. When individuals are too poltroonish to fight, the result is (temporary) calm.

The paradox then: as often as not private virtue combines with that of others at a community level to produce public viciousness. We don't yet know what to do about that. If culture is to continue fueling human evolution, culture must find some way to live with and eventually solve those two impasses.

THE GOOD NEWS

In the face of those two challenges, the two thousand year-old Gospel is fresh Good News. Spiritually molten individuals are exemplars of internal coherence. Those who bathe regularly in radiant goodness emerge with a wry self-acceptance and enjoyment of others. The power of the fear of death dissolves in that washing. The radiant goodness beckons them beyond old doctrinal comforts into risk. That goodness beckons them beyond the urgent rivalries they fall into as they pursue that risk, into an appreciation of the courage displayed and the goodness reflected in commitments other than their own. Eventually that goodness impels them to devote themselves utterly while remaining unattached to specific uniforms.

If the human species is to advance, individuals must get molten in the love God reveals in Jesus Christ. That melting is essential for all the rest of humanity, even for the unmelted. It is a preservative salt. It is the Light of the World.

Likewise, the community of corporations—businesses, sports teams, governments, states—requires the company of molten communities if its members are not to exploit its constituent virtues for vicious ends. The world badly needs the example and challenge of groups so committed to a vision of glory and goodness, so molten in its heat, that they can contemplate their own extinction in God's service. Unless the church is constituted and led by molten individuals, unless she fosters that fluid supple state, the requirements of institutional prestige and survival will always veto any advance towards her goal. By contrast, molten communities are merrily inefficient, outrageously self-risking, insouciant of prestige. Their presence among other human communities both encourages and judges all the rest.

We are so recently evolved as an intelligent cultural species that we can still see our simian cousins, our mammalian second cousins close by, and all our sixth cousins thrice removed further off walking down their own evolutionary forks. And yet at this early stage in our evolution, we can already consciously detect and respond to the Presence of God. The recently evolved response to God's Presence is our highest achievement as individuals and as cultures.

◆　◆　◆　◆　◆

The molten soul begins with bodily sensations, swiftly followed with the realization that we are not alone in the room. We feel awe, joy, embarrassment, relief, and exaltation in that Presence. It takes us out of the ordinary into some pretty strange company. Later, with the help of others, we compress and twist ourselves in order to get that Presence under control, to modify it, to exploit it without being consumed by it. And in so doing, we lose access to it. Yet that Presence will not be denied or blocked. God comes for us again and again, each time leaving us changed. Where will it end? We sense that it will not end, that it will lead us ultimately, after all manner of missteps, into what we presently can only awkwardly name—Glory.

THE CHARISMATIC MOVEMENT

The term "Charismatic" refers to the entry of Pentecostalism into mainline denominations and groups outside the Holiness tradition.

Pentecostalism began on New Year's Day 1901, in Topeka, Kansas, at Charles Parham's Holiness Bible School. A student named Agnes Ozman stayed up all night praying about the reports found in the New Testament of being "filled" or "baptized" in the Holy Spirit. Some of the passages she studied include:

> Later he appeared to the eleven themselves as they were sitting at the table; and he upbraided them for their lack of faith and stubbornness, because they had not believed those who saw him after he had risen. And he said to them, "Go into all the world and proclaim the good news to the whole creation. The one who believes and is baptized will be saved; but the one who does not believe will be condemned. And these signs will accompany those who believe: by using my name they will cast out demons; they will speak in new tongues; they will pick up snakes in their hands, and if they drink any deadly thing, it will not hurt them; they will lay their hands on the sick, and they will recover." So then the Lord Jesus, after he had spoken to them, was taken up into heaven and sat down at the right

hand of God. And they went out and proclaimed the good news everywhere, while the Lord worked with them and confirmed the message by the signs that accompanied it. (Mk. 16:14–20)

So when they had come together, they asked him, "Lord, is this the time when you will restore the kingdom to Israel?" He replied, "It is not for you to know the times or periods that the Father has set by his own authority. But you will receive power when the Holy Spirit has come upon you; and you will be my witnesses in Jerusalem, in all Judea and Samaria, and to the ends of the earth." (Acts 1:6–8)

When the day of Pentecost had come, they were all together in one place. And suddenly from heaven there came a sound like the rush of a violent wind, and it filled the entire house where they were sitting. Divided tongues, as of fire, appeared among them, and a tongue rested on each of them. All of them were filled with the Holy Spirit and began to speak in other languages, as the Spirit gave them ability. (Acts 2:1–4)

While Apollos was in Corinth, Paul passed through the interior regions and came to Ephesus, where he found some disciples. He said to them, "Did you receive the Holy Spirit when you became believers?" They replied, "No, we have not even heard that there is a Holy Spirit." Then he said, "Into what then were you baptized?" They answered, "Into John's baptism." Paul said, "John baptized with the baptism of repentance, telling the people to believe in the one who was to come after him, that is, in Jesus." On hearing this, they were baptized in the name of the Lord Jesus. When Paul had laid his hands upon them, the Holy Spirit came upon them, and they spoke in tongues and prophesied–altogether there were about twelve of them. (Acts 19:1–7)

To each is given the manifestation of the Spirit for the common good. To one is given through the Spirit the utterance of wisdom, and to another the utterance of knowledge according to the same Spirit, to another faith by the same Spirit, to another gifts of healing by the one Spirit, to another the working of miracles, to another prophecy, to another the discernment of spirits, to another various kinds of tongues, to another the interpretation of tongues. All these are activated by one and the same Spirit, who allots to each one individually just as the Spirit chooses. (1 Cor. 12:7–11)

By contrast, the fruit of the Spirit is love, joy, peace, patience, kindness, generosity, faithfulness, gentleness, and self-control. There is no law against such things. (Gal. 5:22–23)

Those are the passages Charismatics usually cite. Agnes Ozman took all those passages literally. She was puzzled to see no evidence of such phenomena around her. She stayed up all night praying to know what it was all about. At breakfast the next morning she was visibly joyous, reporting that she had received the Baptism in the Holy Spirit, manifested in the "Gift of Tongues." The interested responses of her colleagues launched Pentecostalism.

The Charismatic Movement is the entry of Pentecostalism into the denominational mainstream and outside of the Holiness tradition. The term comes from the Greek word *charisma*, referring to a gift of the Holy Spirit, which Charismatics and Pentecostals rely upon. Charismatics believe that the coming of the Holy Spirit upon Jesus' disciples in the Upper Room in Acts 2 (with the resulting peculiar behavior such as speaking in tongues, prophesy, and miraculous healing) is an accurate description of the way God operated back then. Evangelicals, Fundamentalists, and conservative Roman Catholics hold the same belief with no apparent difficulty. What marks Charismatics as different is the expectation that God intends to operate within the church today in the same manner. Consequently Charismatics stress the ministries of healing, prayer with spontaneously emerging unknown syllables, miracles, and transformed personalities.

Whatever else all that entails, it clearly adds up to a relationship with God experienced and reported as personal and energetic. Faith for a Charismatic is not intellectual assent to particular doctrines. It is relatedness to Jesus on similar terms as might apply between married partners, close friends, or cordial employers and employees. It is heavily experiential, occasionally impatient with too much dogmatizing. Because it is experiential, it offers a route into something like mystical experience to ordinary people.*

---

* I regard the latter as its most fruitful promise to the church at large.

FORGIVING OTHERS

Years ago I was late to a meeting in a distant city. I arrived just as lunch was beginning, discovering that the only empty seat was across from the chairman. I said something like, "Forgive me for being late." His reply seemed gracious: "Oh, that's all right. We didn't get much done this morning anyway. I'm sometimes late myself." Another man across the table remarked, "Did you notice that he didn't forgive you?"

That remark produced an awkward conversational do-si-do in which I asked again and he replied that he indeed forgave me—then we sort of mused on what had just taken place. I drove home realizing that I had not understood those transactions, likely because I had no understanding of forgiveness.

Jean and I discussed forgiveness that night—gingerly, as it turned out, since by then we had accumulated gunnysacks full of grievances that such a discussion might tear open. I recall that after discussion, we prayed together that the next few days or weeks would allow an answer to assemble itself. So it happened.

The problem posed itself this way. Forgiveness appears to mean being loving and accepting of someone who has hurt you. But that is close to imposture and verges on being an Iago-like setup for revenge. How can you forgive someone and mean it? Isn't that pretending to feel one way while feeling another?

Yet in the Gospels Jesus commands forgiveness, as though it were an action within the scope of our wills, not just a passive emotional reflex to another's actions. If forgiveness is really a decision, an act of will, what do you decide?

Five different components emerged from Jean's and my struggle with that question. I find they work best initially if done in solitude in the company of God.

> 1. Assess and acknowledge the damage you have received without posturing as too tough to be vulnerable. You let yourself say "Ouch!" This may take a while—perhaps months—and can helpfully occur in the disciplined setting of counseling or psychotherapy. To rush over this step invites failure.

> 2. Renounce revenge—in thought, word, deed, or inference. That is a promise you make to God. It includes: dropping lawsuits; abandoning critical gossip; arresting vengeful trains of thought, turning them into prayers; quitting acting or speaking in such a way as to enlist others to be vengeful on your behalf. It hurts to do.

> 3. Refuse to use the other's action as an excuse for your own. (Renounce secondary benefits of your pain.) If you misbehave in response to another's misbehavior, you will seek God's forgiveness without using the other person's offense as your excuse. This hurts to do as well.

> 4. Pray to God to prosper the one who hurt you. It is important to pray for prosperity rather than blessing, as blessings can easily get ambiguous. ("Bless my sister with insight into the effect she has on people!") Prosperity is surer. When you see your "enemy" prosper," you will know God has heeded your prayer; you will not mess that up with your voodoo, so to speak. This hurts too.

---

* If my wife starts serving me cold casseroles for dinner (likely resentful that I still think the cooking is her province) that does not warrant my stopping off for a few short ones after work; the police officer issuing the DUI does not want to hear about my wife's cooking.

At this juncture you will rediscover the purpose of unforgiveness. Your sense of vulnerability, of the unfairness of it all, alerts you to how you have used your resentment as a burglar alarm to stay aware of the possibility of future harm. To complete forgiveness, you have to address your vulnerability.

> 5. You ask God to heal your heart toward the other, sharing God's own pleasure in their creation with you so you can agree with it. When you feel God's safety and God's love for the one you resent, it is as though you have been taken up a couple of stories above the conflict and can see it whole—and see that it is over.

There are some obvious games you should not play here. For one thing, you do this in private or with a deeply trusted companion for encouragement and guidance. You do not necessarily in all cases rush up to your former antagonist and announce that you have forgiven him—that can be prideful posturing, vengeful in itself. At some proper time, you may likely make an overture to announce that the offense is settled, assuming that he even was or needs to be aware that there was an offense.

Likewise, you do not always assume that your need to forgive another means that they have done wrong. For example, I silently forgive my physician after physical exams (that escalate in degradation each passing year) in order that I will be willing to return in twelve months.

I have placed this discussion at the tail end of this book for the simple reason that the procedure must be done in the presence of God. Apart from that Presence, any attempt at forgiveness is likely to wind up a pretentious, ultimately futile, legalism. In that Presence, it is an action that expands the very universe itself.

BIBLIOGRAPHY

Abelard, Peter. "Exposition of the Epistle to the Romans." In *A Scholastic Miscellany: Anselm to Ockham*, edited by Eugene R. Fairweather. Philadelphia: Westminster, John Knox Press, 1956.

Achtemeier, Elizabeth Rice. "Righteousness in the Old Testament." In *The Interpreter's Dictionary of the Bible: An Illustrated Encyclopedia Identifying And Explaining All Proper Names And Significant Terms And Subjects*, edited by George Butterick, et. al. Vol. 4. Nashville: Abingdon Press, 1962.

Anselm of Canterbury. "*Cur deus homo?*" In *A Scholastic Miscellany: Anselm to Ockham*, edited by Eugene R. Fairweather. Philadelphia: Westminster, John Knox Press, 1956.

Armstrong, Karen. *A History of God: The 4,000-Year Quest of Judaism, Christianity and Islam.* New York: Ballantine Books, 1993.

Augustine. *Confessions.* Garden City: Doubleday & Co. Inc., Image Books, 1960.

Barton, John. *People of the Book? The Authority of the Bible in Christianity.* Louisville: Westminster, John Knox Press, 1988.

Bataille, Georges. *Eroticism: Death & Sensuality.* San Francisco: City Lights Books, 1986.

Becker, Ernest. *The Denial of Death.* New York: Free Press, 1973.

——*Escape From Evil.* New York: Free Press, 1975.

Bennett, Dennis. *Nine O'clock in the Morning.* South Plainfield: Bridge Publishing, 1984.

Berger, Peter L. *The Sacred Canopy; Elements of a Sociobiological Theory of Religion.* Garden City: Doubleday & Company, Inc., Anchor Books, 1969.

——*A Rumor of Angels: Modern Society and the Rediscovery of the Supernatural.* Garden City: Doubleday & Company, Inc., Anchor Books, 1990.

——and Thomas Luckmann. *The Social Construction of Reality: A Treatise in the Sociology of Knowledge.* Garden City, Anchor Books, Doubleday & Company, Inc., 1966.

Berkhof, Louis. *Systematic Theology.* Grand Rapids: Wm. B. Eerdmans Publishing Co., 1941.

Bernard of Clairvaux. "On the Love of God"; "Of the Three Ways in Which We Love God"; "That the Soul, Seeking God, Is Anticipated by Him." In *Late Medieval Mysticism,* edited by Ray C. Petry. Philadelphia, Westminster Press, 1957.

Bethune-Baker, J. F. *An Introduction to the Early History of Christian Doctrine.* London: Methuen & Co. Ltd., 1951.

Bettenson, Henry, ed. *Documents of the Christian Church.* New York: Oxford University Press, 1961.

The Book of Common Prayer 1979. New York: The Church Hymnal Corporation, 1979.

The Book of Common Prayer 1928. New York: The Church Hymnal Corporation, 1929.

Brock, Rita Nakashima. *Journeys By Heart: A Christology of Erotic Power.* New York: Crossroad, 1991.

Brown, Raymond E. *The Churches the Apostles Left Behind.* Ramsey: Paulist Press, 1984.

Calvin, Jean. *Institutes of the Christian Religion.* Edited by John T. McNeill. Philadelphia: Westminster Press, 1960.

Charles, Robert Henry, ed. *Apocrypha and Pseudepigrapha of the Old Testament in English,* Vol. 2. London: Oxford Press, 1964.

Chesterton, G. K. *The Everlasting Man.* New York: Dodd, Mead, and Company, 1953.

Chrysostom, John. "Easter Homily." In *Handbook of American Orthodoxy.* Cincinnati: Forward Movement Publications, 1972.

Dhammapada. Translated by P. Lal. New York: Farrar, Straus, and Giroux, 1967.

Dörner, Dietrich. *The Logic Of Failure: Why Things Go Wrong and What We Can Do to Make Them Right.* Translated by Rita and Robert Kimber. New York: Henry Holt and Company, Metropolitan Books, 1996.

Dostoyevsky, Fyodor. *The Idiot.* Translated by David Margarshack. New York: Penguin, 1956.

Erikson, Erik H. *Childhood And Society.* New York: Norton, 1950, 1963.

Fairweather, Eugene R., ed. *A Scholastic Miscellany: Anselm to Ockham,* Vol. 10, Philadelphia: Westminster, John Knox Press, 1956.

Fischer, David Hackett. *Historians' Fallacies: Toward a Logic of Historical Thought.* New York: Harper Torchbooks, 1970.

Fowler, James W. *Stages of Faith: The Psychology of Human Development and the Quest for Meaning.* New York: HarperCollins, 1981.

Goethe, Johann Wolfgang von. *Faust.* Edited by Heffner, Rehder, & Twaddell. Madison: University of Wisconsin Press, 1955.

The Gospel According to Saint Matthew. 1964. 140 min. Rome: Arco Film; Paris: Lux-C.C.F.

Griffiths, Bede. *The Marriage of East and West.* Springfield: Templegate, 1982.

Groome, Thomas H. *Christian Religious Education: Sharing our Story and Vision.* New York: HarperCollins, 1980.

Heim, Karl. *Christian Faith and Natural Sciences.* New York: Harper Torchbooks, 1953.

Heinlein, Robert A. *Stranger In A Strange Land*. New York: Ace Books, 1995.

Hoffstaeder, Douglas. *Gödel, Escher, Bach: An Eternal Golden Braid*. New York: Random House Vintage Books, 1980.

Hooker, Richard, "Of The Laws of Ecclesiastical Polity." In *Hooker's Works* (The Works of That Learned And Judicious Divine, Mr. Richard Hooker: with an Account of His Life and Death by Isaac Walton). Arranged by The Rev. John Keble, M.A. Fifth Edition Vols. 1, 2, 3. Oxford: Clarendon Press, 1868.

Huxley, Aldous. *The Genius and the Goddess*. New York: Bantam Books, 1956.

The Hymnal 1940. New York: The Church Hymnal Corporation, 1940.

Jesus of Nazareth. 1977. 371 min. United Kingdom: Incorporated Television Company; Italy: Radio televisione Italiana.

Johnston, Luke Timothy. *The Real Jesus: The Misguided Quest for the Historical Jesus and the Truth of the Traditional Gospels*. San Francisco; HarperSanFrancisco, 1996.

Johnston, William. *Being In Love: A Practical Guide to Christian Prayer*. London: Harper Collins, 1988.

Julian of Norwich. *Revelations of Divine Love*. London: Methuen & Co. Ltd., 1952.

Keen, Sam. "The Heroics of Everyday Life, A Conversation with Ernest Becker." In *Voices and Visions*. New York: Harper and Row, Perennial Library, 1974.
———*To a Dancing God*. New York: Harper & Row, 1970.

Kipling, Rudyard. *The Jungle Book*. New York: The Century Company, 1919.

Koestler, Arthur *Janus: A Summing Up*. London: Picador, 1977.
———*Darkness At Noon*. New York: Random House, 1978.

Lao Tsu. *Tao Te Ching*, translated by Gia-Fu Feng & Jane English. New York: Random House Vintage Books, 1972.

*The Last Temptation of Christ.*1988. 164 min. United States: Cineplex Odeon Films; Universal Pictures.

Lawrence, T. E. *Seven Pillars of Wisdom.* New York: Dell Publishing Co. Inc., 1962.

Levinson, Daniel J., with C. N. Darrow, E. B. Klein, M. H. Levinson, B. McKee. *The Seasons of a Man's Life.* New York: Ballantine Books, 1978.

Lewis, C.S. *The Weight of Glory And Other Addresses.* Grand Rapids: Wm. B. Eerdmans Pub. Co., 1972.

Lindsell, Harold. *The Battle for the Bible.* Grand Rapids: Zondervan Publishing House, 1976.

Lowen, Alexander, M.D. *Pleasure: A Creative Approach to Life.* Penguin, 1975.

MacDonald, George. "The Consuming Fire." In Rolland Hein, ed., *George MacDonald: Creation in Christ* (Wheaton, Illinois: Harold Shaw Publishers, 1976).
————*The Princess and the Goblin.* New York: Penguin Books, Ltd., Puffin Books, 1979.
————*The Princess and Curdie.* New York: Penguin Books, Ltd., Puffin Books, 1979.
————*The Lost Princess.* Elgin: Chariot Books, 1979.

Mac Lean, Paul D. *The Triune Brain in Human Evolution.* New York: Plenum Press, 1990.

McCurdy, Harold G. *The Personal World: An Introduction to the Study of Personality.* New York: Harcourt, Brace & World, Inc., 1961.

Merton, Thomas. *The Asian Journals of Thomas Merton.* Edited by Naomi Buarton, Partick Hart, James Laughlin. New York: New Directions, 1973.
————*Contemplative Prayer.* Garden City: Doubleday IMAGE, 1971.

Muggeridge, Malcolm. *Christ and the Media.* New York: Harcourt Brace, 1950.

Phillips, J.B. *Your God Is Too Small.* New York: Macmillan Publishing Co., Inc., 1997.

Plato. *The Symposium.* Edited by B. Jowett. New York: Charles Scribner's Sons, 1911.

Polanyi, Michael. *Tacit Dimension.* New York: Doubleday and Company, 1966.

The Q'ran. Edited by N.J. Dawood. New York: Viking Penguin, 1974.

Richards, I.A. *Practical Criticism: A Study of Literary Judgment.* New York: Harcourt Brace, 1950.

Rilke, Rainer Maria. "Archäischer Torso Apollos." In *Ausgewählte Gedichte.* Frankfort am Main, Suhrkamp Verlag, 1966.

Sayers, Dorothy L. "The Dogma Is the Drama." In *The Whimsical Christian*, New York: Macmillan Publishing Co., Inc., 1978.

Schumacher, E.F. *A Guide for the Perplexed.* New York: Harper & Row, 1977.

Shakespeare, William. *As You Like It.* London: Arden Shakespeare, 2000.

Sheehy, Gail. *Passages.* New York: Bantam, 1984.

Sherrill, John L. *They Speak With Other Tongues.* Grand Rapids: Chosen Books, 1985.

Sims, Bennett J. *Servanthood: Leadership for the Third Millenium.* Cowley Publications, 1997.

Solzhenitzyn, Alexander. *The First Circle.* Evanston: Northwestern University Press, 1997.

Steere, Douglas V. "Foreword." In *Contemplative Prayer* by Thomas Merton. Garden City: Doubleday & Co. Inc., Image Books, 1971.

Steinberg, Leo. *The Sexuality of Christ in Renaissance Art and in Modern Oblivion.* New York; Random House, Pantheon Books, 1983.

Suurmond, Jean-Jacques. *Word and Spirit at Play: Toward a Charismatic Theology.* Translated by John Bowden. Grand Rapids: Wm. B. Eerdmans Pub. Co., 1995.

Taylor, Kenneth N. *Taylor's Bible Story Book.* Illustrated by Richard and Frances Hook. Wheaton: Tyndale House, 1978.

Tillich, Paul. *The Courage to Be.* New Haven: Yale University Press, 2000.

Twain, Mark. *Huckleberry Finn.* Garden City: Harper & Brothers, 1954.
———*Letters From the Earth.* New York: Harper & Row, 1962.

Verduin, Leonard. *The Reformers And Their Stepchildren.* Grand Rapids: Wm. B. Eerdmans Pub. Co., 1964.

Wallace, Ronald S. "Principles of Biblical Interpretation." In New American Standard Bible: Study Edition. New York: A.J. Holman Company, 1975.

Wright, Robert. *The Moral Anima Why We Are the Way We Are; The New Science of Evolutionary Psychology.* New York: Random House, Vintage Books, 1994.

All passages from the Bible are taken from the New Revised Standard Version. Word changes for emphasis and editorial omissions are noted where they occur.